Eighth Edition

Keeping the Books

Basic Recordkeeping and Accounting for the Successful Small Business

Linda Pinson

published by

OM..IM

**Out of Your Mind...
and Into the Marketplace™**

Author: Linda J. Pinson

Assistant Publisher: Ndaba Mdhlongwa

Editor: Julie Filppi

Interior and cover design: Linda Pinson

Cover Photo: The cover photo is used by permission and copyrighted by the photographer, Kurhan. (© Kurhan. Image from BigStockPhotos.com)

Published by: **OUT OF YOUR MIND...AND INTO THE MARKETPLACE™**

13381 White Sand Drive
Tustin, CA 92780-4565

714-544-0248 (Information)
800-419-1513 (Orders)
www.business-plan.com

Pinson, Linda.
    Keeping the books: basic recordkeeping and accounting for the successful small business / Linda Pinson—8th ed.
        p.   cm.
    Includes bibliographical reference and index.
    ISBN-13: 978-0-944205-57-0
    ISBN-10: 0-944205-57-7
    1. Bookkeeping. 2. Small Business—United States—Accounting. I. Title
HF5635.P649 2014
657.2—dc22

About the Author

Linda Pinson is an award-winning author, business planning expert, speaker, consultant, and nationally recognized business educator with a specialty in financial management and small business curriculum development. The author of seven popular entrepreneurial books, she has also developed and published the bestselling business plan software program, Automate Your Business Plan. Linda's books are widely used as curriculum in colleges and universities. They have been translated into several foreign languages including Spanish, Chinese, and Italian.

Linda served for seven years on the Small Business Financial Development Corporation Executive Board of Directors and for nine years on its Loan Committee. She also served for several years on the Tri County SBDC Board of Directors and as a member of the Entrepreneurial Advisory Committee at California State University at Fullerton. Her dedication to the small business community has been recognized through awards from the U.S. Small Business Administration, the National Association of Women Business Owners, and the State of California. Linda served as a delegate and tax issue chair at the White House Conference on Small Business.

Linda resides in Tustin, California with her husband Ray. She is an avid golfer (one hole-in-one) and bowler, paints watercolors, and loves to fish. Linda and Ray have two sons, two daughter-in-laws, two grandsons, and one granddaughter (all great, of course).

Dedication

It is with a great deal of pleasure that I dedicate this book to Virginia Haverty, a wonderful friend who is now gone, but never forgotten. Her gifts of encouragement and confidence live on in this book and in my life.

Acknowledgments

During the writing and revising of eight editions of *Keeping the Books*, it has been my good fortune (and the readers') to have input from many business associates whose expertise in certain areas admittedly exceeds my own. I would like to acknowledge three of those individuals here.

- **Judee Slack,** Enrolled Agent and owner of SlackTax, Inc., in Fountain Valley, CA (www.slacktax.com) has been instrumental in keeping me on track through more than 20 years of changes in accounting practices and IRS tax regulations. She never fails to take the time out of her own busy schedule to help with each new revision of *Keeping the Books.*

  Judee also worked with me in the development of two chapters that make the book even more valuable to small business owners. She wrote Appendix I, Independent Contractors: Facts vs. Myths and worked with me on the writing of Chapter 3, Cash Accounting Versus Accrual Accounting.

- **Ndaba Mdhlongwa,** owner of Business Plan Solutions in Dallas, Texas (www.businessplanprofessionals.com) has worked with me for fifteen years on book and software tasks, including the development of great Instructor's Manuals for *Keeping the Books, Steps to Small Business Start-Up, and Anatomy of a Business Plan.* Ndaba is a delight to work with and never asks what he will get in return.

- **Julie Filppi**, my able and enthusiastic assistant, has worked by my side putting editions of our books and versions of our software together – in addition to everything else she does on a day-to-day basis to keep us up and running.

Thank you, Judee, Ndaba, and Julie. *Keeping the Books* is a better book because of you. I thank you — and I know that my readers would also thank you personally if they had the chance.

Thank You, Educators!

Over the past 27 years, we have received great support and encouragement from the many universities, colleges, entrepreneurial schools, and technical institutes that have adopted our business books and business plan software as required course material for their classes. With each semester (or term) that passes, we are always happy to receive new inquiries and orders from dedicated educators throughout the United States.

One of our ongoing objectives has been to continually provide you with up-to-date resources that will spur students to success in their business ventures. We are pleased to let you know that we have new 2014 editions of our three most popular books (and eBooks) and also our business plan software. Each of the books has an up-to-date instructor's manual (free for you) with lesson plans for each chapter, extensive presentation slides and printable handouts, and two basic tests with answer keys. The books can be adopted individually or as a series package.

Once again, we are happy to offer you the latest materials and information for teaching your entrepreneurship courses. We hope that, through the continued utilization of our books and software, you can help your students and clients to launch their businesses, familiarize themselves with small business accounting and tax issues, develop a marketing plan, and put it altogether by writing a winning business plan that will serve as a lifetime guide for their companies.

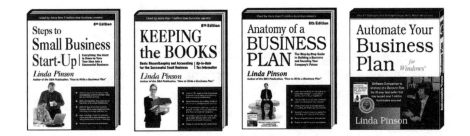

Thank You to All of Our Educators!

We would like to take this time and space to extend a special thank you to each and every one of you – and to wish you and your students continued success. You are highly valued and it is an honor to serve you.

Table of Contents

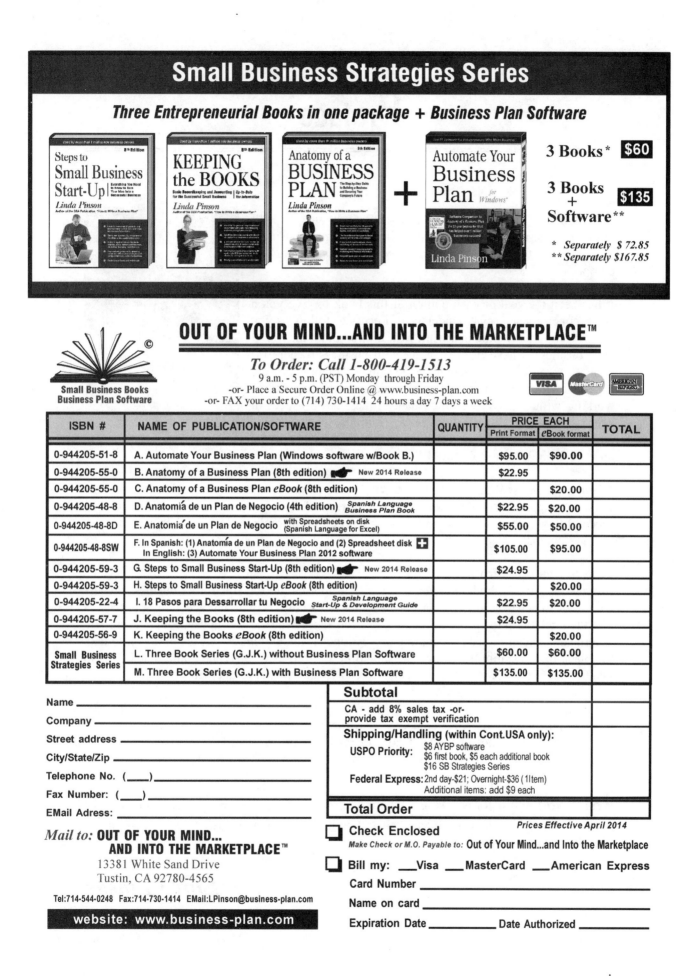

Preface

Thank you for choosing *Keeping the Books* to use as your guide for learning about recordkeeping and small business accounting. I think you will be pleased with this new *eBook* edition.

It has been the goal of each edition of this book to give you a clear, concise, and easy-to-understand process to follow as you set up your bookkeeping and work with it throughout the life of your business. I have been working with business owners for many years and most of them have the same problem—they are experts in their industries, but are novices when it comes to working with financials. In fact, many times, the prospect of keeping financial information is so formidable that some business owners avoid it until tax time when they have to come up with the information for the IRS.

Keeping the Books should provide you with a clear, concise, and easy-to-understand process for setting up, understanding, and attending to recordkeeping and accounting. If I have been successful, you should be able to follow that process, customize it for your business, and set up a system that will greatly benefit your company.

Who is this book for?

I frequently get asked who *Keeping the Books* is appropriate for. It is for all business owners who need to better familiarize themselves with the recordkeeping and accounting processes and their relationship to tax accounting – even those who hire in-house bookkeepers and accountants and/or outside accounting professionals. *Keeping the Books* is not meant to take the place of accounting software, but should be utilized as a reference guide that will help you to better understand and utilize general records and financial statements.

The purpose of accounting is not just to provide the IRS with information at tax time. Its main benefit is to boost your company's profitability through periodic financial statement analysis. If you do not understand how to read and utilize profit & loss statements and balance sheets, you are forfeiting one of the most valuable tools at your disposal.

Thank you again for choosing *Keeping the Books* to help you accomplish your financial goals. I appreciate your confidence that it will help you and wish you success in the operation of your businesses.

Linda Pinson

Recordkeeping Basics

The keeping of accurate records is imperative if you are going to succeed at business. From time to time, I have had students in my small business classes who have wonderful ideas for products or services, but who do not want to be bothered with the details of recordkeeping/accounting. Their businesses are already doomed to failure. This book was written with the assumption that you are starting from scratch and know nothing about small business accounting. I have tried to solve the puzzle for you. By the time you have finished applying the principles in the book, I hope that you will understand how all of the pieces fit together to develop a simple, but accurate recordkeeping and accounting system.

Functions of Recordkeeping

The first, and most important, function is to provide you with information that will help you to see the trends that are taking place within your operation. You will see, as you study this book, that a complete and simple set of accounting records will make it possible to tell at a glance what is happening with your business – which areas are productive and cost-effective and which will require the implementation of changes. The second function of accounting records is to provide you with income tax information that can be easily retrieved and verified.

Who Should Do Your Bookkeeping?

You, the business owner, should be personally involved rather than simply delegating this job to an outsider. Keeping your own books and important records in house will make you doubly aware of what is going on in your business and it will also save you money that can be used to benefit your business in other areas. For example, you may now be able to afford a piece of effective advertising that will generate more sales. Even if time will not allow you to personally do your own bookkeeping and you assign the task to someone else, it will be a major benefit to you to make every attempt to understand how your records are organized and to learn how to read and use them to make decisions in your business.

1

Do You Need an Accountant?

Absolutely! I do not advocate the elimination of an accounting professional. In fact, end-of-the-year tax accounting requires special expertise and will best be handled by an accountant who can maximize your tax benefits. You will have to decide whether to use a Certified Public Accountant (CPA), Enrolled Agent (tax accountant), or non-certified bookkeeper/tax preparer. The first two are empowered to represent you at an IRS audit.

All accounting professionals are dependent on the financial information that you provide. To ensure the most profitable results for your business, you will need to set up and maintain general records as the source of financial data. You should also work with the accountant to establish a good line of communication and a smooth flow of that data.

Depending on the size and scope of your business, you will have to decide which of the accounting chores you can handle and which ones should be delegated to an expert. For instance, you may be able to do all of your accounting except for payroll, which is very exacting and will probably be more effectively handled by your accountant. You may also decide that you would like to use an accountant at the end of the month to generate your financial statements. In fact, if the scope of your business becomes very large, it may become necessary to turn over your entire accounting operation to an expert. If so, it will still be imperative that you understand the process, so you will be able to use your financial information to make sound business decisions.

Accounting Software

One of the most frequently asked questions is about which accounting software application is the best and easiest to use. There are many accounting software programs on the market today that will adequately take care of your needs. However, if you do not understand accounting basics, you will not know how to input the proper information in order to effectively utilize the software for your business. In the start-up stage of your business, you may best be served by beginning with a few spreadsheets that emulate a manual system. You can always transfer the information into your accounting application when the time is right. At that time, if you are working with an accountant, it will probably be best to use the accounting software application that he or she suggests and one that will easily interface with what is currently being used in that office. Coordinating with your tax accountant may even enable you to work together via Internet transmissions.

Every Business Is Unique

The system you use should be tailored to the needs of your business. Obviously a service-oriented business will not use the same accounts as a retail operation. Because no two businesses will have exactly the same concerns, it is imperative that you set up the right records and accounts. You will have to consider any information that will be used by your particular venture and set up your records according to those needs.

When Does Recordkeeping Begin?

Your business commences as soon as you begin to refine your idea. You do not have to wait until you have a license and are open for business to start with your recordkeeping. In fact, you will do yourself a great disservice if you are not keeping track of financial information at this very moment. Many of your initial expenses are deductible if you have begun to actively pursue your business. A good way to begin is as follows:

- **Deductible Expenses**
  The first thing you should do is familiarize yourself with the expenses that are commonly deductible for a business. When you are doing things that relate to your business begin to think of the costs involved and record them for future use. (See: Chapter 2, "Income and Expenses.")

- **Diary**
  Buy yourself a hardbound journal at your local stationers – or start a journal on your computer. Keep a diary of your thoughts and actions related to your new business. If you use a hardbound journal, number the pages, write in pen, and initial any corrections you make. Your journal will serve to protect your idea as well as provide you with a record of your contacts and the information you gather for the future. You can also list any expenses incurred and file away your receipts. Be sure to date all entries.

- **Beginning Journal**
  I like to utilize the last few pages of the journal to keep a record of income and expenses during the planning stages of a business. It need not be complicated. You can set it up like the sample Beginning Journal provided on page 4. On your computer, you can set up a simple spreadsheet of the same type.

Simplicity is the Key

Simplicity is the key to small business accounting. Your records must be complete, but not so complicated that they cannot be read and interpreted.

It will be the function of this book to introduce you to the terminology and forms necessary to set up an accounting system for your business. My goal is for you to clearly understand how a good accounting system works to provide you with the information you need to satisfy tax requirements, examine trends, make decisions, and implement changes that will make your business venture more profitable and rewarding.

Beginning Journal for ABC Company

Date	1. Check # 2. Cash 3. C/Card	Paid To or Received From	Explanation of Income or Expense	Income		Expense	
1/7/15	Pers. Check 1475	Coastline Community College	Registration for "Small Business Start-Up"			65	00
1/09/15	Cash	Tam's Stationers	Office Supplies			25	63
1/17/15	Cash	Ace Hardware	Tools			71	80
2/03/15	VISA	A-1 Computer	Toshiba Desktop Computer w/Samsung Monitor			821	34
2/03/15	Pers. Check 1493	Office Depot	Epson Printer			328	10
2/29/15	Pers. Check 1493	AT&T	Business Telephone Calls (Jan-Feb)			52	00

 Remember: All expenses relating to your new business endeavor should be recorded. A few examples are as follows:

1. Conference, seminar and workshop fees

2. Mileage to and from business pursuits

3. Meals related to business (see tax rulings)

4. Books, tapes, videos, etc. purchased for business

5. Office supplies (notebooks, journals, pens, etc.)

6. Telephone calls relating to business

7. Professional organizations (dues, fees, etc.)

8. Materials used for developing your product

9. Tools or equipment purchased for your business

There are many other business expenses, including those mentioned under the pages on "Common Deductible Expenses." A good rule of thumb is that when a purchase or activity seems to have any possible bearing on your business, journalize it, keep receipts, look up tax rulings, and then utilize the information accordingly.

Income and Expenses

Accounting for small businesses is based on one premise. Every transaction that takes place involves: 1. money that is earned by the business, 2. money paid out by the business for ordinary and necessary costs, 3. money infused into the business, or 4. money taken out of the business. Earnings and monies paid for ordinary and necessary costs fall under one of two classifications – income or expenses. Before you set up your accounting system, you need to understand some basic facts about the two terms.

Income

Ordinary business income is money earned by your business in any given period of time. It is made up of monies derived from retail and wholesale sales of products, sales of services, interest income, and any miscellaneous income. Money infused by the business owners as a loan or capital contribution is not earned business income and needs to be deposited separately.

All income must be deposited. Do not mix income with money paid out. Under no circumstance do you use part of the money received as income to purchase goods or services (or spend otherwise) and subsequently deposit the remainder.

Expenses

Ordinary and necessary business expenses are the costs of carrying on a trade or business, and they are usually deductible if the business is operated to make a profit. They include expenses paid by check, cash, or credit card. It should be noted that credit card transactions are recorded as expenses when they are charged, not when the bill is paid. All require careful recording.

Expenses fall into distinct categories:

Cost of Goods Sold (Inventory)
- The cost of the merchandise (inventory) sold during an accounting period.
  Cost of goods sold = beginning inventory + purchases – ending inventory.

- Includes material and labor or the purchase price of manufactured goods.

Variable (Selling) Expenses
- Those expenses directly related to the selling of your product or service.
- Includes marketing costs, production salaries, shipping, research and development, packaging, sales commissions, non office salaries, vehicle expenses, travel expenses, vehicle expense and depreciation, machinery and equipment repairs and maintenance and depreciation, and various other product or service overhead.

Fixed (Administrative) Expenses
- These are costs not directly related to your production or rendering of services. They are the type of expenses that all businesses have in common.
- These expenses include normal office overhead such as accounting and legal, bank charges, office salaries, payroll expenses, rents, licenses, office equipment and depreciation, office supplies, telephone, utilities, insurance, etc. Administrative expenses are those that generally remain constant if your business suddenly ceases production or services for a period of time.

Other Expenses
- Interest Expense
- Includes monies paid out for interest on purchases, loans, etc.

Note: Some categories of expense may be divided into both selling (variable) and administrative (fixed). Examples are:

- **Utilities.** Those used for production as differentiated from utilities consumed in the office, heating, restrooms, etc.

- **Telephone.** Telemarketing and advertising are selling expenses. Monthly charges and office telephone charges are administrative expenses.

- **Freight and Postage.** Shipping of your product is a selling expense. Postage used as office overhead is an administrative expense.

The categories into which certain expenses should be placed can be confusing. The important thing to remember is that all expenses must be recorded somewhere. If you erroneously record a selling expense as an administrative expense, it will not carry any serious consequence. However, if you can properly classify expense information, you will have a good basis for analyzing your business and implementing changes.

What Are "Deductible" Expenses?

Deductible expenses are those expenses that are allowed by the IRS when you are computing the net profit (loss) or taxable income at the end of your business tax year. In order to pay the least amount of income tax and maximize your own profits, you need to become familiar with those expenses that you are allowed by law to deduct.

Common Deductible Expenses

The list on the next page will help you to identify many of those items which are normally deductible for income tax purposes. The new business owner should become familiar with those appropriate to the business. DO NOT wait until tax preparation time to look at this list. Knowing ahead of time which expenses are deductible will help you to better utilize them to your advantage while keeping proper records for income tax verification and business analysis. DO keep in mind that this is only a partial list. There may very well be additional deductible expenses relating to your business. Call or visit the IRS. They have free publications that will answer many of your questions. Another source of information is your accounting professional. Be sure to have documentation for all expenses so you can verify them if you are audited.

Fully Deductible or Depreciable?

Expenses fall into two major categories: (1) Those that are deductible in their entirety in the year in which they are incurred, and (2) Those items that are depreciated and deducted over a fixed number of years.

- **Fully deductible expenses.** All expenses incurred in the operation of your business are deductible in their entirety in the year in which they occur and reduce your net income by their amount unless they are major expenses that fall in the depreciable assets category. Expenses will have to be itemized for tax purposes and receipts should be easily retrievable for verification.

- **Depreciable expenses.** If you buy business property that has an expected life in excess of one year and that is not intended for resale, it is considered depreciable property. The cost (generally in excess of $100) can either be expensed in the current year or it can be spread over more than one year and the depreciation deductions claimed over the useful life or recovery period of the property. Depreciable assets generally include such tangible assets as buildings, vehicles, machinery, and equipment, and also intangible properties such as copyrights or franchises. Depreciation is taken at a fixed rate. The portion allowed for the current year is deducted as an expense.

    Under Code Section 179, you can elect to treat all or part of the cost of certain qualifying property as an expense rather than as a depreciable asset. The total cost you could elect to deduct was $500,000 for 2010 thru 2013. The 2014 limit has dropped to $25,000. This maximum applies to each taxpayer and not to each business operated by a taxpayer.

 Caution! *Be sure that you do not list the same costs of any purchase as both a deductible expense and a depreciable asset. For example, if you have purchased a computer for $1,500 and you are depreciating it, be sure that it is not also listed as a fully deductible expense under office equipment. It is wise to keep a separate list of all purchases that might be depreciable. Rules relating to depreciation are complicated. Let your tax accountant make the final determination as to which items should be depreciated or expensed under Section 179.*

Home office expenses. In order for your home to qualify as a business expense, that part of your home used for business must be used "exclusively and on a regular basis." There are also some additional requirements relating to where your income is earned, where you see your clients, etc. For further information on what is and is not allowed, download the free IRS Publication #587, ***Business Use of Your Home.***

Common Deductible Expenses

👉 *There may be other deductible expenses that apply to your business. The ones listed below are the most common.*

DEDUCTIONS TO BE EXPENSED

Advertising - yellow pages, newspaper, radio, direct mail, etc.

Bank Charges - checks, etc.

Books & Periodicals - business-related

Car & Truck Expenses - gas, repair, license, insurance, maintenance (when mileage is not elected)

Commissions - to sales reps.

Contract Services - independent

Convention Expenses

Display & Exhibit Expenses

Donations

Dues - professional

Educational Fees & Materials

Electric Bills

Entertainment of Clients

Freight - UPS, FedEx, Postal, etc.

Gas Bills

Improvements - under $100.00

Insurance - business-related

Interest Paid Out

Laundry/Cleaning - uniforms, etc.

Legal & Professional Fees

License Fees - business license

Maintenance - material & labor

Office Equipment - under $100

Office Furniture - under $100

Office Supplies

Parking Fees

Pension & Profit-Sharing Plans

Postage

Printing Expenses

Professional Services

Promotional Materials

Property Tax

Publications

Rent

Repairs

Refunds, Returns & Allowances

Sales Tax - sales tax collected is offset by reimbursement to the State Board of Equalization

Sales Tax Paid - on purchases

Subscriptions

Telephone

Tools - used in trade and with a purchase price under $100

Uniforms Purchased

Utilities - see gas, electric, and telephone

Wages Paid Out

TO BE DEPRECIATED*

*** Section 179 Deductions:**
You may elect to expense rather than depreciate all or part of qualifying fixed assets purchased during a tax year ($500,000 for 2013; $25,000 for 2014). Be sure to utilize your accountant for depreciation.

Business Property - not land

Office Furniture - over $100

Office Equipment - over $100

Production Machinery

Tangible Purchases - used for business and costing over $100 (not intended for resale)

Tools - purchase price over $100

Vehicles - percentage used for business purposes only

Cash Accounting
Versus Accrual Accounting

There are two different accounting methods based on the timing of the recording and reporting of the income and expenses you learned about in the last chapter. Selecting the method to be used by your company is an important decision that must be made very early in the life of your business. Once it has been established, it is difficult to change due to IRS legalities.

The two methods are (1) cash accounting and (2) accrual accounting. In the following pages, I will explain the difference between the two methods, show you how and when income or expenses would be recorded using each method, and give you some of the pros and cons associated with each method.

"Cash" and "Accrual" Accounting Defined

- **Cash Accounting**
  The reporting of your income (revenues) and expenses at the time they are actually received or paid. A company that uses the cash accounting method is considered to have made a transaction when the cash is physically received or paid out for services or products.

- **Accrual Accounting**
  The recognition of income and expenses at the time they are earned or incurred, regardless of when the cash for the transaction is received or paid out.

Examples Illustrating the Difference

1. Sales/Income Transaction:

On January 16th, ABC Company billed XYZ Company $500 for consulting services. XYZ Company paid the invoice on February 5th.

Accounting Method Used:

- **Cash Basis**
  On January 16th, no recordkeeping entry is required because there has been no cash exchanged between the two companies. ABC Company will not record the sale until it receives payment in February. It will then be recorded and will be considered as a February sale.

- **Accrual Basis**
  On January 16th, the sale is recorded by ABC Company even though no cash has been exchanged. ABC Company is considered to have earned the income on January 16th (the invoice date), even though they will not receive the cash until February 5th. In other words, it is a January sale.

2. Purchase Transaction:

On January 25th, ABC Company purchased $125.32 of office supplies from Office Super Store. Office Super Store bills ABC Company at the end of the month. ABC Company pays the invoice on February 10th.

Accounting Method Used:

- **Cash Basis**
  On January 25th, no recordkeeping entry is made by ABC Company because they did not exchange cash with Office Super Store. ABC Company will not record the expense until they make payment on February 10th. The transaction will be reflected as a February expense.

- **Accrual Basis**
  On January 25th, the expense is recorded by ABC Company even though they did not exchange cash with Office Super Store. ABC Company is considered to have incurred the expense on January 25th when it purchased the office supplies, even though it will not pay for them until February 10th. The transaction will be reflected as a January expense.

Which Method Will You Be Required To Use?

The most popular method used by businesses is the cash basis because it is the most simple and direct to deal with. However, the IRS requires that certain types of businesses use the accrual basis of accounting.

According to the IRS, taxpayers that maintain inventories (i.e. retail stores, wholesalers, manufacturers, etc. whose revenues are generated from the sale of products) must use the accrual method to account for purchases and sales. However, small businesses with average annual gross receipts of $1 million or less are allowed to use the cash method.

There are other circumstances under which accrual accounting is generally used. Also by IRS specifications, C Corporations and businesses that have gross receipts of over $5 million generally use the accrual method of accounting as their overall method of accounting for tax purposes.

In addition, there are a few specific circumstances under which a company may be required to use or exempted from using this method.

Check with Your Tax Accounting Professional

I will give you some of the pros and cons of both methods. However, to make the most intelligent determination as to whether your business should use the accrual basis or the cash basis for your recordkeeping and reporting method, it would be wise to check with your tax accounting professional who can clarify the requirements and help you make your decision.

Pros and Cons of the Two Methods

Pros:

1. Cash Basis:

- Easier of the two methods
- Allows for use of single entry accounting
- Taxes paid only on cash actually received

2. Accrual Basis:

- Provides a better analytical tool because it closely matches income and expenses to the actual period in which the transactions occurred

Cons:

1. Cash Basis:

- Does not closely match income and expenses to the actual period in which the transactions occurred

2. Accrual Basis:

- Requires a more complex double entry system of accounting
- Income tax is paid on income invoiced out, but not yet received

Can You Change Methods from Year to Year?

For IRS purposes, you must choose a method and stay with it. Again, my advice would be to consult with your tax professional before setting up your accounting and select the method that will do the best job for you and satisfy the IRS when you file your tax returns.

Summary

At this point you have taken only the first step in learning about recordkeeping and accounting for your business. The introduction of the accrual and cash accounting methods may very well seem confusing to you at this point. However, because the selection of the appropriate method is an early decision that you will have to make in regard to the timing of the recording and reporting of your income and expenses, I felt that this was a good time to familiarize you with the concept.

Once you have selected either the accrual or cash basis for your accounting, you will be ready to go on to the next section where you will learn about the general records that you will maintain for your company.

Essential General Records for Small Business

In this chapter you will learn about the general records that are used to track the daily transactions of your business. You will also be introduced to single entry and double entry accounting and you will learn how to develop a chart of accounts that is customized to your business. Also in this chapter you will learn about some of the advantages to be gained by using accounting software.

The most common general records are as follows:

- Cash in Bank*
- Income & Expense Journal*
- Invoices & Sales Receipts*
- Petty Cash Record*
- Inventory Records
- Fixed Assets Log*
- Accounts Receivable*
- Accounts Payable*

- Independent Contractor Record
- Payroll Records
- Mileage Log
- Travel & Entertainment Logs
- Customer Records/Database
- Business Checkbook**
- Filing System

Cash in Bank is the accounting software equivalent for the Income & Expense Journal used in manual bookkeeping. Invoicing can be generated and tracked in the software. Petty Cash and Fixed Assets expenditures will be entered in your accounting software. Accounts Receivable and Payable can also be tracked in the application.

**A physical business checkbook will be used for manual bookkeeping. Most accounting software provides for checks to be written and printed directly from within the software. However, if a business prefers, it may use a physical checkbook in preference to, or in addition to, utilizing the check-printing feature.*

Again, I would like to emphasize the need to keep your records as simple as possible. You will need to think about all the things that will pertain to your business and then determine the simplest way to have the information at your fingertips. All of the above records will be discussed and you will learn how they can be used to help you with your business. You will also be shown a filled-in example of each of the records.

In Appendix II, you will find blank forms that you can use as general records for your own business. You may need to customize some of the records to serve your particular industry. You should also eliminate unnecessary records. For instance, if you are a repair business and your customers always pay you when you perform your service, you will not need an "Accounts Receivable" record. You may also wish to develop new records that will help you to keep track of information that will make your business more effective.

☞ **Keep To Standard Formats.** *All of your records will be utilized in the development of your financial statements. For this reason, it will be important to use forms that have been developed using an accepted format. The forms discussed in this section will provide you with records that are easy to use and interpret both by you and by anyone else who has occasion to retrieve information pertaining to your business.*

Single & Double Entry Accounting

There are two basic bookkeeping methods: (1) Single Entry and (2) Double Entry. In the past, only double entry accounting was thought to be proper for businesses. However, it is now generally recognized that a single entry system will adequately serve many very small (micro) businesses. As the business grows and becomes more complex, it will be necessary to move into double entry accounting (best accomplished through the use of accounting software) in which each transaction is posted as a debit to one account and a credit to another. In the past this was done manually through the use of ledger and journal entries utilizing debits and credits. Manual double entry systems have now been replaced by accounting software.

Single Entry

This is a term referring to a bookkeeping system that uses only income and expense accounts. Its main requirement is an Income & Expense Journal that you maintain on a daily basis for recording receipts and expenditures. You will also need to keep General Records in which you record petty cash, fixed assets, accounts payable and receivable, inventory, mileage, travel and entertainment and customer information. (Note: Payroll will be discussed later and should be handled by your accountant.) Single Entry bookkeeping is the easier of the two systems to understand and maintain with a set of individual spreadsheets (or manually) and can be extremely effective and 100% verifiable. However it is seldom used except for very small businesses.

Double Entry

This is an accounting method by which every transaction is recorded in equal amounts as debits and credits. It is based on the premise that every transaction has at least two sides.

A cash purchase of a computer, for example, would be both a receipt of equipment and a payment to the seller. On your Balance Sheet, the receipt of the equipment (the computer) increases your fixed assets and would be recorded as a debit (increase of assets), while the payment to the seller for the computer would decrease your cash in the bank and would be recorded as a credit (reduction of assets).

The two halves of the double entry always have to be equal. Through the utilization of accounting software, the process has been simplified for the user because the transaction is easily entered and matched to its primary account. The software then automatically debits or credits the proper corresponding accounts.

Although, accounting software streamlines the small business accounting process, it still adheres to the adage, "*Garbage In – Garbage Out*". A smart business owner needs to learn the basics of bookkeeping before attempting to set up and utilize accounting software. Even better, have your accountant help with the initial setup to be sure that your chart of accounts is correct – and to ensure that your accounts are properly linked.

Be Sure To Read This!

In the next nine pages, you will be introduced to basic information on double entry accounting and the utilization of accounting software. If your business is small and very simple, you may choose to set up a single entry accounting system and keep your books manually or on a set of spreadsheets. Talk to your accountant if you are in doubt.

★ Micro Businesses Planning to Start with Single Entry Accounting
Skip to Single Entry Bookkeeping on page 25

Note: *Even though you do not plan to immediately utilize software for your business, it would be a wise move to familiarize yourself with the accounting principles presented on pages 16-19 before skipping ahead to the "Income & Expense Journal" where you will begin setting up your own bookkeeping system as described in the rest of the chapter.*

★ Businesses Planning to Use Accounting (Double Entry) Software
Continue to page 16

Important: *If you are a larger, more complex business, you will use accounting software. The next few pages (pages 16-24) will give you a basic understanding of the underlying principles of accounting. Armed with this knowledge, you will be better prepared to work with your accountant to tailor the software setup for your business.*

Before you attempt to set up and use accounting software, you will find it worthwhile to read about the general records that are discussed on pages 26 through 59. It is important to understand what these records are and what information is required by the IRS for each type of deduction. If you take the time to study them, you will find it easier to understand and utilize your accounting software.

Flow of Accounting Data

After a transaction is completed, the initial record of that transaction, or of a group of similar transactions, is evidenced by a business document such as a sales ticket, a check stub, or a cash register tape. On the basis of the evidence provided by that document, transactions are then entered in chronological order in the Accounting Software. The amounts of the debits and the credits are automatically transferred to the proper accounts within the software. The flow of data from transaction to individual accounts may be diagrammed as follows:

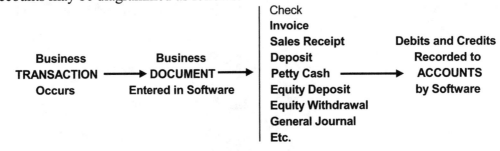

Chart of Accounts

Double Entry/Software Accounting requires that you set up a chart of accounts. These accounts are used when recording transactions in the Software in order that they will be posted to the proper accounts. In the next chapter of this book, we will be discussing Financial Statements. Two of these statements, the Balance Sheet and Income Statement (Profit & Loss), can be automatically generated by your software. The nice thing is that most accounting software will allow you to do so on any day and for any time period you choose. The information utilized to generate a Balance Sheet and Income Statement is derived from the chart of accounts you set up in your software.

Major Divisions of a Chart of Accounts

All accounts in the bookkeeping are divided into the following major divisions:

- ✓ ASSETS
- ✓ LIABILITIES
- ✓ CAPITAL (Net Worth/Equity)
- ✓ INCOME (Revenue)
- ✓ COST OF GOODS SOLD
- ✓ EXPENSES

Each division contains its own individual accounts. Each of these accounts may also be further divided down into sub accounts.

Setting Up a Chart of Accounts

On the following page, I have developed a sample chart of accounts for a fictitious business. Your own accounts will match your operation. Also, as your business progresses, new accounts may be necessary in order to better reflect your company's transactions. Software has the advantage of permitting the later insertion of these new accounts in their proper sequence without disturbing the original setup.

Chart of Accounts For a Fictitious Business	
Balance Sheet Accounts	**Income Statement Accounts**
ASSETS Cash in Bank Petty Cash Accounts Receivable Inventory Prepaid Expenses Fixed Assets Land Buildings Equipment Furniture Vehicles Accumulated Depreciation **LIABILITIES** Notes Payable Accounts Payable Credit Cards Payable Payroll Taxes Taxes Payable **CAPITAL (Equity/Net Worth)** John Jones, Capital John Jones, Drawing Year-to-Date Net Income	**INCOME (REVENUE)** Product Sales, Taxable Product Sales, Non-taxable Services Income **COST OF GOODS SOLD** Material & Labor (Manufacturer) -or- Products Purchased for Resale **EXPENSES** Accounting, Legal, Licenses Bank Charges Commissions on Sales Insurance Interest Expenses Marketing/Advertising Payroll Taxes Salaries/Wages Rent Repair & Maintenance Taxes Travel & Entertainment Utilities Vehicle Expenses

 Your Chart of Accounts Must Match Your Business. *If you have been in business for a period of time, it will be fairly easy to set up your chart of accounts. It will be the categories of assets, liabilities, capital, income, cost-of-goods and expenses that you have been keeping track of in the past. If you are a new business, deciding on your initial chart of accounts will take some thought. I suggest that you look at each category and determine what things you will be dealing with in your business. Assets, liabilities, and capital will be fairly standard and match those you will use in a balance sheet. Income, cost of goods, and expenses will be according to the kind of business you are operating. Income accounts will be the major types of products and/or services you offer. Cost of goods accounts are the costs related to the products you will sell. Expenses accounts are determined by the kinds of selling and administrative expenses that your company will have. Your accountant is the best person to help you with the chart of accounts setup.*

Debits & Credits

All double-entry accounting – and all accounting software – is based on the premise that every transaction affects at least two accounts. For every entry you make, one account(s) will be debited and the other(s) will be credited. And the debits <u>must</u> equal the credits.

Computer software will automatically take care of both sides of this entry. When you enter the transaction as a check or into a check register the software will credit (decrease) your bank account (asset) and you will record the account to which the expense applies, office supplies. Office supplies (expense) will then be debited (increased).

What are debits and credits? When you are recording transactions in an accounting application, you will be asked to choose the account (from your chart of accounts) to which the transaction applies. Your choice will trigger the software to debit and credit the proper accounts. For this reason, it is not imperative that you have a clear understanding of the terms "debit" and "credit". However, taking time to learn how debits and credits work in the background, will help you to better understand what is happening in the accounting process.

There is a well-known accounting equation that must always remain true in your business bookkeeping. The equation is as follows:

Assets-Liabilities = Net Worth (Equity/Capital)

The accounting equation is kept in balance through the double entry system. In the sample Chart of Accounts we set up six categories. Increases and decreases in each of these accounts are represented by debits or credits (generally) as follows:

	Increase	**Decrease**
Assets	Debit	Credit
Liabilities	Credit	Debit
Net Worth (Equity/Capital)	Credit	Debit
Income (Revenue)	Credit	Debit
Cost of Goods Sold	Debit	Credit
Expenses	Debit	Credit

Example 1: When you buy office supplies with a check you must credit (decrease) your bank account (an asset) and you will debit (increase) your office expense account (expense). One is debited and the other is credited in an equal amount.

Example 2: Another example of the accuracy of double entry accounting would be the purchase of an asset with borrowed funds. You purchase $10,000 worth of office furniture and equipment, you make a down payment of $1,000 and take a loan for the $9,000 balance. The correct (double entry) entry for this transaction would be:

	Debit	Credit
Office Furniture (Increase – Asset)	$10,000	
Loan (Increase – Liability)		$9,000
Cash in Bank (Decrease –Asset)		$1,000

Note: *The Debits and the Credits balance ($10,000), but the "increases" and the "decreases" do not have to balance. This can be confusing to many small business owners.*

The next step in this transaction would be the loan payment. If your payment is $300 per month, this payment consists of two parts, principal payment (decrease liability) and interest (increase expense). If this entry is correctly reported each month your balance sheet will correctly reflect the balance due on your loan.

Why didn't I think of this? Thanks to Peter Hupalo, author of *Thinking Like an Entrepreneur* (HMC Publications), I have learned a simple rule that makes the understanding of debits and credits much easier. It is this: The one giving in the transaction is the credit(or), and the one receiving in the transaction is the debit(or). For example, if you sell one hour of your service, Service Income is the giver (so it's credited) and Cash in the Bank is the receiver (so cash is debited) and increased.

– A Peek into Software Accounting –

The next few pages will give you a glimpse as to how the use of Software/Double Entry Accounting can be used to streamline the flow of information from transaction to financial reporting. Although I have not targeted the use of software to micro businesses, it is equally as appropriate for the smallest of companies. The choice between manual and computer accounting is strictly by choice.

I have chosen QuickBooks Pro® by Intuit as the application I will use to illustrate some of the tasks that can be accomplished by using accounting software. This is not to be construed as an endorsement of QuickBooks Pro® in preference to other accounting software applications. I do use it in my own business and have found it to be effective for my company. It is my understanding that most popular accounting software packages will perform the same basic functions.

If you do not use a computer and you intend to set up a manual bookkeeping system, feel free to skip this section. Move ahead to the "Income & Expense Journal" and start there with the setting up of your accounting records.

★ An Overview of Four Accounting Tasks
Using QuickBooks Pro®

1. Invoicing

Invoicing is the process of billing a customer for sales or services that are provided, ***but not due to be paid until a future time***. If you use the accrual method of accounting, these invoices are your "Accounts Receivable".

The Invoice is entered in your accounting software on a screen that will look similar to the one below:

In this case Sophia Carrillo, the customer, purchased $110 in custom landscape design services, to be paid Net 30. When the invoice information is entered and saved (11/15/2014), accounts receivable will automatically be debited (increased) for $110 (the amount of the invoice). The software will credit the matching income account (custom landscape design) in an equal amount.

When the invoice is paid (12/15/2014) and the funds are entered either as an undeposited check or a deposit to cash in bank, the invoice will automatically be marked as paid. At that time, the software will credit (decrease) accounts receivable in the amount of $110 and debit undeposited checks or cash in bank.

By the time the sale has been invoiced, recorded as paid, and subsequently deposited, the information will also automatically have been factored into the company's profit & loss (income) statement and balance sheet – perfectly completing the accounting process.

2. Entering a Sales Receipt

Sales Receipts are entered for sales or service transactions that are *paid for with cash, checks, or credit cards at the time of purchase.* After entering the information, a sales receipt can be printed as an original and copy for you and your customer or you can enter the information after the fact strictly as an accounting task.

The Sales Receipt screen in your accounting software might look similar to the one below:

In this case the customer, John Smith, purchased $100 in tree removal service and paid with a check.

When the sales receipt information is input and the transaction saved, undeposited funds will automatically be debited (increased) for $100 (the amount of the sales receipt. At the same time the software will credit the matching account (tree removal service) in an equal amount.

When the check is later deposited to cash in bank, the software will credit (decrease) undeposited funds in the amount of $100 and debit (increase) cash in bank for an equal amount.

Again, the information will also automatically have been factored into the company's profit & loss (income) statement and balance sheet, completing the accounting process.

3. Writing a Check

Your company's checks can be written, printed, and the amount recorded (debited and credited) to the proper accounts in a single operation.

The Check Writing window in your accounting software might look similar to this QuickBooks© screen:

In this case the Computer Services by DJ charged the company $243.57 for installing a new version of Windows® and for reinstalling and setting up the company's other software applications.

A check was written to pay for the service. During input, Repairs: Computer Repairs was selected as the account related to the expense. The software then debited that account (increased computer repair expense account). At the same time the software credited (decreased) the matching account, Cash in Bank, also in the amount of $243.57.

The check was also printed out, complete with address to insert in a windowed envelope, ready to stamp and mail to DJ Computers.

As before, the information will also automatically have been factored into the company's profit & loss (income) statement and balance sheet to complete the accounting process.

4. Cash in Bank
(Software Check Register)

When you deposit or transfer funds, write checks, earn interest, record bank charges during reconciliation, or record any other transaction that either adds or removes money from your bank account, it will automatically be reflected in your Cash In Bank account.

This account serves the same purpose as your check register in a bound checkbook. At any time, you can review the checks you have written and deposits or withdrawals that have been made to your account.

The Cash in Bank window may look similar to the screen below:

Date	Number / Type	Payee / Account	Memo	Payment	✓	Deposit	Balance
12/15/2014	DEP	-split-	Deposit			4,035.00	42,661.06
12/15/2014	DEP	Undeposited Funds	Deposit **1**			110.00	42,771.06
12/15/2014	DEP	Washinton Mutual Bank	Deposit			15.00	42,786.06
12/15/2014	Transfer CHK	Undeposited Funds	Deposit **2**			100.00	42,881.06
12/15/2014	1459 CHK	DJ's Computers	Repairs:Computer Re Inv. 7032245 **3**	243.57			42,637.49
12/15/2014	To Print BILLPMT	Middlefield Nursery	Accounts Payable 09876	240.00			42,397.49
12/15/2014	To Print BILLPMT	Patio & Desk Designs	Accounts Payable DE-0918	1,275.00			41,122.49

Ending balance   34,612.49

Splits   ☐ 1-Line   Sort by [Date, Type, Number/Rel ▼]   Record   Restore

To show the flow of information from the preceding three transactions described through to Cash in Bank, I have marked them 1, 2, and 3 to correspond with each of the transactions.

Note: In reality, the company would have grouped any undeposited funds together and made one deposit. For purposes of this example, each of the transactions has been entered and deposited separately so that you would be able to follow them more easily.

Summary: Accounting Software

The information on the preceding pages has been meant to serve as an introduction to accounting software. The days of manually posting transactions to journals and ledgers are gone. Computer technology has ushered accounting into a new generation. The benefit for business owners is the opportunity to participate at a higher level in the financial administration of their businesses.

Invoicing, Sales Receipts, Check Writing, and the subsequent flow of information into a Cash in Bank Register are among the important basic features found in most accounting software applications. However, these processes represent only a small portion of the accounting procedures that can now be done electronically. It has already been mentioned, that various accounting software applications can enable you to generate an income (profit & loss) statement and balance sheet at any time and for any chosen period. Some other advantages available include such things as:

- Accounts receivable tracking
- Accounts payable tracking
- Petty cash accounting
- Bank statement reconciliation
- Customer reports
- Generation of 1099 information
- Inventory tracking

Choosing the Right Software for Your Business

There are many different accounting software packages on the market. Some are designed as general accounting applications and some are designed for specific industries. Some have basic packages as well as more advanced ones with modules added to accomplish certain tasks.

It is up to you to select the software that is most appropriate for your business. However, I would suggest that you work with your accountant to find the accounting package that will best accommodate both of you. Your accountant can then help you with the setup, work with problem solving throughout the year, and easily transfer your end-of-year information at tax reporting time. The end result will be the maximizing of profits for your business.

 Important Note to Accounting Software Users:
If you are planning to use accounting software, you can skip pages 25-29. However, on pages 30-60, you will learn about the various general records that a business is required to keep. **Don't skip this section.** There is a lot to learn that will be of value to you as you use the accounting software of your choice.

This Is the Beginning
of
* Single Entry Bookkeeping *

This is where you will begin if you are going to maintain your records by the single entry accounting method. At this point you will begin to set up your General Records as presented in the remainder of the chapter, beginning with the Income & Expense Journal.

Flow of Accounting Data

If you read the information on double entry/software accounting, you learned that when business transaction occurs, that transaction is recorded within the software, debiting and crediting related accounts selected from your Chart of Accounts.

You should remember that there are six major types of accounts (Assets, Liabilities, Capital/Equity, Income/Revenue, Cost of Goods Sold, and Expenses). These same accounts will be used in your manual bookkeeping system. You will develop a better understanding of these divisions as you progress through the General Records. They should become even clearer by the time you complete the Financial Statement Section of the book.

The advantage of single entry bookkeeping for micro business owners is that the recording of transaction is accomplished by simply entering income and expenses on a single form and requires no formal accounting education. You are still required to keep those general records pertinent to your business (such as Petty Cash, Accounts Receivable and Payable, Fixed Assets, Travel and Entertainment, Inventory, etc.), but in a very simple and logical way that can still provide for perfect retrieval of needed tax and business analysis information.

With this method the flow of accounting data will be as follows:

		Entry
Business	**Business**	**Recorded in**
TRANSACTION ⟶	**DOCUMENT** ⟶	**INCOME & EXPENSE JOURNAL**

Now you are ready to setup your bookkeeping system. I will take you a step at a time through the entire process and explain each of the general records that you will need. Turn to the next page and begin with the *Income & Expense Journal.*

★ Income & Expense Journal

The Income & Expense Journal is used to record the transactions of a business that involve earnings and ordinary expenses. They are recorded as income and expenses.

1. **Income** transactions are those for which money that your business has earned is received. Equity and loan fund deposits are not income. Record equity deposits in your checkbook deposits, but not in the Income & Expense Journal.

2. **Expenses** are ordinary and necessary transactions for which monies are paid out. Owner draws and principal payments on business loans are not expenses. Record only the interest payment on the loan and reference the check number used for the payment in the Revenue & Expense Journal. The check with the actual amount of the payment will be recorded in your checkbook register.

To make your accounting more effective, you will need to have enough columns in the Income & Expense Journal to cover major categories of income and expenses (or create two separate forms (i.e., one for income and one for expenses). If you have done your homework and figured out the areas of direct and indirect expenses, these divisions will serve as headings in your journal. Usually, a 12-column journal will suffice for most small businesses, but feel free to use more or less, as long as your report is clear and easy to interpret.

Avoiding Errors

The Income & Expense Journal is an important part of your bookkeeping. On this form, **each entry is recorded twice** to help with checks and balances at the end of each month. If you will look on the sample form, the first two columns are headed "Income" and "Expense". Every transaction is entered in one of these two columns. The next groups of three and five columns are breakdowns of revenues and expenses. The entry is first recorded as an income or expense and then entered in its corresponding breakdown column.

For example, an advertising expense of $100 would be entered under the heading, "Expense" and also under the expense breakdown heading, "Advertising". When the columns are totaled, the amount under "Expense" will equal the sum of all expense breakdown columns. The "Income" total will equal the sum of all income breakdown columns. This serves as a check for accuracy and will save hours of searching your records for errors when attempting to balance your books.

Headings in the Income & Expense Journal

The column headings in the income & expense journal for any business will follow the same format. The first five columns headings are:

1. **Check No.**
2. **Date**
3. **Transaction**
4. **Income**
5. **Expense**

The remaining columns are used for individual income and expense categories that will reflect the most common sources of your business deposits for earned income and the kinds of ordinary business expenses for which you most frequently write checks.

1. **Income breakdown columns** will be divided by source (e.g., as a book publisher and teacher, I might choose these categories: Sales, Sales Tax, Royalties, Seminar Fees, etc.).

2. **Expense breakdown columns** reflect the categories for which you most frequently write a check (e.g., Inventory Purchases, Shipping, Advertising, Office Supplies, Utilities, Vehicle Expenses, etc.). The last column heading should be "Miscellaneous" (see two paragraphs below).

The headings for the individual income and expense columns will vary from business to business. Every business is different and it may take some time to determine the categories that will best reflect the transactions of your particular venture.

If you are coordinating your bookkeeping with a tax accountant, you might ask that person to help you develop your headings. The best rule of thumb is to devote a column to each type of expense for which you frequently write a check.

Miscellaneous Column

The last column in the Income & Expense Journal should be Miscellaneous. This column serves as a catchall for any expense that does not fall under a main heading. For example, insurance may be paid only once a year and, therefore, a heading under that title would not be justified. Record that transaction first under Expense and secondly under Miscellaneous with an explanation either under the Transaction Column or in parenthesis next to the amount in the Miscellaneous Column.

For example, you write only one check every six months, in the amount of $500, for insurance. You enter it as "$500 (insurance)". The explanation is a must. This will allow you to group infrequent expenses under one column and still be able to allocate them to the proper expense categories at the end of the month when you do a Profit & Loss (or Income) Statement.

Totals

Each column should be totaled at the bottom of each journal page. (Remember to check accuracy. The sum of all income breakdown columns = the sum of the column headed "Revenue" and the sum of all expense breakdown columns = the sum of the columns headed "Expense".) All totals are then transferred to the top of the next page and added in until you have completed a month.

At the end of the month, the last page is totaled and checked. The breakdown revenue and expense totals are transferred to your Profit and Loss Statement and a new month begins with a clean page and all zero balances.

Sample Income & Expense Journal

In order for you to better understand how to develop and make entries in your own Income & Expense Journal, we will: (1) create headings for a fictitious company, (2) enter six transactions, and (3) total the page.

1. **The headings are determined:**

    a. The first five and the last column are standard: (Check No., Date, Transaction, Income, Expense and Miscellaneous)

    b. The individual income headings are determined. (Our company sells and services computers. We want to know how much of our income comes from sales and how much comes from service. We also want to know how much sales tax is collected. The column headings are: Sales, Sales Tax and Service)

    c. The individual expense columns are determined. (Checks are most frequently written to purchase inventory, advertise, ship orders and purchase office supplies. The column headings are: Inventory Purchases, Advertising, Freight and Office Supplies)

2. **The transactions are as follows:**

    a. This is the second journal page used for the month of July. The totals from the first page are brought forward and entered on the line entitled "Balance forward".

    b. The new transactions to be entered are as follows:

    (1) Check 234, dated July 13th, was written to J.J. Advertising to pay for an advertising promotion. ($450.00)

    (2) Check 235, dated July 13th, was written to T & E Products to buy a computer to resell to a customer. ($380.00)

    (3) Check 236, dated July 16th, was written to Regal Stationers for office supplies. ($92.50)

    (4) $1232.00 was deposited in the bank. ($400.00 + $32.00 sales tax came from taxable sales, $165.00 in sales were sold to an out-of-state customer; $370.00 was for a sale to another reseller; $265.00 was received for repairing a customer's computer)

    (5) The bank statement was reconciled on July 19th. (The bank charged $23.40 for new checks)

    (6) Check 237 dated July 19th was written to Petty Cash. ($100.00 was deposited to the Petty Cash Account)

3. **The journal page is full. Total and check columns:**

    a. Add individual income columns and check to see that the sum of their totals equals the total of the Income column. ($3,058.00)

    b. Add individual expense columns and check to see that the sum of their totals equals the total of the Expense column. ($1,880.90)

ABC Company
Income & Expense Journal

July 2014, page 2

CHECK NO.	DATE	TRANSACTION	INCOME	EXPENSE	SALES	SALES TAX	SERVICES	INVENTORY PURCHASES	ADVERTISING	FREIGHT	OFFICE SUPPLIES	MISCELL
		Balance forward—	1,826 00	835 00	1,218 00	98 00	510 00	295 00	245 00	150 00	83 50	61 50
234	7/13	J. J. Advertising		450 00					450 00			
235	7/13	T & E Products		380 00				380 00				
236	7/16	Regal Stationers		92 50							92 50	
***	7/17	Deposit:	1,232 00									
		1. Sales (taxable)			400 00	32 00						
		2. Sales (out of state)			165 00	O.S.						
		3. Sales (resale)			370 00	Resale						
		4. Services					265 00					
O.K. BANK	7/19	Bank charges		23 40								(bank chg) 23 40
237	7/19	Petty Cash deposit		100 00								(p/cash) 100 00
		TOTALS	3,058 00	1,880 90	2,153 00	130 00	775 00	675 00	695 00	150 00	176 00	184 90

★ Petty Cash Record

Petty cash refers to all the small business purchases made with cash or personal funds instead of with a business check. These purchases may account for several thousand dollars by the end of the year. Failure to account for them can result in a false picture of your business and additional cost in income taxes. It is imperative that you keep an accurate record of all Petty Cash Expenditures, that you have receipts on file, and that you record them in a manner that will enable you to categorize these expenses at the end of an accounting period.

Where Do Petty Cash Funds Come From?

In order to transfer cash into the Petty Cash Fund, you must first draw a check and expense it to Petty Cash in the Income & Expense Journal (See entry in Income & Expense Journal). That same amount is entered in the Petty Cash Record as a deposit. When cash purchases are made, they are entered in the Petty Cash Record as Expenses. When the balance gets low, another check is drawn to rebuild the fund. At the end of the tax year, you can let the balance run as a negative, write a final check in that amount and deposit it to Petty Cash to zero out the fund. The end result will be that you will have deposited an amount that is exactly equal to your petty cash expenditures for the year.

Petty Cash Format

The two purposes of Petty Cash Accounting are: (1) To account for personal expenditures relating to business; and (2) To provide information that will classify those expenses for income tax retrieval and for business analysis. Any accountant will warn you that a large miscellaneous deduction will be suspect and may very well single your return out for an IRS audit. Dividing your Petty Cash Record into the following categories will provide for individual purchases to be summarized, combined with expenses on the Income & Expense Journal, and entered on the Profit & Loss Statement.

- **Date of transaction**
- **Paid to whom**
- **Expense account debited**
- **Deposit**
- **Amount of expense**
- **Balance**

 Sample petty cash record. On the next page you will see how deposits and expenses are recorded. If a cash expense also needs to be entered in another record (Inventory, Fixed Assets, etc.), do so at the same time to keep the record current and eliminate omissions.

ABC Company

Petty Cash Record

PETTY CASH - 2014					Page 6	

DATE		PAID TO WHOM	EXPENSE ACCOUNT DEBITED	DEPOSIT		AMOUNT OF EXPENSE		BALANCE	
		BALANCE FORWARD						10	00
July	19	✳✳ Deposit (Ck. 237)		100	00			110	00
	20	ACE Hardware	Maintenance			12	36	97	64
	23	Regal Stationers	Office Supplies			20	00	77	64
	23	U.S. Postmaster	Postage			19	80	57	84
	31	The Steak House	Meals			63	75	(5	91)
Aug	1	✳✳ Deposit (Ck. 267)		100	00			94	09

Toward the end of the year, you can let the Petty Cash account run a minus balance. On December 31st, a check is written for the balance and the account is zeroed out.

The amount of cash spent during the year will be exactly equal to the amount deposited into the Petty Cash Account from your checking account.

Note:
1. Save all receipts for cash purchases.
2. Exchange receipt for cash from petty cash drawer.
3. Use receipts to record expenses on petty cash form.
4. File receipts. You may need them for verification.
5. Be sure to record petty cash deposits.

★ Inventory Record

The term inventory is used to designate: (1) Merchandise held for sale in the normal course of business; and (2) Materials in the process of production or held for such use. The recording of inventories is used both as an internal control and as a means of retrieval of information required for the computation of income tax.

The Great Inventory Myth

Before proceeding with the mechanics of keeping your inventory, I would like to clear up a misconception about the pros and cons of the relationship of inventory size and income tax due. Any business that has had to deal with inventory will almost certainly have heard the statement, "Put your cash into inventory. The larger it is, the few taxes you will have to pay." Conversely, you may also hear that if your inventory is reduced, your taxes will also be reduced. Both are nonsense statements, and I will prove it to you mathematically. The fact is that your net profit remains the same regardless of the amount reinvested in inventory. Ten thousand dollars is $10,000 in your checking account or on the shelves as saleable goods. This can be proved as follows:

Companies A & B: 1. Both had beginning inventories of $25,000.

2. Both had gross sales of $30,000.

3. Both sold their product at 100% markup and reduced their beginning inventory by $15,000.

Company A: Reinvested $20,000 in inventory and deposited $10,000. This gave them an ending inventory of $30,000.

Company B: Reinvested $5,000 in inventory and deposited $25,000. The result was an ending inventory of $15,000.

Net Profit is arrived at by subtracting deductible expenses from your Gross Profit. The following computation will prove that Companies A & B will in fact have the same Gross Profit (and will not have their Net Profit affected by the amount of reinvestment in inventory):

	Company A	Company B
1. Beginning Inventory	$25,000	$25,000
2. Purchases	$20,000	$ 5,000
3. Add lines 1 & 2	$45,000	$30,000
4. Less Ending Inventory	$30,000	$15,000
5. Cost of Goods Sold (sub 4 from 3)	$15,000	$15,000
6. Gross Receipts or Sales	$30,000	$30,000
7. Less Cost of Goods Sold (line 5)	$15,000	$15,000
8. GROSS PROFIT (line 6 minus 7)	**$15,000**	**$15,000**

The Gross Profits Are Exactly The Same!

It is very important that you understand the above concept. Inventory only affects your net profit as a vehicle to greater sales potential. How much or how little you stock at tax time will neither increase nor decrease your taxes. Companies A and B will both have a gross profit of $15,000 and will be taxed the same. Some states, however, may have inventory taxes and this could enter in as a factor.

Inventory Control

Keeping records for the IRS is actually the lesser reason for keeping track of inventory. I personally know of two companies that nearly failed due to a lack of inventory control. One was a restaurant whose employees were carrying groceries out the back door at closing time. Although, the restaurant enjoyed a good clientele and followed sound business practices for the food industry, their year-end profit did not justify their existence. A careful examination of their records showed a failure to properly inventory their stock. By instituting strict inventory control, pilferage was ended and the next years increase in profit saved the business. Inventory control in a retail business can help you to see such things as turnover time, high and low selling periods, and changes in buying trends. Periodic examinations of your inventory and its general flow may be the meat of your existence.

Format for Inventory Records

Basic inventory records must contain the following information in order to be effective.

- **Date purchased**
- **Item purchased** (include stock no.)
- **Purchase price** (cost)
- **Date sold**   (Information on sale date and selling price are helpful for
- **Sale price**   determining shelf life and market value trends for your product.)

If your inventory is at all sizeable, you will want to use some sort of Point of Sale (P.O.S.) inventory system. However, it is possible to keep it in hand-written form based on two premises: (1) You begin immediately; and (2) You keep it current and do it regularly. My husband owns a clock shop with approximately two thousand items for sale. On any given day, he knows how long he has had each item, which items are selling repeatedly and what time periods require the stocking of more inventory. Keep in mind that all businesses differ.

Compile your inventory according to your specific needs. Be sure that it is divided in such a way as to provide quick reference. I sort mine out by using separate pages for each company from which I make my purchases. Another method might be to separate pages by type of item. The important thing is to make your inventory record work for you.

Common Kinds of Inventory

- Merchandise or stock in trade
- Raw materials
- Work in process
- Finished products
- Supplies (that become a part of a product intended for sale)

To arrive at a dollar amount for your inventory, you will need a method for identifying and a basis for valuing the items in your inventory. Inventory valuation must clearly show income and, for that reason, you must use this same inventory practice from year to year.

Cost Identification Methods

There are three methods that can be used to identify items in inventory. They are as follows:

1. **Specific Identification Method.** In some businesses it is possible to keep track of inventory and to identify the cost of each inventoried item by matching the item with its cost of acquisition. In other words, there is specific identification of merchandise and you can determine the exact cost of what is sold. There is no question as to which items remain in the inventory. Merchants who deal with items having a large unit cost or with one-of-a-kind items may choose to keep track of inventory by this method.

For those businesses dealing with a large quantity of like items, there must be a method for deciding which items were sold and which remain in inventory.

2. **FIFO (first-in-first-out)** assumes that the items you purchased or produced first are the first sold. This method most closely parallels the actual flow of inventory. Most merchants will attempt to sell their oldest inventory items first and hopefully will have the last items bought in current inventory.

3. **LIFO (last-in-first-out)** assumes that the items of inventory that you purchased or produced last are sold first. You must check tax rules to qualify before electing this method. (See regulations under section 472 of the Internal Revenue Code.)

The FIFO and LIFO methods produce different results in income depending on the trend of price levels of inventory items. In a period of rising prices, valuing your inventory by the LIFO method will result in a higher reported cost of goods sold and a lower reported net income. This is because it is assumed that you sold goods purchased at the higher price. Conversely, in a period of falling prices, the LIFO method would result in a lower reported cost of goods sold and a higher reported net income than the FIFO method.

Valuing Inventory

The two common ways to value your inventory if you use the FIFO method are the specific cost identification method and the lower of cost or market method. If at the end of your tax year the market price of items in your inventory decline, you may elect to use the following method of evaluation:

- **Cost or market, whichever is lower.** At inventory time, if your merchandise cannot be sold through usual trade channels for a price that is above its original cost, the current market price is determined and compared to your accepted costing method (FIFO, LIFO, or Specific Identification). The lower figure, "cost" or "market" is selected. This is especially useful for outdated inventory. If you use this method you must value each item in the inventory.

- **You must be consistent.** As a new business using **FIFO**, you may use either the cost method or the lower of cost or market method to value your inventory. However, you must use the same method consistently and, again, you must use it to value your entire inventory. You **may not** change to another method without permission of the IRS.

Physical Inventories

You must take physical inventories at reasonable intervals and the book figure for inventory must be adjusted to agree with the actual inventory. The IRS requires a beginning and ending inventory for your tax year.

 Sample Inventory Records

The sample inventory record on the next page is for the "Specific Identification Method" of taking inventory. Remember, it is for inventory of those products which differ from each other and can be individually accounted for as to purchase date, description and cost.

The sample inventory record two pages ahead is for "Non-Identifiable Inventory". An example would be the purchase or production of 2,000 units of a like item -- the first thousand being produced at a unit cost of $5 and the second at a unit cost of $6. It would be impossible to determine which remain in inventory. They must be identified by the FIFO or LIFO method and valued accordingly to figure taxable income.

More information on inventory rules. Please read "Cost of Goods" in the IRS Publication 334, *"Tax Guide for Small Business"*.

ABC Company
Inventory Record — Identifiable Stock

WHOLESALER: _All Time Clock Company_   **Page** _1_

PURCH DATE	INVENTORY PURCHASED		PURCH. PRICE		DATE SOLD	SALE PRICE		NAME OF BUYER (Optional)
	Stock #	Description						
9/23/13	25-72-D	Oak Gallery (25")	352	00				
11/19/13	24-37-A	Desk Alarm (1)	18	00	12/08/13	28	50	N/A
		(2)	18	00				
		(3)	18	00				
2/21/14	26-18-C	"The Shelby" GF	1,420	00	4/20/14	1,865	00	J. Kirkland
3/19/14	25-67-D	Mahog. Regulator	27	00				
5/04/14	26-18-C	"The Shelby" GF	1,420	00				

Note: 1. Use this record for keeping track of identifiable goods purchased for resale. If your inventory is very large, it may be necessary to use some sort of *Point-of-Sale* inventory system.

2. Each page should deal with either: (1) purchases in one category, or (2) goods purchased from one wholesaler.

3. Use the name of the wholesaler or the category of the purchase as the heading.

ABC Company
Inventory Record—Non-Identifiable Stock

DEPARTMENT/CATEGORY: _Ski Hats / Headwear_

PRODUCTION OR PURCHASE DATE	INVENTORY PURCHASED OR MANUFACTURED		NUMBER OF UNITS	UNIT COST		VALUE ON DATE OF INVENTORY (Unit Cost X Units on Hand)	
	Stock #	Description				Value	Date
2/05/13	07-43	Knitted Headbands	5,000	2	50	0	1/13
3/25/13	19-12	Face Masks	3,000	5	12	450.80	1/13
9/14/13	19-10	Hat/Mask Combo	1,200	7	00	3,514.00	1/13
4/18/14	19-09	Hats, Multi-Colored	10,500	4	00	5,440.00	1/13
8/31/14	19-07	Gortex (w/bill)	10,000	8	41	50,460.00	1/13
BEGIN 2015							
2/01/15	19-12	Face Masks	2,500	4	80		
2/28/15	19-09	Hats, Multi-Colored	10,300	4	00		

Note: 1. This record is used for inventory of like items that are manufactured or purchased in bulk. It is a good idea to divide your records by department, category, or by manufacturer.

2. Inventory of these items is done by a physical count or by computer records. A physical inventory is required at the close of your tax year.

3. Inventory is valued according to rules that apply for **FIFO** or **LIFO** (*first in first out* or *last in first out*). The selected method must be used consistently. In order to understand and apply rules for inventory evaluation, refer to IRS Publication 334, *Tax Guide for Small Business.*

★ Fixed Assets Log

At the end of each tax year you will have to provide your accountant with a list of all assets for which depreciation is allowed. Many different kinds of property can be depreciated, such as machinery, buildings, vehicles, furniture, equipment. These are items purchased for use in your business usually at a cost in excess of $100.

What Can Be Depreciated?

In general, property is depreciable if it meets these requirements:

- It must be used in business or held for the production of income.
- It must have a determinable life and that life must be longer than one year.
- It must be something that wears out, decays, gets used up, becomes obsolete or loses value from natural causes.

You can never depreciate land, rented property or the cost of repairs that do not increase the value of your property. You cannot depreciate your inventory or any item that you intend for resale.

Section 179 Deduction

You can elect to treat all or part of the cost of certain depreciable property as an expense rather than as a capital expenditure. The total cost you can elect to deduct for a calendar tax year was increased to $500,000 for 2013. In January 2014, that amount was restored to its original limit of $25,000 plus an adjustment for inflation. In lay terms, instead of depreciating assets placed in service during the current year, you may be allowed to directly expense them up to the limit for that year. There are some restrictions that apply and you will need the help of your accountant to make the final decision for tax purposes.

Keeping Track Of Fixed Assets

You will need to keep an inventory of depreciable purchases made during the current tax year. You will also have to be able to tell your accountant if any of these purchases were entered in your Income & Expense Journal to avoid double-expensing. Be aware that you are also accountable for disposition of these items. If you have depreciated an automobile down to $2,000 and then sell it for $3,500, you will have to report a profit of $1,500. Depreciation can be very tricky and the laws change. Your job is to be able to provide your accountant with basic information. Your accountant must then apply the law to maximize your benefits.

 Sample fixed assets log. The form that follows will help you to do your part and have a general overview of what assets you have that fall in this category.

ABC Company
Fixed Assets Log

COMPANY NAME: _____ABC Company_____

ASSET PURCHASED	DATE PLACED IN SERVICE	COST OF ASSET	% USED FOR BUSINESS	RECOVERY PERIOD	METHOD OF DEPRECIATION	DEPRECIATION PREVIOUSLY ALLOWED	DATE SOLD	SALE PRICE
2010 Dodge Van	1/08/10	18,700 00	80%	5 yr.	MACRS	15,469 00	12/05/14	8,500 00
IBM Computer	7/15/12	6,450 00	100%	5 yr.	MACRS	3,620 00		
Canon Copier	2/29/12	3,000 00	100%	5 yr.	MACRS	1,469 00		
Fence	6/17/12	4,500 00	100%	15 yr.	MACRS	600 00		
2014 Lexus 350	12/05/13	51,500 00	80%	5 yr.	MACRS			
Desk (Office)	3/15/14	1,500 00	100%	5 yr.	MACRS			

Note: See IRS Publication 334, *Tax Guide for Small Business,* for more detailed information on depreciation. Also see Publications 534, 544, and 551.

★ Accounts Receivable

An accounts receivable record is used to keep track of money owed to your business as a result of extending credit to a customer who purchases your products or services. Some businesses deal in cash transactions only. In other words, the product or service is paid for at the time of the sale. If this is the case in your business, you will not need accounts receivable records. However, if you do extend credit, the amount owed to you by your credit customers will have to be collected in a timely manner to provide you with the cash needed for day-to-day operations. It will be essential to have detailed information about your transactions and to always know the balance owed to you for each invoice. This can be accomplished by setting up a separate accounts receivable record for each customer.

Format for Accounts Receivable

In order to ensure that you have all the information needed to verify that customers are paying balances on time and that they are within credit limits, the form used will need to include these categories:

1. **Invoice Date.** This will tell you the date the transaction took place and enable you to age the invoice.

2. **Invoice Number.** Invoices are numbered and can be filed in order. If you need to refer to the invoice, the number makes it easy to retrieve.

3. **Invoice Amount.** Tells how much the customer owes for each invoice.

4. **Terms.** Tells the time period allowed until invoice is due and also if a discount applies. (Ex: "Net 30 / 2% Net 10" means the invoice is due in 30 days, but a 2% discount will be allowed if payment is made in 10 days.)

5. **Date Paid.** Shows when the invoice was paid.

6. **Amount Paid.** Shows whether the customer made a partial payment or paid the invoice in full.

7. **Invoice Balance.** Tells what portion of the invoice is not paid.

8. **Header Information.** The customer's name, address and phone number will tell you where to send statements and how to make contact.

At the end of a predetermined billing period, each open account will be sent a statement showing their invoice number and amounts, balance due and preferably age of balances (over 30, 60, or 90 days). The statement should also include terms of payment. When the payment is received, it is recorded on the accounts receivable record. The total of all the outstanding balances in Accounts Receivable is transferred to Current Assets when preparing a Balance Sheet for your business.

 Sample accounts receivable record. The form on the next page contains a sample form to show you how it should be filled out. There is a blank form in Appendix II for you to copy and use.

Accounts Receivable
Account Record

CUSTOMER: _T-Quarter Circle Outfitters_

ADDRESS: _222 Bridge Street_
Winnemucca, NV 89502

TEL. NO: _(775) 555-2222_   ACCOUNT NO. _1016_

INVOICE DATE	INVOICE NO.	INVOICE AMOUNT		TERMS	DATE PAID	AMOUNT PAID		INVOICE BALANCE	
6/09/14	3528	247	00	Net 30	7/02/14	247	00	0	00
7/14/14	4126	340	00	Net 30	8/15/14	340	00	0	00
9/26/14	5476	192	00	N30/2%10	10/02/14	188	16	0	00
10/03/14	5783	211	00	N30/2%10	11/01/14	109	00	102	00
10/12/14	6074	386	00	N30/2%10				386	00

★ Accounts Payable

Those debts owed by your company to your creditors for goods purchased or services rendered. Having open-account credit will allow your company to conduct more extensive operations and use your financial resources more effectively. If you are going to have a good credit record, the payment of these invoices must be timely and you will need an efficient system for keeping track of what you owe and when it should be paid. When your accounts payable are not numerous and you do not accumulate unpaid invoices by partial payments, you may wish to eliminate accounts payable records and use an accordion file divided into the days of the month. Invoices Payable may be directly filed under the date on which they should be paid, taking into account discounts available for early payment.

Format for Accounts Payable

If your Accounts Payable are stretched over a longer period, you will need to keep separate records for the creditors with whom you do business. The form used will need to include these categories:

1. **Invoice Date.** This will tell you when the transaction took place.

2. **Invoice Number.** If you need to refer to the actual invoice, the number makes it easy to retrieve. File unpaid invoices behind the record.

3. **Invoice Amount.** Tells the amount of the transaction.

4. **Terms.** Tells the time period allowed until invoice is due and if a discount applies. (e.g., "Net 30 / 2% Net 10" means the invoice is due in 30 days, but a 2% discount will be allowed if payment is made in 10 days.)

5. **Date Paid.** Shows when you paid the invoice.

6. **Amount Paid.** Shows whether you made a partial payment or paid the invoice in full.

7. **Invoice Balance.** Tells what potion of the invoice is not paid.

8. **Header Information.** The creditor's name, address and phone number will tell you where to send payments and how to make contact.

You will be billed regularly for the balance of your account, but the individual records will help you to know at a glance where you stand at any given time. They should be reviewed monthly and an attempt should be made to satisfy all your creditors. After the invoice is paid in full and the payment is recorded, mark the invoice paid and file with the rest of your receipts. At the end of your accounting period, the total for Accounts Payable should be transferred to the Current Liabilities portion of the Balance Sheet.

 Sample accounts payable record. The next page contains a sample form showing how it should be filled out. A blank form is located in Appendix II for you to copy and use.

ABC Company

Accounts Payable

Account Record

CREDITOR:: *Charles Mfg.*

ADDRESS: *1111 E. Trenton Road*

Tarrington, NH 03928

TEL. NO: *(800) 555-7201*

ACCOUNT NO. *2072*

INVOICE DATE	INVOICE NO.	INVOICE AMOUNT		TERMS	DATE PAID	AMOUNT PAID		INVOICE BALANCE	
2/16/14	10562	1,500	00	Net 15	2/24/14	1,500	00	0	00
2/25/14	11473	870	00	Net 30	2/18/14	870	00	0	00
3/17/14	12231	3,200	00	N30/2%10	3/25/14	3,136	00	0	00
7/02/14	18420	2,400	00	N30/2%10	8/01/14	1,800	00	600	00
8/15/14	19534	2,600	00	N30/2%10				2,600	00

★ Payroll Records

The decision to add employees should not be taken lightly. In addition to having a responsibility to the employees you hire, you also acquire the responsibility to withhold, report and pay taxes to the federal, state and sometimes your local government. The next four pages will be devoted to taking you through the necessary steps of putting employees on your payroll, paying them, making payroll tax deposits, completing quarterly payroll tax returns and making year end reports.

At the end of this section, I will make a suggestion as to how you might work with an accounting professional to make sure that everything is done according to requirements.

FEIN, W-4, Form I-9, Official Notice

If you decide to hire employees, you will have to do the following:

1. **FEIN.** When you decide you will hire employees, you must file for a Federal Employer Identification Number (FEIN). This is done by completing Form SS-4 and sending it to the Internal Revenue Service. You will receive a packet that includes Circular E, *Employer's Tax Guide.* This publication contains the charts you will use to determine the amount of Federal Income Tax to be withheld from your employees' paychecks. In addition to registering as an employer with the IRS, you will need to determine your state and local government requirements.

2. **W-4's.** Your new employees **MUST** complete a Form W-4, furnishing their full names, addresses, social security numbers, marital status and number of withholding allowances to be claimed, all of which you must have to compute your employees' first and succeeding paychecks.

3. **Forms I-9.** Employers are required to verify employment eligibility for all of their employees. This is accomplished by completing Form I-9, *Employment Eligibility Verification.* When you register as an employer, the "Handbook for Employers", (containing complete instructions), will be sent to you.

4. **Official Notice.** As an employer, you will be required to adhere to regulations regarding minimum wage, hours and working conditions, and workers compensation insurance. Again, as part of your "registration", you will receive the Official Notice describing these regulations. The Notice must be posted for all employees to read. Now is the time for you to familiarize yourself with these regulations.

Paying Your Employees

You can determine how often you want to pay your employees: weekly, bi-weekly, semi-monthly or monthly. Your employees can be paid by the hour, job or commission.

1. **Determine Gross Wage.** Since taxes to be withheld will be based on the employee's gross wage, your first step is to determine that amount. For example, if your employee is hired to work 40 hours and the agreed upon hourly rate is $10.00, that employee's gross wage is $400.

2. **FICA (Social Security).** FICA is calculated as a percent of the employee's gross wages. The percentage (7.65% in 2013) is a combination of old-age, survivors, and disability insurance (OASDI at 6.2%) and hospital insurance (Medicare at 1.45%). This tax is also imposed in an equal amount on the employer and applies to the wage base $117,000 for 2014 for OASDI and no limit for Medicare tax. Beginning in 2013, employee wages in excess of $200,000 ($250,000 married, filing jointly) are subject to an additional 0.9% medicare tax.

3. **Federal Income Tax.** Based upon the employee's marital status and the number of withholding allowances claimed on Form W-4, Federal Income Tax must be withheld from each employee's paycheck. Publication 15, Circular E, *Employer Tax Guide* contains the charts used to calculate the amount of withholding. Separate charts are used according to frequency of payment (weekly, bi-weekly, semi-monthly or monthly) and marital status of the employee.   **Note: State and local taxes may also apply.** *It is your responsibility to determine these requirements.*

Payroll Tax Deposits

The taxes that are withheld from employees' paychecks must be turned over to the IRS. In fact, you are liable for the payment of these taxes to the federal government whether or not you collect them from your employees.

1. **Open a Separate Account.** To avoid "accidentally" spending these funds, you should open a **separate** bank account for withheld taxes. When you write your employees' paychecks, calculate your tax liability (FICA and Federal Income Tax withheld and the employer's matching share of FICA) and immediately deposit that amount into that account.

2. **When Tax Liability** equals or exceeds $2,500. If, at the end of any quarter, your total tax liability is $2,500 or more, you must make monthly deposits of the income tax withheld and the FICA taxes using the Electronic Federal Tax Payment System (EFTPS). All corporations must use EFTPS and can set up for payments by going to the EFTPS website to provide business information and authorization for payments from the business checking account. New companies receive automatic enrollment to EFTPS when they file an application for an Employer Identification Number (EIN). Payments can be made at anytime of the day or night, from any location by computer or phone. For further information, call 800-555-4477 or 800-945-8400 or go online to: *www.eftps.gov*.

Quarterly Payroll Tax Returns

At the end of each quarter (March, June, September and December), you must send quarterly payroll tax returns to the IRS.

1. **Social Security and the Withholding of Income Taxes.** You will have to report to the IRS the total amount of wages you paid throughout the quarter, as well as the amount of taxes you withheld from your employees. This reporting is done on Form 941. Any monthly deposits you made will be reported on this form and will be applied to your tax liability. Any balance due (less than $2,500) must be paid with your return.

2. **FUTA (Unemployment Tax) Deposits.** If, at the end of any calendar quarter, you owe but have not yet deposited, more that $100 in Federal Unemployment (FUTA) Tax for the year, you must make a deposit by the end of the next month. Most states have reporting requirements that are similar to the IRS and that also include unemployment insurance payments. Contrary to popular belief, unemployment insurance is not deducted from your employees' paychecks. It is an expense of the employer.

Year End Reports

The end of the year is a busy time for payroll reporting. Since it is also the end of a quarter, all of the quarterly tax returns described above are also due at the same time.

1. **ANNUAL FUTA RETURN.** Form 940 *Employer's Annual Federal Unemployment (FUTA) Tax Return* must be completed. This return reports each employee's wages that are subject to unemployment tax. Any quarterly deposits will be applied to the total tax liability.

2. **FORM W-2.** This form must be prepared for each employee. Form W-2 reports the total wages paid for the year and itemizes the total of each type of tax withheld from his or her paychecks. Multiple copies of these forms must be prepared. A packet of three or four are sent to the employee to be attached to his or her personal returns. You must send a copy to the Social Security Administration and additional copies to your state and local government agencies.

Accuracy in Reporting

It is vitally important that information reported on the Form W-2's, Form 941 *Employer's Quarterly Federal Tax Return* and Form 940 *Employer's Annual Federal Unemployment (FUTA) Tax Return* agrees. The Internal Revenue Service and Social Security Administration regularly compare information and will send notices to employers that have submitted conflicting information.

Can You Take the Responsibility?

The IRS, Social Security, State and local agencies require that all of your reporting be exact. This can be a very heavy burden. The amount of paperwork alone requires many hours of work. The fact that you cannot afford to make a mistake makes it even more frightening.

Many small business owners buy a computer program, which supposedly makes the job easy. However, I have spoken with several of them that still find themselves not knowing what they are doing. Some hire an in-house employee to do the job. This too can be costly. My suggestion is this:

Hire a Professional!

You can have your payroll done by your accountant or by a payroll service for a very nominal fee. You will pay your employees and report wages paid to your payroll service. They will work with you, take the responsibility for collecting the proper information from you on wages paid and see that all of the required reports are prepared and filed in a timely manner.

Note*: Be aware that the business owner is responsible for the payment of the taxes even if they have a payroll service that collected the taxes but didn't pay them into the government agencies.*

For More Information

The Tax Section of the book, (Chapter 7), will give you more information on tax reporting requirements for employees. There are also examples of Forms W-2, W-3, W-4, FUTA and FICA returns. It would be good to read about and familiarize yourself with the requirements. Then you can make a decision as to whether you wish to do your own or hire a professional.

For detailed information, see IRS Publication 334, *Tax Guide for Small Business* and Publication 15, *Employer's Tax Guide* (Circular E)

★ Independent Contractors

One of the major problems that you, as a small business owner, must deal with is that of determining the status of people and/or companies that you hire to provide specific services for your company. Are they *independent contractors* (non-employees) or are they, in fact, *employees* of your company?

- **If the service providers are independent contractors,** they are not eligible for unemployment, disability, or workers' compensation benefits. Also, you as the hiring firm do not have to pay employee-employer taxes or provide workers' compensation insurance, and you are usually not liable for the contractor's actions.

- **If the service provider is, in fact, an employee of your company** rather than an independent contractor, the opposite is true. They are eligible for unemployment, disability, and workers' compensation benefits and you, as the hiring firm must pay employee-employer taxes, provide workers' compensation insurance, and will be liable for the contractor's actions.

Who Determines the Proper Classification of Service Providers?

The IRS and the laws of individual states determine whether a worker is an independent contractor or an employee. A contract between the hiring firm and the service provider is not proof of an Independent Contractor relationship. Workers are employees unless the hiring firm can prove otherwise.

The government looks negatively at the misclassification of bona-fide employees as Independent Contractors for two reasons: (1) Independent Contractors are responsible for withholding their own taxes and Social Security. Many do not report their earnings and thus rob the system and other taxpayers of tax dollars; (2) The government wants to protect workers. They do not want businesses to circumvent the Social Security, disability, and unemployment insurance programs (and their costs) simply by calling their workers Independent Contractors.

Penalties for Misclassification

If your firm misclassifies an employee as an independent contractor, you will be assessed 1.5% of the gross wages (federal withholding, 20% of the amount that would have been the employee's share of FICA taxes, and the appropriate employer's share of FICA. This is providing that information returns (form 1099-MISC) were filed and the failure to deduct was not intentional disregard of the requirement. If you fail to file information returns or fail to provide W-2s to employees, the penalty is doubled.

20 Common Law Factors

The IRS has a "List of the 20 Common Law Factors" that are used to evaluate the status of the provider. Independent contractors do not have to satisfy all 20 factors. The courts have given different weights for each factor according to the industry and jobs. If you are planning to use independent contractors, it would pay you to familiarize yourself with the 20 factors and avoid misclassification and costly penalties.

Recordkeeping and Reporting

If you have hired Independent contractors, you will need to keep accurate records as to how much you paid each of them for the services performed for your company.

- Keep a record of each independent contractor and record the dates, check numbers, and amounts paid for each service performed.

- Keep a record of the independent contractor's name, company, address, telephone number, and social security/EIN number.

- Before January 31st of the new year, send each independent contractor a form1099MISC. (See Chapter 7, *"Taxes & Recordkeeping"* for more information)

- By February 28th, send in your forms 1099-MISC and transmittal form 1096 to the government. (See Chapter 7, *"Taxes & Bookkeeping"* for more information)

Independent Contractors

Facts vs. Myths

Appendix I of *Keeping the Books* will provide you with more comprehensive information regarding independent contractors. The section, entitled "Independent Contractors: Facts vs. Myths," includes:

- ♦ The "List of 20 Common Law Factors"

- ♦ Basic rules regarding independent contractor status.

- ♦ Benefits and risks of hiring independent contractors

- ♦ Benefits and risks to the independent contractor.

★ Transportation, Entertainment, and Travel Expenses

You will have to prove your deductions for travel, transportation, and entertainment business expenses by adequate records or by sufficient evidence that will support your claim. Records required should be kept in an account book, diary, statement of expense, or similar record. In the following paragraphs, I will discuss general information pertaining to transportation expenses, meal and entertainment expenses and travel expenses. It is important that these expenses be recorded as they occur. It is difficult to remember them accurately after the fact.

Transportation Expenses

These are the ordinary and necessary expenses of getting from one work place to another in the course of your business (when you are not traveling away from home). They *do* include the cost of transportation by air, rail, bus, taxi, etc., and the cost of driving and maintaining your car. They *do not* include transportation expenses between your home and your main or regular place of work, parking fees at your place of business or expenses for personal use of your car.

Vehicle expenses

If you use your vehicle for business purposes, you may be able to deduct vehicle expenses. You generally can use one of these two methods to figure these expenses:

1. **Actual Expense.** Gas, oil, tolls, parking, lease or rental fees, depreciation, repairs, licenses, insurance, etc.

2. **Standard Mileage Rate.** Instead of figuring actual expenses, you may choose to use the standard mileage rate, which means that you will receive a deduction of a specific amount of money per mile (56.5 cents in 2013 and decreased to 56 cents in 2014) of business use of your car. Standard Mileage Rate is allowed if you own or lease the car or if you operate only one car at a time for business. Standard Mileage Rate is not allowed if you use the car for hire, operate two or more cars at the same time, or claimed depreciation in previous years using MACRS depreciation, or a Section 179 deduction.

☛ Mileage log

You are required to record business miles traveled during the year. A filled-in form is provided on the next page, and a blank one is available in Appendix II for your use – or you might use a spreadsheet on your smart phone. The first year, it would be a good idea to compare the results of both of the above methods before you make your decision about how to report vehicle expenses. Also, be aware that if the use of the car is for both business and personal use, you must divide your expenses and deduct only the percentage used in business pursuit. For more detailed information get IRS Publication 463, *Travel Entertainment, Gift, and Car Expenses* and IRS Publication 334, *Tax Guide for Small Business.*

ABC Company

Mileage Log

NAME: _ABC Company (John Morgan)_

DATED: From _November 1_ **To** _November 30, 2014_

DATE	CITY OF DESTINATION	NAME OR OTHER DESIGNATION	BUSINESS PURPOSE	NO. OF MILES
11-01	Orange, CA	ExCal, Inc.	Present proposal	67 mi.
11-03	Cypress, CA	The Print Co.	p/u brochures	23 mi.
11-04	Long Beach, CA	Wm. Long	Consultation	53 mi.
11-07	Fullerton, CA	Bank of America	Loan Meeting	17 mi.
11-23	Los Angeles, CA	Moore Corp.	Consultation	143 mi.
11-30	Los Angeles, CA	Moore Corp.	Consultation	140 mi.
			TOTAL MILES THIS SHEET	443

Note: 1. A mileage record is required by the IRS to claim a mileage deduction. It is also used to determine the percentage of business use of a car.

2. Keep your mileage log in your vehicle and record your mileage as it Occurs. It is very difficult to recall after the fact.

Entertainment Expenses

You may be able to deduct business-related entertainment expenses you have to entertain a client, customer or employee. The expense must be ordinary (common and accepted in your field of business) and necessary (helpful and appropriate for your business, but not necessarily indispensable). In addition, you must be able to show that they are (1) directly related to the active conduct of your trade or business, or (2) associated with the active conduct of your trade or business.

- **Expenses that may be deducted.** Entertainment includes any activity generally considered to provide entertainment, amusement, or recreation, and includes meals provided to a customer or client. Examples include entertaining guests at nightclubs; at social, athletic, and sporting clubs; at theaters; at sporting events; on yachts; or on hunting fishing, vacation, and similar trips. Entertainment also may include meeting personal, living or family needs of individuals, such as providing food, a hotel suite or a car to business customers or their families.

- **Expenses that generally may not be deducted.** You generally cannot deduct the cost of entertainment for your spouse or for the spouse of a customer. However, you can deduct these costs if you can show you had a clear business purpose, rather than a personal or social purpose, for providing the entertainment. Generally you cannot deduct any expense for the use of a training facility. You generally cannot deduct club dues and membership fees if the principal purpose of the organization is to conduct entertainment activities for members or their guests or to provide members or guests with access to entertainment facilities.

- **Meals as entertainment.** Entertainment includes the cost of a meal you provide to a customer or client. It does not matter whether the meal is a part of other entertainment or by itself. Generally, to deduct an entertainment-related meal, you or your employee must be present when the food or beverages are provided.

- **50 percent limit.** In general (there are exceptions), you can deduct only 50% of business-related meal and entertainment expenses. You must record these expenses with date, place of entertainment, business purpose, the name of the person entertained and the amount spent.

 Sample Entertainment Expense Record. There is a filled-in example of this form on the next page. We have also provided a blank form in the Appendix to help you record all information required to justify entertainment expenses. Be sure to fill in all categories. Keep all receipts for verification and file for easy retrieval. For more detailed information see IRS Publication 463, *Travel, Entertainment, Gift, and Car Expenses* and Publication 334, *Tax Guide for Small Business.*

ABC Company

Entertainment Expense Record

NAME: _____John Kelley_____

DATED: From ___11-01-14___To___11-30-14___

DATE	PLACE OF ENTERTAINMENT	BUSINESS PURPOSE	NAME OF PERSON ENTERTAINED	AMOUNT SPENT	
11-04	The 410 Club	Consulting	William Long	46	32
11-23	Seafood Chef	Consult w/attorney	Thomas Moore	23	50
11-27	The Cannon Club	Staff Dinner	Company Employees	384	00

Note: For more information on Meals and Entertainment, please refer to IRS Publication 463, *Travel, Entertainment and Gift Expenses.*

Travel Expenses

Deductible travel expenses include those ordinary and necessary expenses you incur while traveling away from your home on business. The following lists provide general guidelines:

Expenses that can be deducted

- **Transportation fares.** The cost of traveling between home and business destination.
- **Taxi, commuter bus, and limousine fares.** The fare between the airport and your hotel or temporary work site.
- **Baggage and shipping.** Actual costs between regular and temporary work locations.
- **Car expenses.** Includes leasing expenses, actual expenses or the standard mileage rate (56.5 cents in 2013 and 56 cents in 2014).
- **Lodging.** If the trip is overnight, or long enough to require rest to properly perform duties.
- **Meals.** Actual or standard meal allowance if business trip qualifies for lodging.
- **Cleaning and laundry expenses.** Cost of cleaning your business clothes while away from home overnight.
- **Telephone expenses.** Telephone usage including fax and other communication devices.
- **Tips.** Related to any of the above services.
- **Other business-related expenses.** Any expenses connected with your travel (i.e., computer rental).

Expenses you cannot deduct

- That portion of travel, meals and lodging for your spouse – unless a real business purpose for your spouse's presence.
- Investment travel (such as investment seminars or stockholders' meetings).
- Amounts you spend for travel to conduct a general search for, or preliminary investigation of, a new business.

Special rulings

You will need to study special rulings. For instance, when your trip is not entirely for business purposes, you will have to properly allocate the expenses. Treatment of expenses depends on how much of your trip was business-related and what portion occurred within the United States. Also, if you are not traveling for the entire 24-hour day, you must prorate the standard meal allowance and claim only one-fourth of the allowance for each 6-hour quarter of the day during any part of which you are traveling away from home.

 Travel Record. When you travel away from home on business, keep records of all the expenses you incur. The Travel Record on the next page shows information that you will be required to keep. A blank form is located in Appendix II. You will also need to keep documentation such as receipts, canceled checks, or bills to verify your expense. For more information, see IRS Publication 463, *Travel, Entertainment, Gift, and Car Expenses.*

ABC Company
Travel Record

TRIP TO: _Dallas, Texas_

Dated From: _6-15-14_   To: _6-18-14_

Business Purpose: _Technology Expo (show exhibitor)_

No. Days Spent on Business: _6_

DATE	LOCATION	EXPENSE PAID TO	MEALS Breakfast	MEALS Lunch	MEALS Dinner	MEALS Misc.	HOTEL	TAXIS, ETC.	AUTOMOBILE Gas	AUTOMOBILE Parking	AUTOMOBILE Tolls	MISC EXP
6-15	Phoenix, AZ	Mobil Gas				640			2100			
6-15	Phoenix, AZ	Greentree Inn		1250								
6-15	Chola, NM	Exxon							2350			
6-15	Las Cruces, NM	Holiday Inn			2700		4900					
6-16	Las Cruces, NM	Exxon							1900			
6-16	Taft, TX	Molly's Cafe		1625								
6-16	Dallas, TX	Holiday Inn			1875		5400					
6-17	Dallas, TX	Expo Center								800		
6-17	Dallas, TX	Harvey's Eatery		2100								
6-17	Dallas, TX	Holiday Inn			2450		5400					
6-18	Dallas, TX	Holiday Inn	950									(Fax) 900
6-18	Dallas, TX	Expo Center		1400						800		
6-18	Dallas, TX	Holiday Inn			1620		5400					
6-19	Pokie, TX	Texaco							2100			
6-19	Pokie, TX	Denny's		1850								
6-19	Chola, NM	Holiday Inn			2700		4800					
6-20	Chola, NM	Holiday Inn	1275									
6-20	Flagstaff, AZ	Texaco							2200			
TOTALS →			2225	8225	11345	640	25900		10650	1600		900

Attach all receipts for Meals, Hotel, Fares, Auto, Entertainment, etc. Details of your expenses can be noted on the receipts. File your travel record and your receipts in the same envelope. Label the envelope as to trip made. File all travel records together. When expenses are allocated, be sure not to double expense anything. (Ex: Gas cannot be used if you elect to use mileage as the basis for deducting your car expenses.)

★ Customer Information Records

To help a business deal more effectively with its customers, it can be very beneficial to develop a system to keep track of customer information. Without technology to enable them to reach out through databases and information services, many businesses have no way to keep specialized information on customers due to volume or change in clientele. Small businesses in the service industry and in specialty retail sales are finding that if they can incorporate specialized customer records into their operations, they have a better chance of retaining customers. Service businesses strive for repeat and referral business plus new customers who come to them through commercial advertising. Specialty retail sales shops also look for repeats and referrals as their primary source of business.

By keeping a database that can selectively draw out information, the customer can be better served. For those without the electronic advantage, a file of 3" x 5" index cards – one for each customer – provides the business owner with ready information at his fingertips. In my husband's clock shop, he has effectively used a manual system of this type to service a customer list of approximately 10,000. The types of things that can be recorded and some uses of that information are as follows:

Service Industry

- **Include:** Name, address, telephone numbers (work and home), service performed, charges, special advice to customer, guarantees given and any other information that you feel may be helpful.

- **Some uses of Information.** Protection of the business from customers' claims that services were performed which were not recorded, information as proof of dates of warranty service (benefiting both customer and business owner), and information to help business owners remember customers and give them specialized attention.

Specialty Retail Sales Business

- **Include:** Name, address, telephone numbers (work and home) sales information, special interests of customer.

- **Some uses of Information.** Use as a mailing list for special sales; when customers call, use card to jog your memory as to their interests, what they have already purchased and what they might like. Your customers like to be remembered and receive personalized service.

 Sample Customer Files. See the next page for examples of customer files: (1) for a Service Industry business (2) for a Specialty Retail Sales business.

Sample

Customer Data Files

Service Industry

Jones, John W.   (H) (714) 555-2489
123 W. 1st Street   (W) (714) 555-1234
Anywhere, CA 97134

1. *Ridgeway G/F Clock (IHS) a. Repaired pendulum, rep.*
   $55.00 8/19/11   susp. sprg., serviced.

2. *S/Thomas O.G. a. Cleaned, bushed movement, balanced.*
   $155.00 6/07/12 Guarantee: 1 year

3. *Waltham L/WW (antique) a. Stem, clean, repair hspg.*
   $45.00 7/11/14

Specialty Retail Sales

Smith, Henry L. (D.D.S)   (W) (201) 555-1304
76 Main Street, Suite X
Somewhere, CA 96072
                                  Birthday: May 3rd
*Buys for wife's (Ann) collection: Anniversary: Oct. 21st

1. *08 CM M/Box w/"Lara's Theme" 1/18 (Rosewood burl)*
   $55.00 + Tax   4/28/12

2. *789 BMP 3/72 w/"Phantom of the Opera"*
   $675.00 + Tax 10/17/12

3. *Novelty M/B - Bear w/Heart $32.00 + Tax 2/13/14*

★ Business Checkbook

Your business checkbook is not just a package of preprinted forms that represents your business bankroll. It is also the initial accounting record showing when, where, and what amount of money was dispersed and when, from what sources and how much money was received by your company. This information is all kept on the recording space provided in your checkbook.

What Type of Checkbook Is Most Effective?

Don't get a pocket-size checkbook. This type of checkbook does not provide enough space for entry of information (and it is also easily misplaced). Some points to consider when selecting your business checkbook are:

- **Size.** A business-size checkbook is best. There is a personal desk type with three standard size checks on each right-hand page and a register (recording) page of equal size on the left. Instead of one line of check register for each transaction, you will have room to record such things as invoice numbers and descriptions of purchases. You can divide amounts paid with one check into separate expenses. For instance, the payment of an invoice to an office supply store may involve $15 for office supplies and $45 for exhibit materials. Deposits can be divided into types of income received. These and other notations will be invaluable when you do your weekly bookkeeping because you will not have to look for paperwork to supply missing information.

- **Duplicate Feature.** Many business owners number among the ranks of those people who do not automatically record information when they write checks. To eliminate the frustration created by this unfortunate habit, banks can provide checkbooks made with carbonless copies underneath each check. If you fail to record a check at the time you write it, a copy will remain in your checkbook. I don't use one, but lots of people swear by them.

- **Pre-printing and Numbering of Checks.** Your checks should be pre-printed with your business name, address and telephone number. They should also be numbered. Some businesses will not even deal with you if you try to use personal checks or ones without pre-printed information. Some venders with which you wish to do business perceive them as a possible danger signal and indicator of a lack of your credibility.

- **Deposit Record.** There is one last feature that I like when it comes to my banking supplies. Instead of deposit slips that can get lost, I like to use a Deposit Record Book. It is a bound book of deposit slips arranged in sets of two. The original goes to the bank and the duplicate stays in your book and is dated stamped and initialed by the teller. The book can be kept in your bank bag and is ready to use for the next deposit. It ensures that you have a permanent record of all of your deposits.

 Note: *You can print your own checks on your computer. It requires that you buy check stock and use check writing software (accounting or specialty).*

Balancing Your Checkbook Manually

Once a month your bank will send you a statement of your account, showing a summary of your activity since the last statement date. It will list all deposits, check withdrawals, ATM activity, bank charges and interest earned. You will need to reconcile it with your checkbook on a timely basis. This is one of those chores that is frequently ignored. "I will catch it up later when I have more time." This is the kind of attitude results in undiscovered errors and overdrawn accounts. It is not difficult to balance your checkbook if you follow these steps:

1. Update your checkbook

Add: Interest earned.
Deposits not recorded.
Automatic credits unrecorded.

Subtract: Service Charges
Checks not recorded.
Automatic debits unrecorded.
Payments not recorded.

Mark Off: Amount of all checks paid against statement.
Amount of all deposits shown.
All ATM and electronic transactions that are recorded.

2. List and total

- All deposits made and other credits not shown on the statement.

- All outstanding checks not shown on current or previous statements.

3. Balance

- Enter statement balance as indicated.

- Add the total of all deposits and other credits not shown on current or previous statements.

- Subtract items outstanding.

Total should agree with checkbook balance

BALANCE FORM

Statement Balance		
Add Deposits made and not shown on this statement		
Total	$	
Subtract Outstanding Items		
Total Should agree with your checkbook balance	$	

Outstanding Items

Check number or Date	Amount	Check number or Date	Amount	
Total	$	**Total**	$	

If you are not in balance. Recheck your addition and subtraction in the checkbook. Check amounts in checkbook against those in statement. Look for uncashed checks from previous statements and be sure they are not still outstanding. Check amount you are off and see if it matches amount on any of your checks. Be sure that you did not add a check when you should have subtracted. Be sure that you recorded and subtracted all ATM withdrawals in your checkbook.

Recording Bank Statement Information

When you are doing your bookkeeping, **you must remember** that you will have to record all bank charges (service charges, check orders, returned check charges, returned checks, etc.) in your Income & Expense Journal. If you do not, your expenses will be understated and you will pay more taxes. Also be sure to record interest earnings.

 Note: *If you are using accounting software, you will perform a **bank reconciliation** within the software at the end of each month. It is easily done utilizing the information on your bank statement.*

★ Receipt Files

It is required by the IRS that you be able to verify deductions. For that reason alone, you must have a filing system that insures that your receipts are easy to retrieve. This is also very important for your own benefit. There will be many times that you will need to find information on a transaction for any one of innumerable reasons. If your filing system is a mess, you are lost.

Where Do You Keep Receipts?

For most businesses, an accordion file divided into alphabet pockets will be the most efficient way of filing your receipts. These files also come with pockets divided into months, but I think it becomes cumbersome for retrieval. Picking out all of your utility bills, for example, would require that you pick from 12 different pockets. With the alphabet file, it would require only one. You will probably also need one or more two-drawer file cabinets for systematic filing of other paperwork.

One of the most frequent questions I get asked is how to determine what letter of the alphabet you file the receipt under. The easiest way is to use the first letter entered in a record. If you record a meal in Petty Cash as paid to cash because you don't know the name of a seller, file the receipt under "C". I do keep all the meal receipts in one envelope marked "Meals" and file it under "M" because that is an item frequently audited and I can pull all of the receipts quickly. I also keep all the records for a trip in a single envelope and mark it with the occasion and date. Then I file all travel records under "T" for the same reason. You may wish to keep a separate file for Petty Cash Receipts. I use the same one for those paid by check and by cash.

At the End of the Year

When the tax year is closed, you can add your bank statements, income & expense journal, a copy of your tax return, and any other pertinent information for that year. All are put away in the one accordion file and labeled with the year. If, at a later date, you need information for a tax audit or for another purpose, everything is in one place.

* This ends the General Records section *

You have now completed the General Records Section of the book and you should have a better understanding of the most common financial records that are necessary for your business – and that are required by the IRS for tax reporting.

In the next section of this book you will learn about Financial Statements and how they are generated from the general records with which we have just been concerned.

Financial Statements

In the four previous chapters of this book, you have been introduced to the functions and types of recordkeeping and some simple accounting terminology. You were also introduced to double and single entry accounting and taken through the process of setting up essential general records for your business.

Now it is time to see how financial statements are developed from your general records and how the use of those financial statements can help you to see the financial condition of your business and to identify its relative strengths and weaknesses. Business owners who take the time to understand and evaluate operations through financial statements over the life of the business will be far ahead of enthusiastic entrepreneurs who concern themselves only with their products or services.

What Are Financial Statements?

Financial Statements show past and projected finances. These statements are both the source of your tax information (discussed in Chapter 7) and the means by which you analyze your business (Chapter 6). They are developed from your General Records and fall into two main categories: Actual Performance (Historical) Financial Statements and Pro Forma (Projected) Financial Statements. Before you proceed further, it is best to understand what financial statements are and which ones you will use for your business.

Actual Performance (Historical) Statements

These are historical financial statements reflecting the past performance of your business. If you are planning a new business, you have no history. However, as soon as you have been in business for even one accounting period, you will have the financial information to generate two financial statements, both of which will prove to be invaluable to you in making decisions about your business. They are:

1. Balance Sheet
2. Profit & Loss Statement (Income Statement)

I will also introduce you to a Business Financial History, which is a composite of the Balance Sheet, Profit & Loss Statement, and legal structure information. It is sometimes used as a loan application.

Pro Forma (Projected) Statements

The word pro forma in accounting means projected. These are the financial statements that are used for you to predict the future profitability of your business. Your projections will be based on realistic research and reasonable assumptions, trying not to overstate your revenues or understate your expenses. The pro forma statements are:

- Cash Flow Statement (or Budget)
- Quarterly Budget Analysis (means of measuring projections actual performance within budget)
- Three-Year Projection (Pro Forma Income Statement)
- Break-Even Analysis

How to Proceed

Each of the above financial documents will be discussed as to:

- Definition and use
- How to develop the statement
- Sources of needed information

Every business owner will need to understand and generate Profit & Loss (Income) Statements, Balance Sheets, and Pro Forma Cash Flow Statements. Information from these three statements will then be utilized to perform a Quarterly Budget Analysis on a regular basis. Some additional financial statements will be required for a business plan and will serve as useful financial planning tools. The following are four guidelines for preparing financial statements for differing situations.

1. **If you are a new business and you are going to seek a lender or investor.** You will be required to write a business plan. You will need to create all Pro Forma Statements included in this chapter. You will have no financial history and cannot include Actual Performance Statements.

2. **If you are a new business and you are not going to seek a lender or investor.** You should still think about writing a business plan. You will include all Pro Forma Statements. Even if you decide not to write one, it is especially important to plan your cash flow (budget).

3. **If you are an existing business and you are going to seek a lender or investor.** You will be required to write a business plan. You will include all financial documents discussed in this chapter, plus other elements. (See our book, *Anatomy of a Business Plan.*)

4. **If you are an existing business and you are not seeking a lender or investor.** All financial statements are beneficial. The Profit & Loss, Balance Sheet, and Pro Forma Cash Flow Statement are a must.

Now You Are Ready to Learn to Develop
Actual Performance (Historical) Statements

Balance Sheet

What Is a Balance Sheet?
The Balance Sheet is a financial statement that shows the financial position of the business as of a fixed date. It is usually done at the close of an accounting period. The Balance Sheet can be compared to a photograph. It is a picture of what your business owns and owes at a given moment and will show you whether your financial position is strong or weak. By regularly preparing this statement, you will be able to identify and analyze trends in the financial strength of your business and thus implement timely modifications. A sample Balance Sheet is shown on page 65.

Format
The Balance Sheet must follow an accepted format and contain the following three categories so anyone reading it can readily interpret it. The three categories are related in that, at any given time, a business' assets equal the total contributions by its creditors and owners.

> **Assets** = Anything your business owns that has monetary value.
>
> **Liabilities** = Debts owed by the business to any of its creditors.
>
> **Net Worth (Capital)** = Amount equal to the owner's equity.

The relationship between these three terms is simply illustrated in a mathematical formula. It reads as follows:

Assets - Liabilities = Net Worth

Examined as such, it becomes apparent that if a business possesses more assets than it owes to creditors, its net worth will be a positive. Conversely, if the business owes more money to creditors than it possesses in assets, the net worth will be a negative.

Sources of Information
If you (or your accountant) use accounting software for your business, it should generate a Balance Sheet on command. If you do your accounting manually, the figures come from your general records. Each of the categories on the next page is defined to help you understand how its dollar amount is arrived at.

 An **Explanation of Balance Sheet Categories** and a **Sample Balance Sheet** are provided for you on the next two pages.

Explanation of Categories
Balance Sheet

ASSETS. Everything owned by or owed to your business that has cash value.

Current Assets. Assets that can be converted into cash within one year of the date on the Balance Sheet.

Cash - Money you have on hand. Include monies not yet deposited.

Petty Cash - Money deposited to Petty Cash and not yet expended.

Accounts Receivable - Money owed to you for sale of goods and/or services.

Inventory - Raw materials, work in process and goods manufactured or purchased for resale.

Short-Term Investments – (Assets expected to be converted to cash within one year) Stocks, bonds, CD's. List at cost or market value, whichever is less.)

Prepaid Expenses - Goods or services purchased or rented prior to use. (i.e., rent, insurance, prepaid inventory purchases, etc.)

Long-Term Investments. Stocks, bonds, and special savings accounts to be kept for at least one year.

Fixed Assets. Resources a business owns and does not intend for resale.

Land - List at original purchase price.

Buildings - List at cost less any depreciation previously taken..

Equipment, Furniture, Autos/Vehicles - List at cost less depreciation. Kelley Blue Book can be used to determine value of vehicles.

LIABILITIES. What your business owes; claims by creditors on your assets.

Current Liabilities. Those obligations payable within one operating cycle

Accounts Payable - Obligations payable within one operating cycle.

Notes Payable - Short-term notes; list the balance of principal due. Separately list the current portion of long-term debts.

Interest Payable - Interest accrued on loans and credit.

Taxes Payable - Amounts estimated to have been incurred during the accounting period.

Payroll Accrual - Current Liabilities on salaries and wages.

Long-Term Liabilities - Outstanding balance less the current portion due. (i.e., mortgage, vehicle)

NET WORTH (also called "capital" or "owner equity"). Claims of the owner or owners on the assets of the business. (document according to the legal structure of your business)

Proprietorship or Partnership. Each of the owner's original investment plus earnings after withdrawals.

Corporation. The sum of contributions by owners or stockholders plus earnings retained after paying dividends.

Balance Sheet

Business Name: *ABC Company*   **Date: September 30, 2014**

ASSETS

Current Assets

Cash	$	8,742
Petty Cash	$	167
Accounts Receivable	$	5,400
Inventory	$	101,800
Short-Term Investments	$	0
Prepaid Expenses	$	1,967

Long-Term Investments $ _____0

Fixed Assets

Land (valued at cost)		$	185,000
Buildings		$	143,000
1. Cost	171,600		
2. Less Acc. Depr.	28,600		
Improvements		$	0
1. Cost			
2. Less Acc. Depr.			
Equipment		$	5,760
1. Cost	7,200		
2. Less Acc. Depr.	1,440		
Furniture		$	2,150
1. Cost	2,150		
2. Less Acc. Depr.	0		
Autos/Vehicles		$	16,432
1. Cost	19,700		
2. Less Acc. Depr.	3,268		

Other Assets

1.	$	_____
2.	$	_____

TOTAL ASSETS $ 470,418

LIABILITIES

Current Liabilities

Accounts Payable	$	2,893
Notes Payable	$	0
Interest Payable	$	1,842
Taxes Payable		
Federal Income Tax	$	5,200
Self-Employment Tax	$	1,025
State Income Tax	$	800
Sales Tax Accrual	$	2,130
Property Tax	$	0
Payroll Accrual	$	4,700

Long-Term Liabilities

Notes Payable	$	196,700

TOTAL LIABILITIES $ 215,290

NET WORTH (EQUITY)

Proprietorship	$	_____
or		
Partnership		
John Smith, 60% Equity	$	153,077
Mary Blake, 40% Equity	$	102,051
or		
Corporation		
Capital Stock	$	_____
Surplus Paid In	$	_____
Retained Earnings	$	_____

TOTAL NET WORTH $ 255,128

Assets - Liabilities = Net Worth
and
Liabilities + Equity = Total Assets

Profit & Loss Statement
(Income Statement)

What Is a Profit & Loss (Income) Statement?

This statement shows your business financial activity over a period of time, usually your tax year. In contrast to the Balance Sheet, which shows a picture of your business at a given moment, the Profit & Loss Statement (P&L) can be likened to a moving picture – showing what has happened in your business over a period of time. It is an excellent tool for assessing your business. You will be able to pick out weaknesses in your operation and plan ways to run your business more effectively, thereby increasing your profits. For example, you may find that some heavy advertising that you did in March did not effectively increase your sales. In following years, you may decide to utilize your advertising funds more effectively by using them at a time when there is increased customer spending taking place. In the same way, you might examine your Profit & Loss Statement to see what months have the heaviest sales volume and plan your inventory accordingly. Comparison of your P & Ls from several years will give you an even better picture of the trends in your business. Do not underestimate the value of this particular tool when planning your tactics.

How to Develop a Profit & Loss Statement

The Profit & Loss Statement (Income Statement) is compiled from actual business transactions, in contrast to Pro Forma Statements, which are projections for future business periods. The P & L shows where your money has come from and where it was spent over a specific period of time. It should be prepared not only at the end of the tax year, but at the close of each business month. It is one of the two principal financial statements prepared from the ledgers and the records of a business. Income and expense account balances are used in the P&L Statement. The remaining asset, liability, and capital information provides the figures for the Balance Sheet covered on the last three pages.

If you utilize accounting software (double entry), individual transactions are entered and the balances from income, cost of goods, and expense accounts are used to generate a profit and loss (income) statement. You can generate a profit and loss statement for a specific period of your choice (current month, this fiscal year, last fiscal year, specified dates, etc.) whenever you choose to do so. If an accountant does your bookkeeping, he or she should provide you with a P&L Statement at the end of every month as well as at the end of your tax year. If you set up a manual bookkeeping system (single entry) with General Records discussed in Chapter 4, the P&L Statement is generated by a simple transfer of the end-of-month totals from your Income & Expense Journal.

Format and Sources of Information

The Profit & Loss (or Income) Statement must also follow an accepted accounting format and contain certain categories. The following is the correct format and a brief explanation of the items to be included or computations to be made in each category in order to arrive at "the Bottom Line," or owner's share of the profit for the period.

Profit & Loss (Income Statement)

INCOME

1. **Net Sales (Gross sales less Returns and Allowances):** What were your cash receipts for the period? If your accounting is on an accrual basis, what amount did you invoice out during the period?

2. **Cost of Goods Sold:** See the form on page 69 for computation.

3. **Gross Profit:** Subtract Cost of Goods from Net Sales.

EXPENSES

1. **Variable Expenses (Selling):** What amounts did you actually spend on items directly related to your product or service? (marketing, commissions, freight, packaging, travel, etc.)

2. **Fixed Expenses (Administrative):** What amounts were spent during the period on office overhead? (rent, insurance, accounting, office salaries, telephone, utilities, etc.)

NET INCOME FROM OPERATIONS: Gross profit minus variable and fixed expenses.

Other Income: Interest Received during the period.

Other Expense: Interest Paid Out during the period.

NET PROFIT (LOSS) BEFORE INCOME TAXES: The Net Income from Operations + Interest Received - Interest Paid Out.

Income Taxes: List income taxes paid out during the period (federal, state, local, self-employment).

NET PROFIT (LOSS) AFTER INCOME TAXES: Subtract all Income Taxes Paid Out from the Net Profit (or Loss) Before Income Taxes. This is what is known as "The Bottom Line".

 Sample Forms

The next two pages contain two Profit & Loss forms. The first on page 68 is divided into 12 months. If it is filled in monthly, this form will provide an accurate picture of the previous year's financial activity at the end of the year. The form on page 69 (filled-in) is to be used for either a monthly or an annual Profit & Loss Statement.

Profit & Loss (Income) Statement

ABC Company

For the Year: 2014

	Jan	Feb	Mar	Apr	May	Jun	6-MONTH TOTALS	Jul	Aug	Sep	Oct	Nov	Dec	12-MONTH TOTALS
INCOME														
1. NET SALES (Gross less R&A)	14,400	10,140	10,060	15,658	18,622	12,620	81,500	11,500	9,850	10,150	16,600	29,250	51,000	209,850
2. Cost of Goods to be Sold	2,800	2,900	4,200	7,700	7,350	2,750	27,700	2,959	2,580	2,740	6,250	13,400	23,290	78,919
a. Beginning Inventory	27,000	31,000	48,500	48,600	42,000	35,600	27,000	33,800	40,800	40,900	51,700	53,300	54,700	27,000
b. Purchases	6,800	20,400	4,300	1,100	950	950	34,500	9,959	2,680	13,540	7,850	14,800	12,890	96,219
c. C.O.G. available for sale	33,800	51,400	52,800	49,700	42,950	36,550	61,500	43,759	43,480	54,440	59,550	68,100	67,590	123,219
d. Less ending Inventory	31,000	48,500	48,600	42,000	35,600	33,800	33,800	40,800	40,900	51,700	53,300	54,700	44,300	44,300
3. GROSS PROFIT	11,600	7,240	5,860	7,958	11,272	9,870	53,800	8,541	7,270	7,410	10,350	15,850	27,710	130,931
EXPENSES														
1. Variable (Selling) Expenses														
a. Advertising	900	300	900	250	300	300	2,950	350	300	640	1,300	1,200	1,400	8,140
b. Freight	75	75	75	75	180	70	550	75	75	90	180	300	560	1,830
c. Fulfillment of Orders	300	300	300	400	350	300	1,950	300	280	325	450	600	975	4,880
d. Packaging Costs	2,100	0	0	0	600	0	2,700	0	200	230	0	0	0	3,130
e. Sales Salaries/Commissions	1,400	900	1,300	1,400	1,100	900	7,000	1,400	1,400	1,400	1,400	1,400	1,400	15,400
f. Travel	0	500	700	0	0	400	1,600	0	540	25	80	0	0	2,245
g. Misc. Variable Expense	50	47	73	40	28	62	300	90	73	46	39	74	87	709
h. Depreciation	0	0	0	0	0	0	0	0	0	0	0	0	2,660	2,660
Total Variable Expenses	4,825	2,122	3,348	2,165	2,558	2,032	17,050	2,215	2,868	2,756	3,449	3,574	7,082	38,994
1. Fixed (Admin) Expenses														
a. Financial Administration	75	75	75	475	75	75	850	75	75	75	75	75	75	1,300
b. Insurance	1,564	0	0	0	0	0	1,564	1,563	0	0	0	0	0	3,127
c. Licenses/Permits	240	0	0	0	0	0	240	0	0	0	0	0	125	365
d. Office Salaries	1,400	1,400	1,400	1,400	1,400	1,400	8,400	1,400	1,400	1,400	1,400	1,400	1,400	16,800
e. Rent Expenses	700	700	700	700	700	700	4,200	700	700	700	700	700	700	8,400
f. Utilities	200	200	140	120	80	80	820	75	75	75	90	120	155	1,410
g. Misc. Fixed Expense	54	38	42	57	28	64	283	60	72	31	48	45	89	628
h. Depreciation	0	0	0	0	0	2,660	2,660	0	0	0	0	0	2,660	5,320
Total Fixed Expenses	4,233	2,413	2,357	2,752	2,283	4,979	19,017	3,873	2,322	2,281	2,313	2,340	5,204	37,350
Total Operating Expense	9,058	4,535	5,705	4,917	4,841	7,011	36,067	6,088	5,190	5,037	5,762	5,914	12,286	76,344
Net Income From Operations	2,542	2,705	155	3,041	6,431	2,859	17,733	2,453	2,080	2,373	4,588	9,936	15,424	54,587
Other Income (Interest)	234	240	260	158	172	195	1,259	213	303	300	417	406	413	3,311
Other Expense (Interest)	0	0	0	234	233	232	699	231	230	225	223	222	220	2,050
Net Profit (Loss) Before Tax	2,776	2,945	415	2,965	6,370	2,822	18,293	2,435	2,153	2,448	4,782	10,120	15,617	55,848
Taxes: a. Federal	1,950	0	0	1,950	0	1,950	5,850	0	0	1,950	0	0	0	7,800
b. State	350	0	0	350	0	350	1,050	0	0	350	0	0	0	1,400
c. Local	0	0	0	0	0	0	0	0	0	0	0	0	0	0
NET PROFIT (LOSS) AFTER TAX	476	2,945	415	665	6,370	522	11,393	2,435	2,153	148	4,782	10,120	15,617	46,648

Profit & Loss (Income) Statement
ABC Company

Beginning: January 1, 2014   **Ending: December 31, 2014**

INCOME		
1. Sales Revenues		$ 209,850
2. Cost of Goods Sold (c-d)		78,919
a. Beginning Inventory (1/01)	27,000	
b. Purchases	96,219	
c. C.O.G. Avail. Sale (a+b)	123,219	
d. Less Ending Inventory (12/31)	44,300	
3. Gross Profit on Sales (1-2)		$ 130,931
EXPENSES		
1. Variable (Selling) (a thru h)		38,994
a. Advertising/Marketing	8,140	
b. Freight	1,830	
c. Fulfillment of Orders	4,880	
d. Packaging Costs	3,130	
e. Salaries/Wages/Commissions	15,400	
f. Travel	2,245	
g. Misc. Variable (Selling) Expense	709	
h. Depreciation (Prod/Serv Assets)	2,660	
2. Fixed (Administrative) (a thru h)		37,350
a. Financial Administration	1,300	
b. Insurance	3,127	
c. Licenses & Permits	365	
d. Office Salaries	16,800	
e. Rent Expense	8,400	
f. Utilities	1,410	
g. Misc. Fixed (Administrative) Expense	628	
h. Depreciation (Office Equipment)	5,320	
Total Operating Expenses (1+2)		76,344
Net Income from Operations (GP-Exp)		$ 54,587
Other Income (Interest Income)		3,311
Other Expense (Interest Expense)		2,050
Net Profit (Loss) Before Taxes		$ 55,848
Taxes		
a. Federal	7,800	
b. State	1,400	9,200
c. Local	0	
NET PROFIT (LOSS) AFTER TAXES		$ 46,648

Business Financial History

Your financial history is a financial statement that would be required if you are writing a business plan to go to lender or investor. It is a summary of financial information about your company from its start to the present. The form will generally be provided by the lender.

If You Are a New Business

You will have only projections for your business. If you are applying for a loan, the lender will require a Personal Financial History. This will be of benefit in that it will show him the manner in which you have conducted your personal business, an indicator of the probability of your succeeding in your business.

If You Are an Established Business

The loan application and your Business Financial History are the same. When you indicate that you are interested in obtaining a business loan, the institution considering the loan will supply you with an application. Formats may vary slightly among lenders. When you receive your loan application, be sure to review it and think about how you are going to answer each item. Answer all questions, and by all means be certain that your information is accurate and that it can be easily verified.

Information Needed & Sources

As you fill out your Business Financial History (loan application), will understand why this is the last financial document to be completed. All of the information needed will have been compiled previously in earlier parts of a business plan. To help you with your financial history, the following is a list of information usually included about your business and the source you will refer to for that information:

- **Assets, Liabilities, Net Worth.** You should recognize these three as Balance Sheet terms. You have already completed a Balance Sheet for your company and need only to go back to that record and bring the dollar amounts forward.

- **Contingent Liabilities.** These are debts you may come to owe in the future (for example: default on a co-signed note or settlement of a pending lawsuit).

- **Inventory Details.** Information is derived from your Inventory Record. Also, in the Organizational Section of your plan you should already have a summary of your current policies and methods of evaluation.

- **Profit & Loss Statement.** This is income and expense information. Transfer the information from your Annual Profit & Loss (last statement completed), or from a compilation of several if required by the lender.

- **Real Estate Holdings, Stocks & Bonds.** Refer back to the Business portion of your plan. You may also have to go through your investment records for more comprehensive information.

- **Sole Proprietorship, Partnership, or Corporation Information.** There are generally three separate schedules on the financial history, one for each form of legal structure. You will be required to fill out the one that is appropriate to your business. In the Organizational section, you will have covered two areas that will serve as the source of this information -- Legal Structure & Management. Supporting Documents may also contain some of the information that you will need.

- **Audit Information.** Refer back to the Organizational Section under Recordkeeping. You may also be asked questions about other prospective lenders, whether you are seeking credit, who audits your books, and when they were last audited.

- **Insurance Coverage.** You will be asked to provide detailed information on the amounts of different types of coverage. (i.e. - merchandise, equipment, public liability, earthquake, auto, etc.) The Organizational Section contains information on coverage that can be brought forth to the financial history.

 Sample Forms

Business Financial Statement Form. On the next two pages you will find an example of a Business Financial Statement that might be required by a potential lender or investor.

Personal Financial Statement Form. Following the sample business financial statement, you will find a sample of a personal financial statement form. If you are a new business and need a personal financial statement for your business plan, you can get one from a lender, stationary store, or other supplier of office forms.

Business Financial Statement
INDIVIDUAL, PARTNERSHIP, OR CORPORATION

FINANCIAL STATEMENT OF _____   Received At_____Branch

Name_____   Business_____

Address_____   at Close of Business_____20_____

To

The undersigned, for the purpose of procuring and establishing credit from time to time with you and to induce you to permit the undersigned to become indebted to you on notes, endorsements, guarantees, overdrafts or otherwise, furnishes the following (or in lieu thereof the attached, which is the most recent statement prepared by or for the undersigned) as being a full, true and correct statement of the financial condition of the undersigned on the date indicated, and agrees to notify you immediately of the extent and character of any material changes in said financial condition, and also agrees that if the undersigned or any endorser or guarantor of any of the obligations of the undersigned, at any time fails in business or becomes insolvent, or commits an act of bankruptcy, or if any deposit account of the undersigned with you, or any other property of the undersigned held by you, be attempted to be obtained or held by writ of execution, garnishment, attachment or other legal process, or if any of the representations made below prove to be untrue, or if the undersigned fails to notify you of any material change, as above agreed, or if the business, or any interest therein of the undersigned is sold, then and in such case, at your option, all of the obligations of the undersigned to you, or held by you, shall immediately become due and payable, without demand or notice. This statement shall be construed by you to be a continuing statement of the condition of the undersigned, and a new and original statement of all assets and liabilities upon each and every transaction in and by which the undersigned hereafter becomes indebted to you, until the undersigned advises in writing to the contrary.

ASSETS	DOLLARS	CENTS	LIABILITIES	DOLLARS	CENTS
Cash In_____ (Name of Bank)			Notes Payable to Banks_____		
Cash on Hand_____			Notes Payable and Trade Acceptances for Merchandise_____		
Notes Receivable and Trade Acceptance (Includes $_____ Past Due)___			Notes Payable to Others_____		
Accounts Receivable–$_____ Less Reserves $_____			Accounts Payable (Includes $_____ Past Due)_____		
Customer's . . . (Includes $_____ Past Due)_____			Due to Partners, Employees, Relatives, Officers, Stockholders or Allied Companies____		
Merchandise—Finished—How Valued _____			Chattel Mortgages and Contracts Payable (Describe Monthly Payments) . . . . . $_____		
Merchandise—Unfinished—How Valued _____			Federal and State Income Tax_____		
Merchandise—Raw Material—How Valued _____			Accrued Liabilities (Interest, Wages, Taxes, Etc.)_____		
Supplies on Hand_____			Portion of Long Term Debt Due Within One Year_____		
Stocks and Bonds—Listed (See Schedule B)_____					
TOTAL CURRENT ASSETS			**TOTAL CURRENT LIABILITIES**		
Real Estate—Less Depreciation of: $_____ Net (See Schedule A)			Liens on Real Estate (See Schedule A) $_____		
Machinery and Fixtures— Less Depreciation of: $_____ Net			Less Current Portion Included Above $_____ Net		
Automobiles and Trucks— Less Depreciation of: $_____ Net					
Stocks and Bonds—Unlisted (See Schedule B)_____			Capital Stock—Preferred_____		
Due from Partners, Employees, Relatives, Officers, Stockholders or Allied Companies_____			Capital Stock—Common_____		
Cash Value Life Insurance_____			Surplus—Paid In_____		
Other Assets (Describe_____			Surplus—Earned and Undivided Profit_____		
TOTAL			Net Worth (If Not Incorporated)_____		
			TOTAL		

PROFIT AND LOSS STATEMENT FOR THE PERIOD FROM_____ TO_____			CONTINGENT LIABILITIES (Not Included Above)		
Net Sales (After Returned Sales and Allowances)_____			As Guarantor or Endorser_____		
Cost of Sales:			Accounts, Notes, or Trade Acceptance Discounted or Pledged_____		
Beginning Inventory			Surety On Bonds or Other Continent Liability_____		
Purchases (or cost of goods mfd.)			Letters of Credit_____		
TOTAL			Judgments Unsatisfied or Suits Pending _____		
Less: Closing Inventory			Merchandise Commitments and Unfinished Contracts_____		
Gross Profit on Sales			Merchandise Held On Consignment From Others_____		
Operating Expenses:			Unsatisfied Tax Liens or Notices From the Federal or State Governments of Intention to Assess Such Liens		
Salaries—Officers or Partners			**RECONCILEMENT OF NET WORTH OR EARNED SURPLUS**		
Salaries and Wages—Other			Net Worth or Earned Surplus at Beginning of Period_____		
Rent			Add Net Profit or Deduct Net Loss_____		
Depreciation			Total_____		
Bad Debts			Other Additions (Describe)_____		
Advertising			Total_____		
Interest			Less: Withdrawals or Dividends		
Taxes—Other Than Income			Other Deductions (Explain)_____		
Insurance			Total Deductions_____		
Other Expenses			Net Worth or Capital Funds on This Financial Statement_____		
Net Profit from Operations			**DETAIL OF INVENTORY**		
Other Income					
Less Other Expenses			Is Inventory Figure Actual or Estimated?_____		
Net Profit Before Income Tax			By whom Taken or Estimated _____ When? _____		
Federal and State Income Tax			Buy Principally From_____		
Net Profit or Loss			Average Terms of Purchase_____ Sale_____		
(Total Net Worth or Earned Surplus)_____			Time of Year Inventory Maximum _____ Minimum _____		

Business Financial Statement
INDIVIDUAL, PARTNERSHIP, OR CORPORATION – Page 2

SCHEDULE A   LIST OF REAL ESTATE AND IMPROVEMENTS WITH ENCUMBRANCES THEREON

Description, Street Number, Location	Title in Names of	BOOK VALUE		MORTGAGES OR LIENS		Terms of Payment	Holder of Lien
		LAND	IMPROVEMENTS	MATURITY	AMOUNT		
		$	$		$	$	
TOTALS		$	$		$	$	

SCHEDULE B   STOCKS & BONDS: Describe Fully. Use Supplemental Sheet if Necessary. Indicate if Stocks Are Common or Preferred. Give Interest Rate and Maturity of Bonds.

NO. OF SHARES AMT. OF BONDS	NAME AND ISSUE (DESCRIBE FULLY)	BOOK VALUE	MARKET VALUE	PRICE	VALUE
		LISTED	UNLISTED		
		$	$		$
	TOTALS	$	$		$

SCHEDULE C   Complete if Statement is for an Individual or Sole Proprietorship

Age _____ Number of Years in Present Business _____ Date of Filing _____ Fictitious Trade Style _____

What Property Listed in This Statement is in Joint Tenancy? _____ Name of Other Party _____

What Property Listed in This Statement is Community Property? _____ Name of Other Party _____

With What Other Businesses Are You Connected? _____ Have You Filed Homestead? _____

Do You Deal With or Carry Accounts With Stockbrokers? _____ Amount $ _____ Name of Firm _____

SCHEDULE D   Complete if Statement is of a Partnership

NAME OF PARTNERS (indicate special partners)	Age	Amount Contributed	Outside Net Worth	Other Business Connections
		$	$	

Date of Organization _____ Limited or General? _____ Terminates _____

If Operating Under Fictitious Trade Style, Give Date of Filing _____

SCHEDULE E   Complete if Statement is of a Corporation

	AUTHORIZED	Par Value	OUTSTANDING			ISSUED FOR
			SHARES	AMOUNT	CASH	
Common Stock	$	$		$	$	
Preferred Stock	$	$		$	$	
Bonds—Total Issue	$	$		$	$	
Date Incorporated			Under Laws of State of			

Officers	Age	Shares Owned		Directors and Principal Stockholders	Shares Owned	
		COMMON	PREFERRED		COMMON	PREFERRED
President				Director		
Vice President				Director		
Secretary				Director		
Treasurer						

SCHEDULE F   Complete in ALL Cases   INSURANCE

Are Your Books Audited by Outside Accountants? _____ None _____

Date of Last Audit _____ To What Date Has the U.S. Internal Revenue Department Examined Your Books? _____

Are You Borrowing From Any Other Branch of This Bank? _____ Which? _____

Are You Applying for Credit At Any Other Source? _____ Where? _____

Have You Ever Failed In Business? _____ If So, attach a Complete Explanation and State Basis of Settlement With Creditors _____

Lease Has _____ Years to Run With Monthly Rental of $ _____

Merchandise _____ $ _____

Machinery & Fixtures _____ $ _____

Buildings _____ $ _____

Earthquake _____ $ _____

Is Extended Coverage Endorsement Included? _____

Do You Carry Workmen's Compensation Insurance? _____

Automobiles and Trucks:

Public Liability $ _____ M/$ _____ M

Collision _____ $ _____

Property Damage _____ $ _____

Life Insurance _____ $ _____

Name of Beneficiary _____

STATEMENT OF BANK OFFICER:
Insofar as our records reveal, this Financial Statement is accurate and true. The foregoing Statement is (a copy of) the original signed by the maker, in the credit files as of this Bank.

_____ Assistant Cashier-Manager

The undersigned solemnly declares and certifies that the above statement (or in lieu thereof, the attached statement, as the case may be) and supporting schedules, both printed and written, give a full, true, and correct statement of the financial condition of the undersigned as of the date indicated.

Signature _____

By _____
(Title, If Corporation)

Personal Financial Statement

(DO NOT USE FOR BUSINESS FINANCIAL STATEMENT)

As of _____ 20_____

FINANCIAL STATEMENT OF   Received at _____ Branch

Name_____   Employed by_____

Address_____   Position _____ Age ____ Name of Spouse_____

If Employed Less Than
1 year, Previous Employer

The undersigned, for the purpose of procuring and establishing credit from time to time with you and to induce you to permit the undersigned to become indebted to you on notes, endorsements, guarantees, overdrafts or otherwise, furnishes the following (or in lieu thereof the attached, which is the most recent statement prepared by or for the undersigned) as being a full, true and correct statement of the financial condition of the undersigned on the date indicated, and agrees to notify you immediately of the extent and character of any material changes in said financial condition, and also agrees that if the undersigned or any endorser or guarantor of any of the obligations of the undersigned, at any time fails in business or becomes insolvent, or commits an act of bankruptcy, or dies, or if a writ of attachment, garnishment, execution or other legal process be issued against property of the undersigned or if any assessment for taxes against the undersigned, other than taxes on real property, is made by the federal or state government or any department thereof, or if any of the representations made below prove to be untrue, or if the undersigned fails to notify you of any material change as above agreed, or if such change occurs, or if the business, or any interest therein, of the undersigned is sold, then and in such case, all of the obligations of the undersigned to you or held by you shall immediately be due and payable, without demand or notice. This statement shall be construed by you to be a continuing statement of the condition of the undersigned, and a new and original statement of all assets and liabilities upon each and every transaction in and by which the undersigned hereafter becomes indebted to you, until the undersigned advises in writing to the contrary.

ASSETS	DOLLARS	CENTS	LIABILITIES	DOLLARS	CENTS
Cash in Bank _____ (Branch)			Notes Payable B of _____ (Branch)		
Cash on Hand _____ (Other – give name)			Notes Payable _____ (Other)		
Accounts Receivable-Good _____			Accounts Payable _____		
Stocks and Bonds (Schedule B) _____			Taxes Payable _____		
Notes Receivable-Good _____			Contracts Payable _____ (To Whom)		
Cash Surrender Value Life Insurance _____			Contracts Payable _____ (To Whom)		
Autos _____ (Year-Make) (Year-Make)			Real Estate indebtedness (Schedule A) _____		
Real Estate (Schedule A) _____			Other Liabilities (describe)		
Other Assets (describe)			1. _____		
1. _____			2. _____		
2. _____			3. _____		
3. _____			4. _____		
4. _____			TOTAL LIABILITIES		
5. _____			LESS TOTAL ASSETS		
TOTAL ASSETS			TOTAL NET WORTH		

ANNUAL INCOME			and ANNUAL EXPENDITURES (Excluding Ordinary living expenses)		
Salary_____			Real Estate payment (s)_____		
Salary (wife or husband) _____			Rent_____		
Securities Income_____			Income Taxes _____		
Rentals _____			Insurance Premiums _____		
Other (describe)			Property Taxes _____		
1. _____			Other (describe-include installment payments other than real estate)		
2. _____					
3. _____			1. _____		
4. _____			2. _____		
5. _____			3. _____		
TOTAL INCOME			TOTAL EXPENDITURES		

LESS TOTAL EXPENDITURES

NET CASH INCOME
(exclusive of ordinary expenses) _____

Personal Financial Statement

Page 2

What assets in this statement are in joint tenancy? _____ Name of other Party _____

Have you filed homestead? _____

Are you a guarantor on anyone's debt? _____ If so, give details _____

Are any encumbered assets or debts secured except as indicated? _____ If so, please itemize by debt and security _____

_____

Do you have any other business connections? _____ If so, give details _____

Are there any suits or judgments against you? _____

Have you gone through bankruptcy or compromised a debt? _____

Have you made a will? _____ Number of dependents _____

SCHEDULE A — REAL ESTATE

Location and Type of Improvement	Title in Name of	Estimated Value	Amount Owing	To Whom Payable
		$	$	

SCHEDULE B — STOCKS AND BONDS

Number of Shares Amount of Bonds	Description	Current Market on Listed	Estimated Value on Unlisted
		$	$

If additional space is needed for Schedule A and/or Schedule B, list on separate sheet and attach.

INSURANCE

Life Insurance $_____ Name of Company _____ Beneficiary _____

Automobile Insurance:

Public Liability –   yes ☐   no ☐   Property Damage – yes ☐   no ☐

Comprehensive Personal Liability –   yes ☐   no ☐

STATEMENT OF BANK OFFICER:
    Insofar as our records reveal, this Financial Statement is accurate and true. The foregoing Statement is (a copy of) the original signed by the maker, in the credit files of this Bank.

_____ **Assistant Cashier-Manager**

    The undersigned solemnly declares and certifies that the above statement (or in lieu thereof, the attached statement, as the case may be) and supporting schedules, both printed and written, give a full, true, and correct statement of the financial condition of the undersigned as of the date indicated.

_____
               Date signed   **Signature**

This Is the Beginning of the Section on
Pro Forma (Projected) Financial Statements

Pro Forma Cash Flow Statement

What Is A Cash Flow Statement?

A third or more of today's businesses fail due to a lack of cash flow. You can avoid this trap with careful planning of cash expenditures. The cash flow statement (or budget) projects what your business needs in terms dollars for a specific period of time. It is a pro forma (or projected) statement used for internal planning and estimates how much money will flow into and out of a business during a designated period of time, usually the coming tax year. Your profit at the end of the year will depend on the proper balance between cash inflow and outflow.

The Cash Flow Statement identifies when cash is expected to be received and when it must be spent to pay bills and debts. It also allows the manager to identify where the necessary cash will come from. This statement deals only with actual cash transactions and not with depreciation and amortization of goodwill or other non-cash expense items. Expenses are paid from cash on hand, sale of assets, revenues from sales and services, interest earned on investments, money borrowed from a lender, and influx of capital in exchange for equity in the company. If your business will require $100,000 to pay its expenses and $50,000 to support the owners, you will need at least an equal amount of money flowing into the business just to remain at a status quo. Anything less will eventually lead to an inability to pay your creditors or yourself.

The availability or non-availability of cash when it is needed for expenditures gets to the heart of the matter. By careful planning, you must try to project not only how much cash will have to flow into and out of your business, but also when it will need to flow in and out. A business may be able to plan for gross receipts that will cover its needs. However, if those sales do not take place in time to pay the expenses, a business will soon be history unless you plan ahead for other sources of cash to tide the business over until the income is realized.

Time Period. The cash flow statement should be prepared on a monthly basis for the next tax year. To be effective, it must be analyzed and revised quarterly to reflect your actual performance.

Preparing Your Cash Flow Statement

Before preparing your budget, it might be useful to compile individual projections and budgets. They might be as follows:

- Revenue projections (product and service)
- Inventory purchases
- Variable (selling) expense budget (with marketing budget)
- Fixed (administrative) expense budget

Preplanning Worksheets

Because the cash flow statement deals with cash inflow and cash outflow, the first step in planning can be best accomplished by preparing two worksheets.

- **Cash to Be Paid Out Worksheet.** Cash flowing out of your business; identifies categories of expenses and obligations and the projected amount of cash needed in each category. Use the information from your individual budgets (inventory purchases, variable expenses, fixed expenses, owner draws, etc.). These expenditures are not always easy to estimate. If you are a new business, it will be necessary for you research your market. If you are an existing business, you will be able to combine information from your past financial statements (such as your P&L) with trends in your particular industry.

- **Sources of Cash Worksheet.** Cash flowing into your business; used to estimate how much cash will be available from what sources. To complete this worksheet, you will have to look at cash on hand, projected sales income, assets that can be liquidated, possible lenders or investors, and owner equity to be contributed. This worksheet will force you to take a look at any existing possibilities for increasing available cash.

Sample Worksheets. On the next few pages, you will find examples of the two worksheets (filled in for the fictitious company, ABC Company) with explanatory material to help you better understand how they are developed. (Blank forms for your use are located in Appendix II).

Note that the Cash to be Paid Out Worksheet shows a need for $131,000. It is necessary in projecting Sources of Cash to account for $131,000 without the projected sales, because payment is not expected to be received until November or December (too late for cash needs January through October). Next year, those revenues will be reflected in cash on hand or other saleable assets.

 Be sure to figure all estimates on both your worksheets for the same period of time (annually, quarterly, or monthly).

Explanation of Categories
Cash to Be Paid Out Worksheet

1. Start-Up Costs

These are the costs incurred by you to get your business underway. They are generally one-time expenses and are capitalized for tax purposes.

2. Inventory Purchases

Cash to be spent during the period on items intended for resale. If you purchase manufactured products, this includes the cash outlay for those purchases. If you are the manufacturer, include labor and materials on units to be produced.

3. Variable Expenses (Selling Expenses)

These are the costs of all expenses that will relate directly to your product or service (other than manufacturing costs or purchase price of inventory).

4. Fixed Expenses (Administrative Expenses)

Include all expected costs of office overhead. If certain bills must be paid ahead, include total cash outlay even if covered period extends into the next year.

5. Fixed Assets (Long-Term Purchases)

These are the capital assets that will be depreciated over a period of years (land, buildings, vehicles, equipment). Determine how you intend to pay for them and include all cash to be paid out in the current period.

6. Liabilities

What are the payments you expect to have to make to retire any debts or loans? Do you have any Accounts Payable as you begin the new year? You will need to determine the amount of cash outlay that needs to be paid in the current year. If you have a car loan for $20,000 and you pay $500 per month for 12 months, you will have a cash outlay of $6,000 for the coming year.

7. Owner Equity

This item is frequently overlooked in planning cash flow. If you, as the business owner, will need a draw of $2,000 per month to live on, you must plan for $24,000 cash flowing out of your business. Failure to plan for it will result in a cash flow shortage and may cause your business to fail.

 Note: *Be sure to use the same time period throughout your worksheet.*

Cash to Be Paid Out Worksheet

Business Name: _____   Time Period:_____ to _____

1. **Start-Up Costs:** $ _____
   Business License   _____
   Corporation Filing   _____
   Legal Fees   _____
   Other start-up costs:
      a.   _____
      b.   _____
      c.   _____
      d.   _____

2. **Inventory Purchases**   _____
   Cash out for goods intended for resale

2. **Variable Expenses (Selling)**
      a.   _____
      b.   _____
      c.   _____
      d.   _____
      e.   _____
   Miscellaneous Variable Expense   _____
   Total Selling Expenses   _____

4. **Fixed Expenses (Administrative**
      a.   _____
      b.   _____
      c.   _____
      d.   _____
      e.   _____
      f.   _____
   Miscellaneous Fixed Expense   _____
   Total Operating Expenses   _____

5. **Assets (Long-Term Purchases)**   _____
   Cash to be paid out in current period

6. **Liabilities**   _____
   Cash outlay for retiring debts, loans, and/or
   accounts payable

7. **Owner Equity**   _____
   Cash to be withdrawn by owner

Total Cash to Be Paid Out $ _____

Explanation of Categories
Sources of Cash Worksheet

1. Cash On Hand

Money that you currently have (bank accounts, etc.). Be sure to include petty cash and monies not yet deposited.

2. Sales (Revenues)

This includes projected income from the sale of your products and/or services. If payment is not expected during the time period covered by this worksheet, do not include that portion of your sales. Think about the projected timing of sales. If receipts will be delayed beyond the time when a large amount of cash is needed, make a notation to that effect and take it into consideration when determining the need for temporary financing. Include deposits you require on expected sales or services. When figuring collections on Accounts Receivable, you will have to project the percentage of invoices that will be lost to bad debts and subtract it from your Accounts Receivable total.

3. Miscellaneous Income

Do you, or will you have, any monies out on loan or deposited in accounts that will yield interest income during the period in question?

4. Sale of Long-Term Assets

If you are expecting to sell any of your fixed assets such as land, buildings, vehicles, machinery, equipment, etc., be sure to include only the cash you will receive during the current period.

 Important: At this point in your worksheet, add up all sources of cash. If you do not have an amount equal to your projected needs, you will have to plan sources of cash covered under numbers 5 and 6 below.

5. Liabilities

This figure represents the amount you will be able to borrow from lending institutions such as banks, finance companies, the S.B.A., etc. Be reasonable about what you think you can borrow. If you have no collateral, have no business plan, or you have a poor financial history, you will find it difficult, if not impossible, to find a lender. This source of cash requires pre-planning.

6. Equity

Sources of equity come from owner investments, contributed capital, sale of stock, or venture capital. Do you anticipate availability of personal funds? Does your business have potential for growth that might interest a venture capitalist? Be sure to be realistic. You cannot sell stock (or equity) to a nonexistent investor.

Sources of Cash Worksheet

(Cash Flowing Into Your Business)

Business Name: *ABC Company*

Time Period Covered: From January 1, 2015 to December 31, 2015

1. CASH ON HAND	**$ 20,000**
2. SALES (REVENUES)	
Sales	90,000
Service Income	22,000
Deposits on Sales or Services	0
Collections on Accounts Receivable	3,000
3. MISCELLANEOUS INCOME	
Interest Income	1,000
Payments to be Received on Loans	0
4. SALE OF LONG-TERM ASSETS	0
5. LIABILITIES	
Loan Funds (Banks, Lending Inst., S.B.A., etc.)	40,000
6. EQUITY	
Owner Investments (Sole Prop. or Partnership)	10,000
Contributed Capital (Corporation)	
Sale of Stock (Corporation)	
Venture Capital	35,000
A. Without Product Sales =	**$ 131,000**
TOTAL CASH AVAILABLE	
B. With Product Sales =	**$ 221,000**

Using the Worksheets

When you have completed the worksheets, you will have estimated how much cash will be needed for the year. You also know what sources are available. Now you will break each one-year projection into monthly segments, predicting when the cash will be needed to make the financial year flow smoothly.

Project sales on a monthly basis based on payment of invoices, demand for your particular product or service and ability to fill that demand. Figure the cost-of-goods, fixed and variable expenses in monthly increments. Most will vary. When do you plan to purchase the most inventory? What months will require the most advertising? Are you expecting a rent or insurance increase? When will commissions be due on expected sales? Determine your depreciable assets needs. What are the payments and when will they begin? Fill in as much of the cash flow statement as you can, using any projections that you can comfortably determine.

 Example: Follow ABC Company through January and February.

January Projections

1. ABC projects a beginning cash balance of $20,000.
2. Cash receipts - Product manufacturing will not be completed until February, so there will be no sales. However, service income of $4,000 is projected.
3. Interest on the $20,000 will amount to about $100 at current rate.
4. There are no long-term assets to sell. Enter a zero.
5. Adding 1, 2, 3, and 4 the Total Cash Available will be $24,100.
6. Cash Payments - Product will be available from manufacturer in February and payment will not be due until pickup. However, there will be prototype costs of $5,000.
7. Variable (selling) expenses. Estimated at $1,140.
8. Fixed (administrative) expenses. Estimated at $815.
9. Interest expense. No outstanding debts or loans. Enter zero.
10. Taxes. No profit previous quarter. No estimated taxes would be due.
11. Payments on long-term assets. ABC plans to purchase office equipment to be paid in full at the time of purchase $1139.
12. Loan repayments. No loans have been received. Enter zero.
13. Owner draws. Owner will need $2,000 for living expenses.
14. Total cash paid out. Add 6 through 13. Total $10,494.
15. Cash balance. Subtract Cash Paid Out from Total Cash Available ($13,606).
16. Loans to be received. Being aware of the $30,000.00 to be paid to the manufacturer in February, a loan of $40,000.00 is anticipated to increase Cash Available. (This requires advance planning.)
17. Equity deposit. Owner plans to add $5,000 from personal CD.
18. Ending cash balance. Adding 15, 16, and 17 the result is $58,606.

February Projections

1. February beginning cash balance. January Ending Cash Balance ($58,606).
2. Cash receipts. Still no sales, but service income is $2,000.
3. Interest income. Projected at about $120.
4. Sale of long-term assets. None. Enter zero.
5. Total cash available. Add 1, 2, 3 and 4. The result is $60,726.
6. Cash payments. $30,000 due to manufacturer, $400 due on packaging design.
7. Continue as in January. Don't forget to include payments on your loan.

ABC Company
Partial Cash Flow Statement

	Jan	Feb
BEGINNING CASH BALANCE	20,000	58,606
CASH RECEIPTS		
A. Sales/Revenues	4,000	2,000
B. Receivables	0	0
C. Interest Income	100	120
D. Sale of Long-Term Assets	0	0
TOTAL CASH AVAILABLE	24,100	60,726
CASH PAYMENTS		
A. Cost of Goods to be Sold		
1. Purchases	0	30,000
2. Material	0	0
3. Labor	5,000	400
Total Cost of Goods	5,000	30,400
B. Variable Expenses (Selling)		
1. Advertising	300	
2. Freight	120	
3. Fulfillment of Orders	0	
4. Packaging Costs	270	
5. Sales/Salaries	0	
6. Travel	285	
7. Miscellaneous Selling Expense	165	
Total Variable Expenses	1,140	
C. Fixed Expenses (Administrative)		CONTINUE
1. Financial Admin	80	as in
2. Insurance	125	**JANUARY**
3. License/Permits	200	
4. Office Salaries	500	
5. Rent Expenses	110	
6. Utilities	200	
7. Miscellaneous Administrative Expense	0	
Total Fixed Expenses	1,215	
D. Interest Expense	0	
E. Federal Income Tax	0	
F. Other Uses	0	
G. Long-Term Asset Payments	1,139	
H. Loan Payments	0	
I. Owner Draws	2,000	
TOTAL CASH PAID OUT	10,494	
CASH BALANCE/DEFICIENCY	13,606	
LOANS TO BE RECEIVED	40,000	
EQUITY DEPOSITS	5,000	
ENDING CASH BALANCE	58,606	

Completing Your Pro Forma Cash Flow Statement

This page contains instructions for completing the cash flow statement on the next page. A blank form for your own projections can be found in Appendix II.

- **Vertical columns** are divided by month. The June column is followed by a 6-month total column and the December column is followed by a 12-month total column.

- **Horizontal positions** contain all sources of cash and cash to be paid out. Figures are retrieved from the two previous worksheets and from individual budgets.

To Project Figures for Each Month

Figures are projected for each month, reflecting the flow of cash in and out of your business for a one-year period. Begin with the first month of your business cycle and proceed as follows:

1. Project the Beginning Cash Balance. Enter under "January".

2. Project the Cash Receipts for January. Apportion your total year's revenues throughout the 12 months. Weight revenues as closely as you can to a realistic selling cycle for your industry.

3. Add Beginning Cash Balance and Cash Receipts to determine Total Cash Available.

4. Project cash payments to be made for cost of goods to be sold (inventory that you will purchase or manufacture). Apportion your total inventory budget throughout the year, being sure you are providing for levels of inventory that will fulfill your needs for sales projected.

5. Customize your Variable and Fixed Expense categories to match your business.

6. Project Variable, Fixed, and Interest Expenses for January. Fill out any that you can for each of the 12 months.

7. Project cash to be paid out on Taxes, Long-Term Assets, Loan Repayments, and Owner Draws.

8. Calculate Total Cash Paid Out (Total of Cost of Goods to Be Sold, Variable, Fixed, Interest, Taxes, Long-Term Asset Payments, Loan Repayments, and Owner Draws).

9. Subtract Total Cash Paid Out from Total Cash Available. The result is entered under "Cash Balance/Deficiency". Be sure to bracket this figure if the result is a negative (to avoid errors).

10. Look at Ending Cash Balance for each month and project Loans to be Received and Equity Deposits to be made. Add to Cash Balance/Deficiency to get Ending Cash Balance for each month.

11. The Ending Cash Balance for January is carried forward and becomes February's Beginning Cash Balance (as throughout the spreadsheet, each month's ending balance is the next month's beginning balance).

12. Go to February and input any numbers that are still needed to complete that month. The process is repeated until December is completed.

To Complete the Total Column

1. The Beginning Cash Balance for January is entered in the first space of the 6-month and 12-month "Total" column.

2. The monthly figures for each category (except Beginning Cash Balance, Total Cash Available, Cash Balance/Deficiency, and Ending Cash Balance) are added horizontally and the result entered in the corresponding Total category.

3. The 6- and 12-month Total columns are then computed in the same manner as each of the individual months. If your computations are accurate, the December Ending Cash Balance will be exactly the same as the Total Ending Cash Balance.

 Please Note: *If your business is new, your projections will be based solely on market research and industry trends. If the business is established, you can also use financial statements from previous years.*

Pro Forma Cash Flow Statement

ABC Company

Year: 2015

	Jan	Feb	Mar	Apr	May	Jun	6-MONTH TOTALS	Jul	Aug	Sep	Oct	Nov	Dec	12-MONTH TOTALS
BEGINNING CASH BALANCE	10,360	72,840	54,488	60,346	65,125	79,253	10,360	81,341	71,401	68,974	55,974	54,718	59,032	10,360
CASH RECEIPTS														
A. Sales/Revenues	14,000	9,500	9,500	15,000	18,000	12,000	78,000	9,000	8,000	9,500	16,000	28,000	43,000	191,500
B. Receivables	400	400	300	500	450	425	2,475	500	750	650	600	1,250	8,000	14,225
C. Interest Income	234	240	260	158	172	195	1,259	213	303	300	417	406	413	3,311
D. Sale of Long-Term Assets	2,000	0	4,000	0	0	0	6,000	0	0	0	0	0	0	6,000
TOTAL CASH AVAILABLE	26,994	82,980	68,548	76,004	83,747	91,873	98,094	91,054	80,454	79,424	72,991	84,374	110,445	225,396
CASH PAYMENTS														
A. Cost of Goods to be Sold														
1. Purchases	800	16,500	3,700	200	200	300	21,700	9,000	430	540	6,700	14,000	12,000	64,370
2. Material	2,000	1,430	200	300	250	200	4,380	359	750	5,000	400	300	350	11,539
3. Labor	4,000	2,800	400	600	500	450	8,750	600	1,500	8,000	750	500	540	20,640
Total Cost of Goods	6,800	20,730	4,300	1,100	950	950	34,830	9,959	2,680	13,540	7,850	14,800	12,890	96,549
B. Variable (Selling) Expenses														
1. Advertising	900	300	900	250	300	700	3,350	350	300	640	1,300	1,200	1,400	8,540
2. Freight	75	75	75	75	180	70	550	75	75	90	180	300	560	1,830
3. Fulfillment of Orders	300	300	300	400	350	300	1,950	300	280	325	450	600	975	4,880
4. Packaging Costs	2,100	0	0	0	600	0	2,700	0	200	230	0	0	0	3,130
5. Sales/Salaries	1,400	900	1,300	1,400	1,100	900	7,000	1,400	1,400	1,400	1,400	1,400	1,400	15,400
6. Travel	0	500	700	0	0	400	1,600	0	540	25	80	0	0	2,245
7. Misc. Variable Expense	100	100	100	100	100	100	600	100	100	100	100	100	100	1,200
Total Variable Expenses	4,875	2,175	3,375	2,225	2,630	2,470	17,750	2,225	2,895	2,810	3,510	3,600	4,435	37,225
C. Fixed Expenses														
1. Financial Admin	75	75	75	475	75	75	850	75	75	75	75	75	75	1,300
2. Insurance	1,564	0	0	0	0	0	1,564	1,563	0	0	0	0	0	3,127
3. License/Permits	240	0	0	0	0	0	240	0	0	0	0	0	125	365
4. Office Salaries	1,400	1,400	1,400	1,400	1,400	1,400	8,400	1,400	1,400	1,400	1,400	1,400	1,400	16,800
5. Rent Expenses	700	700	700	700	700	700	4,200	700	700	700	700	700	700	8,400
6. Utilities	200	200	140	120	80	80	820	75	75	75	90	120	155	1,410
7. Misc. Fixed Expense	100	100	100	100	100	100	600	100	100	100	100	100	100	1,200
Total Fixed Expenses	4,279	2,475	2,415	2,795	2,355	2,355	16,674	3,913	2,350	2,350	2,365	2,395	2,555	32,602
D. Interest Expense	0	0	0	234	233	232	699	231	230	225	223	222	220	2,050
E. Federal Income Tax	1,200	1	1	1,200	1	1,200	3,603	0	0	1,200	0	0	0	4,803
F. Other Uses	0	0	0	0	0	0	0	0	0	0	0	0	0	0
G. Long-Term Asset Payments	0	0	0	214	214	214	642	214	214	214	214	214	214	1,926
H. Loan Payments	0	1,111	1,111	1,111	1,111	1,111	5,555	1,111	1,111	1,111	1,111	1,111	1,111	12,221
I. Owner Draws	2,000	2,000	2,000	2,000	2,000	2,000	12,000	2,000	2,000	2,000	3,000	3,000	3,000	27,000
TOTAL CASH PAID OUT	19,154	28,492	13,202	10,879	9,494	10,532	91,753	19,653	11,480	23,450	18,273	25,342	24,425	214,376
CASH BALANCE/DEFICIENCY	7,840	54,488	55,346	65,125	74,253	81,341	6,341	71,401	68,974	55,974	54,718	59,032	86,020	11,020
LOANS TO BE RECEIVED	65,000	0	0	0	0	0	65,000	0	0	0	0	0	0	65,000
EQUITY DEPOSITS	0	0	5,000	0	5,000	0	10,000	0	0	0	0	0	0	10,000
ENDING CASH BALANCE	72,840	54,488	60,346	65,125	79,253	81,341	81,341	71,401	68,974	55,974	54,718	59,032	86,020	86,020

Quarterly Budget Analysis

What Is a Quarterly Budget Analysis?

Your cash flow statement is of no value to you as a business owner unless there is some means to evaluate the actual performance of your company and measure it against your projections. A Quarterly Budget Analysis is used to compare projected cash flow (or budget) with your business' actual performance. Its purpose is to show you whether or not you are operating within your projections and to help you maintain control of all phases of your business operations. When your analysis shows that you are over or under budget in any area, it will be necessary to determine the reason for the deviation and implement changes that will enable you to get back on track.

Example: If you budgeted $1,000 in advertising funds for the first quarter and you spent $1,600, the first thing you should do is look to see if the increased advertising resulted in increased sales. If sales were over projections by an amount equal to or more than the $600, your budget will still be in good shape. If not, you will have to find expenses in your budget that can be revised to make up the deficit. You might be able to take a smaller draw for yourself or spend less on travel. You might even be able to increase your profits by adding a new product or service.

Format and Sources of Information

The Quarterly Budget Analysis needs the following seven columns. Information sources are listed for each column of entries. A blank form is located in Appendix II for your use.

1. **Budget Item.** The list of budget items is taken from headings on the Pro Forma Cash Flow Statement. All items in your budget should be listed.

2. **Budget This Quarter.** Fill in the amount budgeted for current quarter from your Pro Forma Cash Flow Statement.

3. **Actual This Quarter.** Fill in actual your actual income and expenditures for the quarter. These amounts are found in your Profit & Loss Statements, Fixed Assets Log, Owner Draw and Deposit Record, and Loan Repayment Records.

4. **Variation This Quarter.** Amount spent over or under budget. Subtract actual income and expenditures from amounts budgeted to arrive at variation.

5. **Budget Year-To-Date.** Amount budgeted from beginning of the year through and including the current quarter (from Cash Flow Statement).

6. **Actual Year-To-Date.** Actual amount spent or received from beginning of year through current quarter. Again, go to the same records as in 3. above.

7. **Variation Year-To-Date.** Subtract amount spent or received year-to-date from the amount budgeted year-to-date and enter the difference.

 Note: *You will not have any information to input into columns 3, 4, 6, and 7 until you have been in business for at least one quarter. To keep from running out of operating capital early in the year, make your projections, analyze quarterly and revise your budget accordingly.*

All items contained in the Budget are listed on this form. The second column is the amount budgeted for the current quarter. By subtracting the amount actually spent, you will arrive at the variation for the quarter. The last three columns are for year-to-date figures. If you analyze at the end of the 3rd quarter, figures will represent the first nine months of your tax year.

Making Calculations: When you calculate variations, the amounts are preceded by either a plus (+) or a minus (-), depending on whether the category is a revenue or an expenses. If the actual amount is greater than the amount budgeted, (1) Revenue categories will represent the variation as a positive (+).   (2) Expense categories will represent the variation as a negative (-).

Quarterly Budget Analysis

Note: *The numbers for this budget analysis example were not derived from the cash flow statement on page 85.*

Business Name: *ABC Company*   **For the Quarter Ending: September 30, 2014**

BUDGET ITEM	THIS QUARTER			YEAR-TO-DATE		
	Budget	Actual	Variation	Budget	Actual	Variation
SALES REVENUES	145,000	150,000	5,000	400,000	410,000	10,000
Less Cost of Goods	80,000	82,500	(2,500)	240,000	243,000	(3,000)
GROSS PROFITS	65,000	67,500	2,500	160,000	167,000	7,000
VARIABLE EXPENSES						
1. Advertising/Marketing	3,000	3,400	(400)	6,000	6,200	(200)
2. Freight	6,500	5,750	750	16,500	16,350	150
3. Fulfillment of Orders	1,400	950	450	3,800	4,100	(300)
4. Packaging	750	990	(240)	2,200	2,300	(100)
5. Salaries/Commissions	6,250	6,250	0	18,750	18,750	0
6. Travel	500	160	340	1,500	1,230	270
7. Miscellaneous	0	475	(475)	0	675	(675)
FIXED EXPENSES						
1. Financial/Administrative	1,500	1,500	0	4,500	4,700	(200)
2. Insurance	2,250	2,250	0	6,750	6,750	0
3. Licenses/Permits	1,000	600	400	3,500	3,400	100
4. Office Salaries	1,500	1,500	0	4,500	4,500	0
5. Rent	3,500	3,500	0	10,500	10,500	0
6. Utilities	750	990	(240)	2,250	2,570	(320)
7. Miscellaneous	0	60	(60)	0	80	(80)
NET INCOME FROM OPERATIONS	36,100	39,125	3,025	79,250	84,895	5,645
INTEREST INCOME	1,250	1,125	(125)	3,750	3,700	(50)
INTEREST EXPENSE	1,500	1,425	75	4,500	4,500	0
NET PROFIT (Pretax)	35,850	38,825	2,975	78,500	84,095	5,595
TAXES	8,500	9,500	(1,000)	25,500	28,500	(3,000)
NET PROFIT (After Tax)	27,350	29,325	1,975	53,000	55,595	2,595

NON-INCOME STATEMENT ITEMS

	Budget	Actual	Variation	Budget	Actual	Variation
1. Long-term Asset Repayments	2,400	3,400	(1,000)	7,200	8,200	(1,000)
2. Loan Repayments	3,400	3,400	0	8,800	8,800	0
3. Owner Draws	6,000	6,900	(900)	18,000	18,900	(900)

BUDGET DEVIATIONS

	This Quarter	Year-To-Date
1. Income Statement Items:	$1,975	$2,595
2. Non-Income Statement Items:	($1,900)	($1,900)
3. Total Deviation	$75	$695

Three-Year Income Projection

What Is A Three-Year Income Projection?

This pro forma (projected) financial statement differs from a cash flow statement in that the Three-Year Income Projection includes only projected income and deductible expenses. The following examples will illustrate the difference.

- **Example 1.** Your company plans to make loan repayments of $9,000 during the year, $3,000 of which will be interest. The full amount ($9,000) would be recorded on a cash flow statement. Only the interest ($3,000) is recorded on a projected income statement. The principal is not a deductible expense.

- **Example 2.** Your company plans to buy a vehicle for $15,000 cash. The full amount is recorded on your cash flow statement. The vehicle is a depreciable asset and only the projected depreciation for the year will be recorded on the projected income statement.

- **Example 3.** You plan to take owner draws of $2,000 per month. The draws will be recorded on your cash flow statement. They are not a deductible expense and will not be recorded on the projected income statement.

Account for Increases and Decreases

Increases in income and expenses are only realistic and should be reflected in your projections. Industry trends can also cause decreases in both income and expenses. An example of this might be in the computer industry, where constant innovation, heavy competition, and standardization of components have caused decreases in both cost and sale price of related products and services. The state of the economy will also be a contributing factor in the outlook for your business.

Sources of Information

Information for a three-year projection can be developed from your pro forma cash flow statement and your business and marketing analysis. The first year's figures can be transferred from the totals of income and expense items. The second and third years' figures are derived by combining these totals with projected trends in your particular industry. Again, if you are an established business, you will also be able to use past financial statements to help you determine what you project for the future of your business. Be sure to take into account fluctuations anticipated in costs, efficiency of operation, changes in your market, etc.

 Sample Three-Year Income Projection Form. On the next page is a sample form for your use. You may wish to compile all three years on a month-by-month basis. If you are diligent enough to do so, it will provide you with a more detailed annual projection that can be compared with actual monthly performance.

Three-Year Income Projection

Business Name: **Updated: September 26, 2014**

ABC Company	YEAR 1 2015	YEAR 2 2016	YEAR 3 2017	TOTAL 3 YEARS
INCOME				
1. SALES REVENUES	500,000	540,000	595,000	1,635,000
2. Cost of Goods Sold (c-d)	312,000	330,000	365,000	1,007,000
a. Beginning Inventory	147,000	155,000	175,000	147,000
b. Purchases	320,000	350,000	375,000	1,045,000
c. C.O.G. Avail. Sale (a+b)	467,000	505,000	550,000	1,192,000
d. Less Ending Inventory (12/31)	155,000	175,000	185,000	185,000
3. GROSS PROFIT ON SALES (1-2)	188,000	210,000	230,000	628,000
EXPENSES				
1. VARIABLE (Selling) (a thru h)	67,390	84,300	89,400	241,090
a. Advertising/Marketing	22,000	24,500	26,400	72,900
b. Freight	9,000	12,000	13,000	34,000
c. Fulfillment of Orders	2,000	3,500	4,000	9,500
d. Packaging Costs	3,000	4,000	3,500	10,500
e. Salaries/Wages/Commissions	25,000	34,000	36,000	95,000
f. Travel	1,000	1,300	1,500	3,800
g. Miscellaneous Selling Expense	390	0	0	390
h. Depreciation (Prod/Service Assets)	5,000	5,000	5,000	15,000
2. FIXED (Administrative) (a thru h)	51,610	53,500	55,800	160,910
a. Financial Administration	1,000	1,200	1,200	3,400
b. Insurance	3,800	4,000	4,200	12,000
c. Licenses & Permits	2,710	1,400	1,500	5,610
d. Office Salaries	14,000	17,500	20,000	51,500
e. Rent Expense	22,500	22,500	22,500	67,500
f. Utilities	3,000	3,500	3,600	10,100
g. Miscellaneous Fixed Expense	0	0	0	0
h. Depreciation (Office Equipment)	4,600	3,400	2,800	10,800
TOTAL OPERATING EXPENSES (1+2)	119,000	137,800	145,200	402,000
NET INCOME OPERATIONS (GPr - Exp)	69,000	72,200	84,800	226,000
OTHER INCOME (Interest Income)	5,000	5,000	5,000	15,000
OTHER EXPENSE (Interest Expense)	7,000	5,000	4,000	16,000
NET PROFIT (LOSS) BEFORE TAXES	67,000	72,200	85,800	225,000
TAXES 1. Federal, S-Employment	21,700	24,200	28,500	74,400
2. State	4,300	4,800	5,700	14,800
3. Local	0	0	0	0
NET PROFIT (LOSS) AFTER TAXES	41,000	43,200	51,600	135,800

Break-Even Analysis

What Is a Break-Even Point?

This is the point at which a company's costs exactly match their sales volume and at which the business has neither made a profit nor incurred a loss. The breakeven point can be determined by mathematical calculation or by development of a graph. It can be expressed in either of two ways:

Total dollars of income (exactly offset by total costs)
- or -
Total units of production (cost of which exactly equals income derived by their sale)

To apply a break-even analysis to an operation, you will need three projections:

1. **Fixed Costs for the Period** (Administrative Expense + Interest Expense) Many of these costs remain constant even during slow periods. Interest expense must be added to fixed costs for a break-even analysis.

2. **Variable Costs** (Cost of Goods + Selling Expenses). Usually varies with volume of business. The greater the sales volume, the higher the costs.

3. **Total Sales Volume** (Projected sales for same period).

Source of Information

All of your figures can be derived from your Three-Year Projection. Since breakeven is not reached until your total income matches your total expenses, the calculation of your break-even point will require that you add enough years' income (revenues) and expenses together until you see that the total income is greater than the total expenses. Retrieve the figures and plug them into the following mathematical formula. (By now you should be able to see that each financial document in your business plan builds on the ones done previously.)

Mathematically

Sales at break-even point can be computed using the following formula:

B-E Point (Sales) = Fixed Costs + [(Variable Costs/Estimated Revenues) x Sales]

Terms Used: *a. Sales = volume of sales at Break-Even Point*
b. Fixed Costs = administrative expense + interest paid out
c. Variable Costs = cost of goods sold and selling expenses
d. Estimated Revenues = Income (from sales of goods/services)

Figures are: *a. S (Sales at B-E Point) = The Unknown*
b. FC (Fixed Costs) = $25,000
c. VC (Variable Costs) = $45,000
d. R (Estimated Revenues) = $90,000

Using the formula, the computation would appear as follows:
S (at B-E Point) = $25,000 + [($45,000/$90,000) x S]
S = $25,000 + (1/2 x S)
S - 1/2 S = $25,000
1/2 S = $25.000

★ **S = $50,000   (Break-Even Point in terms of dollars of revenue exactly offset by total costs for the same period of time)**

Graphically

Break-Even Point in graph form for the same business would be plotted as illustrated below. There is a blank form for your use in Appendix II.

Break-Even Analysis Graph

Business Name: *ABC Company*   **Date of Analysis: Sept 31, 2014**

NOTE: Figures shown in 10's of thousands of dollars (Ex: 2 = $20,000)

To Complete the Graph. Determine the following projections.

1. **Fixed Costs for Period** - Those costs that usually remain constant and must be met regardless of your sales volume (administrative, rent, insurance, depreciation, salaries, etc.) Also add interest expenses. (i.e., $25,000).

2. **Variable Costs** - Cost associated with the production and selling of your products or services. If you have a product, you will include cost-of-goods (inventory purchases, labor, materials) with your variable costs (freight, packaging, sales commissions, advertising, etc.). If you wish, these costs may be expressed by multiplying the unit cost by the units to be sold for a product. (i.e., $1.50 per unit x 30,000 units = $45,000). For a service having no cost of goods, use total of projected selling expenses.

3. **Total Sales Volume** - This is the figure representing your total projected revenues. You may also calculate revenues by multiplying projected units of product to be sold by the sale price per unit (i.e., 30,000 @ $3.00 = $90,000; for a service, you can multiply your projected billable hours x your hourly rate (i.e., 900 hours x $100 = $90,000).

To Draw Graph Lines.

1. **Draw Horizontal Line** at point representing Fixed Costs (25).

2. **Draw Variable Cost Line** from left end of Fixed Cost Line sloping upward to point where Total Costs (Fixed + Variable) on the vertical scale (7) meet Total Revenues on the horizontal scale (9)

3. **Draw Total Revenues Line** from zero through a point describing total Revenues on both scales (where vertical 9 meets horizontal 9).

Break-Even Point = The point on the graph where the Variable Cost Line intersects the Total Revenue Line. This business projects that it will break even when sales volume reaches $50,000. The triangular area, below and to the left of the intersection point, represents company losses. The triangular area, above and to the right of the point, represents expected company profits.

Summary of Financial Statements

Congratulations!

You have now finished your study of Financial Statements and hopefully will at least feel a little more comfortable about developing a Pro Forma Cash Flow Statement, Profit & Loss Statement and Balance Sheet of your own from your General Records. These three records will be the backbone of your business. The rest of the financial statements you studied will also prove valuable, especially if you are in the process of writing a business plan.

It Takes Time to Learn

Don't expect to remember and absorb all of this information right now. I'm sure that you are overwhelmed. As you set up and work with your records, everything will fall into place. Recordkeeping is not difficult. It is simply a matter of repetitive work that will soon become a matter of habit.

Business Planning

Before we close this chapter, I would like to say another word about business planning. Every now and then, throughout the text, we have mentioned the benefits of writing a business plan. Most entrepreneurs shudder at the thought of having to go through the formal planning process. It is a difficult task, but one that may ultimately make the difference between success and failure. A business plan is required if you are seeking a lender or investor. More importantly, however, it is the guide you will follow during the life of your business. Having learned about recordkeeping and financial statements, you will have made a significant step in the planning process.

If you are inclined to write a business plan for your business, we do have a business plan book, *Anatomy of a Business Plan*, and its companion stand alone software, Automate Your Business Plan. They will lead you step-by-step through the planning process.

What's In The Next Chapter?

In the next chapter, we will show you how to analyze your financial statements in order to make business decisions and implement changes that will make your business more profitable.

CHAPTER

6

Financial Statement Analysis

written by:

Marilyn J. Bartlett, C.P.A.

Marilyn J. Bartlett is a C.P.A. Her success at helping businesses that are in trouble was greatly enhanced by her ability to analyze financial statements and implement the appropriate changes. I would like to thank her for sharing her expertise with me through the contribution of this chapter. Because of her generosity, the user of this book has the opportunity not only to set up and maintain the proper records, but to gain the maximum benefits from those records through financial statement analysis.

Financial Statements

Your financial statements contain the information you need to help make decisions regarding your business. Many small business owners think of their financial statements as requirements for creditors, bankers, or tax preparers only, but they are much more than that. When analyzed, your financial statements can give you key information needed on the financial condition and the operations of your business.

Financial statement analysis requires measures to be expressed as ratios or percentages. For example, consider the situation where total assets on your balance sheet are $10,000.00. Cash is $2,000; Accounts Receivable are $3,000; and Fixed Assets are $5,000. The relationships would be expressed as follows:

	Ratio	Ratio Relationship	Percentages
Cash	.2	.2:1	20%
Accounts Receivable	.3	.3:1	30%
Fixed Assets	.5	.5:1	50%

Financial statement analysis involves the study of relationships and comparisons of (1) items in a single year's financial statement, (2) comparative financial statements for a period of time, and (3) your statements with those of other businesses.

Many analytic tools are available, but I will focus on the following measures that are of most importance to a small business owner in the business planning process:

Liquidity Analysis	**Measures of Investment**
Profitability Analysis	**Vertical Financial Statement Analysis**
Measures of Debit	**Horizontal Financial Statement Analysis**

Let's take a look, on the next few pages, at some ratios that may help you to evaluate your business. To illustrate, we will use the following statements from a small business. We will call it Mary's Flower Shop and we will use small figures that will be easy to examine.

Mary's Flower Shop
Comparative Balance Sheet
12/31/15 and 12/31/14

	2015	2014
ASSETS		
Current Assets		
Cash	$2,000	$5,000
Accounts Receivable	3,000	1,000
Inventory	5,000	3,000
Total Current Assets	$10,000	$ 9,000
Fixed Assets	8,000	5,000
Total Assets	**$18,000**	**$14,000**
LIABILITIES		
Current Liabilities		
Accounts Payable	$4,000	$2,000
Taxes Payable	220	300
Total Current Liabilities	$4,220	$2,300
Long Term Liabilities	10,000	8,000
Total Liabilities	**$14,220**	**$10,300**
OWNER'S EQUITY (NET WORTH)	**$ 3,780**	**$3,700**
TOTAL LIABILITIES + EQUITY	**$18,000**	**$14,000**

Mary's Flower Shop
Comparative Income Statement
For Years Ended 12/31/15 and 12/31/14

	2015	2014
SALES	$8,000	$6,000
Cost of Goods Sold	-6,000	-3,900
GROSS PROFIT	$2,000	$2,100
EXPENSES		
Selling (Variable) Expenses		
Advertising	$ 100	$ 50
Freight	50	40
Salaries	150	150
Total Selling Expenses	$ 300	$ 240
Administrative (Fixed) Expenses		
Rent	$ 450	$ 250
Insurance	150	125
Utilities	150	100
Total Administrative Expenses	$ 750	$ 475
INCOME FROM OPERATIONS	$ 950	$1,385
Interest Income	+ 0	+ 0
Interest Expense	- 620	- 450
NET INCOME BEFORE TAXES	$ 330	$ 935
TAXES	- 60	- 180
NET PROFIT (LOSS) AFTER TAXES	$ 270	$ 755

Now You Are Ready to

Analyze Mary's Financial Statements

Turn the Page to Begin

Liquidity Analysis

The liquidity of a business is the ability it has to meet financial obligations. The analysis focuses on the balance sheet relationships for the current assets and current liabilities.

Net Working Capital

The excess of current assets over current liabilities is net working capital. The more net working capital a business has, the less risky it is, as it has the ability to cover current liabilities as they come due. Let's take a look at the net working capital for Mary's Flower Shop:

Formula	2015	2014
Current Assets	$10,000	$ 9,000
– Current Liabilities	- 4,220	- 2,300
Net Working Capital	$ 5,780	$ 6,700

In both years, net working capital was present, which would indicate a good position. But let's analyze this a bit more to get a clear picture of the liquidity of Mary's Flower Shop.

Current Ratio

The current ratio is a more dependable indicator of liquidity than the net working capital. The current ratio is computed with the following formula:

$$\text{Current Ratio} = \frac{\text{Current Assets}}{\text{Current Liabilities}}$$

For Mary's Flower Shop, the current ratios are:

2015: $\frac{\$10,000}{\$\ 4,220} = 2.37$

2014: $\frac{\$\ 9,000}{\$\ 2,300} = 3.91$

As you can see, the business was in a more liquid position in 2014. In 2015, the business did experience an increase in current assets, but it also had an increase in current liabilities.

There are no set criteria for the **normal** current ratio, as that is dependent on the business you are in. If you have predictable cash flow, you can operate with a lower current ratio.

A ratio of 2.0 is considered acceptable for most businesses. This would allow a company to lose 50% of its current assets and still be able to cover current liabilities. For most businesses, this is an adequate margin of safety.

For Mary's Flower Shop, the **decrease** in the current ratio would cause the owner to investigate further.

Quick Ratio

Since inventory is the most difficult current asset to dispose of quickly, it is subtracted from the current assets in the quick ratio to give a tougher test of liquidity. The quick ratio is computed as follows:

$$\textbf{Quick Ratio} = \frac{\textbf{Current Assets - Inventory}}{\textbf{Current Liabilities}}$$

The quick ratios for our case are:

$$\textbf{2015:} \quad \frac{\$10,000 - 5,000}{\$4,220} = 1.18$$

$$\textbf{2014:} \quad \frac{\$9,000 - 3,000}{\$2,300} = 2.61$$

A quick ratio of 1.00 or greater is usually recommended, but that is dependent upon the business you are in.

From the analysis of the liquidity measures (net working capital, current ratio and quick ratio), we see that the 2015 results are within acceptable limits. The business did experience a decrease in liquidity, and is viewed as more risky than in 2014.

You can use these ratios to see if your business is in any risk of insolvency. You will also be able to assess your ability to increase or decrease current assets for your business strategy. How would these moves affect your liquidity?

Your creditors will use these ratios to determine whether or not to extend credit to you. They will compare the ratios for previous periods and with those of similar businesses.

Profitability Analysis

A Profitability Analysis will measure the ability of a business to make a profit.

Gross Profit Margin

The gross profit margin indicates the percentage of each sales dollar remaining after a business has paid for its goods.

$$\text{Gross Profit Margin} = \frac{\text{Gross Profit}}{\text{Sales}}$$

The higher the gross profit margin, the better. For Mary's Flower Shop, the gross profit margins were:

$$2015: \quad \frac{\$2,000}{\$8,000} = 25\%$$

$$2014: \quad \frac{\$2,100}{\$6,000} = 35\%$$

The **normal** rate is dependent on the business you are in. The Gross Profit Margin is the actual mark-up you have on the goods sold.

In 2015, our case has a 25% contribution margin which means that 25 cents of every dollar in sales is left to cover the variable, fixed, and other expenses. In 2014, there had been a 35% contribution margin, or 35 cents of every dollar in sales left to cover those expenses. Mary's Flower Shop, therefore, can be viewed as "less profitable" in 2015 as compared to 2014.

Operating Profit Margin

This ratio represents the pure operations profits, ignoring interest and taxes. A high operating profit margin is preferred.

$$\text{Operating Profit Margin} = \frac{\text{Income from Operations}}{\text{Sales}}$$

Mary's Flower Shop has the following ratios:

$$\textbf{2015:} \qquad \frac{\$\,950}{\$8,000} \;=\; 11.88\%$$

$$\textbf{2014:} \qquad \frac{\$1,385}{\$6,000} \;=\; 23.08\%$$

Again our case is showing a less profitable position in 2015 than it did in 2014.

Net Profit Margin

The net profit margin is clearly the measure of business success with respect to earnings on sales.

$$\textbf{Net Profit Margin} \;=\; \frac{\textbf{Net Profit}}{\textbf{Sales}}$$

A higher margin means the firm is more profitable. The net profit margin will differ according to your specific type of business. A 1% margin for a grocery store is not unusual due to the large quantity of items handled; while a 10% margin for a jewelry store would be considered low.

Mary's Flower Shop has the following net profit margins:

$$\textbf{2015:} \qquad \frac{\$\,270}{\$8,000} \;=\; 3.4\%$$

$$\textbf{2014:} \qquad \frac{\$\,755}{\$6,000} \;=\; 12.6\%$$

Clearly, Mary's Flower Shop is in trouble. All the ratios indicate a significant decrease in profitability from 2014. The next step is to determine reasons for that decrease.

As a business owner, you can see just how profitable your business is. If the ratios are too low, you will want to analyze why.

- *Are your products and/or services priced high enough? Check your gross profit margin.*

- *Are your operating expenses too high? Check your operating profit margin.*

- *Are your interest expenses too high? Check your net profit margin.*

For Mary's Flower shop, all of the above questions can be answered using the ratios we computed. Your creditors will look at these ratios to see just how profitable your business is. Without profits, a business can't attract outside financing.

Debt Measures

The debt position of a business indicates the amount of other people's money that is being used to generate profits. Many new businesses assume too much debt too soon in an attempt to grow too quickly. The measures of debt will tell a business how indebted it is and how able it is to service the debts. The more the indebtedness, the greater will be the risk of failure.

Debt Ratio

This is a key financial ratio used by creditors.

$$\textbf{Debt Ratio} \ = \ \frac{\textbf{Total Liabilities}}{\textbf{Total Assets}}$$

The higher this ratio, the more risk of failure. For Mary's Flower Shop, the debt ratios are:

$$\textbf{2015:} \quad \frac{\$14,200}{\$18,000} \ = \ 79\%$$

$$\textbf{2014:} \quad \frac{\$10,300}{\$14,000} \ = \ 74\%$$

The acceptable ratio is dependent upon the policies of your creditors and bankers. The rates of 79% and 74% above are excessively high and show a very high risk of failure. Clearly 3/4 of the company is being financed by other peoples' money, and it does not put the business in a good position for acquiring new debt.

If your business plan includes the addition of long-term debt at a future point, you will want to monitor your debt ratio. Will it be within the limits acceptable to your banker or investor?

Investment Measures

As a small business owner, you have invested money to acquire assets, and you should be getting a return on these assets. Even if the owner is taking a salary from the business, he/she also should be earning an additional amount for the investment in the company.

Return on Investment (ROI)

The Return on Investment measures the effectiveness of you as the business owner, to generate profits from the available assets.

$$\text{ROI} = \frac{\text{Net Profits}}{\text{Total Assets}}$$

The higher the ROI, the better. The business owner should set a target for the ROI. What do you want your investment to earn?

For Mary's Flower Shop, the ROI is as follows:

$$2015: \quad \frac{\$\,270}{\$18,000} = 1.5\%$$

$$2014: \quad \frac{\$\,755}{\$14,000} = 5.4\%$$

We do not know Mary's target for ROI, but 1.5% would seem unacceptable. She could put her money in certain types of investments that would be likely to earn 5% or more, so it doesn't appear that a 1.5% return on her investment is good.

Many small business owners have successfully created jobs for themselves, but still don't earn a fair return on their investment. Set your target for ROI, and work towards it.

Vertical Financial Statement Analysis

Percentage analysis is used to show the relationship of the components in a single financial statement.

- **For a Balance Sheet:** Each asset is stated as a percent of total assets, and each liability and equity item is stated as a percent of total liabilities and equity.

- **For an Income Statement:** In vertical analysis of the income statement, each item is stated as a percent of net sales.

A vertical analysis of the income statements for Mary's Flower Shop as shown below.

Mary's Flower Shop
Comparative Income Statement
For Years Ended 12/31/15 and 12/31/14

	2015		2014	
	Amount	Percent	Amount	Percent
Sales	$8,000	100.0%	$6,000	100.0%
Cost of Goods Sold	-6,000	75.0%	-3,900	65.0%
Gross Profit	**$2,000**	**25.0%**	**$2,100**	**35.0%**
Selling (Variable) Expenses				
Advertising	$ 100	1.3%	$ 50	.8%
Freight	50	.6%	40	.7%
Salaries	150	1.9%	150	2.5%
Total Selling Expenses	**$ 300**	**3.8%**	**$ 240**	**4.0%**
Administrative (Fixed) Expenses				
Rent	$ 450	5.6%	$ 250	4.2%
Insurance	150	1.9%	125	2.1%
Utilities	150	3.8%	100	1.7%
Total Administrative Expenses	**$ 750**	**9.3%**	**$ 475**	**8.0%**
Income From Operations	**$ 950**	**11.9%**	**$1,385**	**23.0%**
Interest Income	+ 0	0.0%	+ 0	0.0%
Interest Expense	- 620	7.7%	- 450	7.5%
Net Income Before Taxes	**$ 330**	**4.2%**	**$ 935**	**15.5%**
Taxes	- 60	0.8%	- 180	3.0%
Net Profit (Loss) After Taxes	**$ 270**	**3.4%**	**$ 755**	**12.5%**

Evaluation of Vertical Financial Statement

From the vertical analysis of Mary's income statements, we can see the following:

1. **The components of cost of goods sold and gross showed significant difference.**

    - Cost of goods sold increased from 65% of sales to 75% of sales. This should alert the owner to investigate.

        - Did the cost of the items really increase and the selling price stay the same?

        - Is there a possibility of theft that may have caused the variance?

    - The decrease in gross profit margin from 35% of sales to 25% of sales should also trigger the owner to look at the mark-up.

        - Is the mark-up too low?

        - Will your customers still buy if you raise the selling price on your products?

2. **The composition of variable expenses changed.**

    - The owner would want to evaluate the appropriateness of the increase in advertising and the decrease in salaries.

3. **The composition of fixed expenses would alert the owner to evaluate the increase in rent.**

    - Why did this occur?

    - Is it necessary or are there other alternatives?

4. **The increase in interest should be analyzed.**

    - The most likely reason for the increase would probably be an increase in debt.

Horizontal Financial Statement Analysis

Horizontal analysis is a percentage analysis of the increases and decreases in the items on comparative financial statements (i.e., balance sheets or income statements).

The increase or decrease of the item is listed, and the earlier statement is used as the base. The percentage of increase or decrease is listed in the last column.

A horizontal analysis of the income statements for Mary's Flower Shop can be seen below.

Mary's Flower Shop
Comparative Income Statement
For Years Ended 12/31/15 and 12/31/14

	2015	2014	Increase/Decrease	
	Amount	Amount	Amount	Percent
Sales	$8,000	$6,000	$2,000	33.3%
Cost of Goods Sold	6,000	3,900	2,100	53.8%
Gross Profit	**$2,000**	**2,100**	**($ 100)**	**(4.8%)**
Selling (Variable) Expenses				
Advertising	$ 100	$ 50	$ 50	100.0%
Freight	50	40	10	25.0%
Salaries	150	150	same	same
Total Selling Expenses	**$ 300**	**$ 240**	**$ 60**	**25.0%**
Administrative (Fixed) Expenses				
Rent	$ 450	$ 250	$ 200	80.0%
Insurance	150	125	25	20.0%
Utilities	150	100	50	50.0%
Total Administrative Expenses	**$ 750**	**$ 475**	**$ 275**	**57.9%**
Income From Operations	**$ 950**	**$1,385**	**(435)**	**(31.4%)**
Interest Income	0	0	0	0.0%
Interest Expense	620	450	170	37.8%
Net Income Before Taxes	**$ 330**	**$ 935**	**($ 605)**	**(64.7%)**
Taxes	60	180	(120)	(66.7%)
Net Profit (Loss) After Taxes	**$ 270**	**$ 755**	**($ 485)**	**(64.2%)**

Evaluation of Horizontal Financial Statement

From the horizontal analysis of Mary's income statements, we should evaluate the following:

1. **The 33.3% increase in sales resulted in a 4.8% decrease in gross profit.**
    - This would alert the owner that something is wrong.
    - Is the mark-up sufficient?
    - Was there an according adjustment?

2. **The 100% increase in advertising expense was steep.**
    - Did this expense increase sales?
    - Was it justified?

3. **The 80% rent increase and 50% utilities increase should be looked at.**
    - Are they justified?

4. **The 60% interest increase is most likely a result of increased debt.**
    - The owner would want to analyze the components.
    - Decide if the interest level is correct.
    - Decide if some debt should be retired.

5. **The 64.2% decrease in net profit is not acceptable.**
    - A serious decrease will require that the owner re-evaluate the business.

Summary

Now, you can see how financial statement analysis can be a tool to help you manage your business.

- If the analysis produces results that don't meet your expectation or if the business is in danger of failure, you must analyze your expenses and your use of assets. Your first step should be to cut expenses and increase the productivity of your assets.

- If your return on investment is too low, examine how you could make your assets (equipment, machinery, fixtures, inventory, etc.) work better for your benefits.

- If your profit is low, be sure that your mark up is adequate, analyze your operating expenses to see that they are not too high, and review your interest expenses.

- If your liquidity is low, you could have a risk of becoming insolvent. Examine the level and composition of current assets and current liabilities.

The vertical and horizontal financial statement analysis will reveal trends and compositions that signify trouble. Using your management skills, you can take corrective action.

Keeping the Books, Chapter 6, Financial Statement Analysis

CHAPTER

7

Taxes & Accounting

Warning!

DISCLAIMER

The information in this chapter is presented with the understanding that I am in no way rendering legal, accounting, or other professional services. My purpose is to introduce you to some of the common tax forms and publications and to provide you with a general guide for use in recordkeeping. Detailed information, along with legal advice, will have to be obtained from your accountant, attorney, or the IRS.

Accounting ◄──► U.S. Tax System

If you are going to be in command of your business recordkeeping, it will be necessary for you to have a good basic understanding of the relationship between your finances and income tax accounting.

When the federal income tax came into being, it was structured according to accounting principles. This has served a double purpose.

- **Accounting → Taxes.** Your financial records enable you to retrieve the necessary information for filing taxes at the close of your tax year.

- **Taxes → Accounting.** By the same token, the tax forms that you will be required to submit will provide you with important clues as to how your accounting can be set up, not only in a usable format, but in a manner that will make it practical for you to analyze your financial statements and determine what changes will have to be implemented for future growth and profit.

Using Tax Information for Business Analysis

In order for you to better comprehend the relationship between the tax system and analyzing your business, I will give you two examples of tax forms and how you can benefit from understanding those forms.

1. **Schedule C (Form 1040)**

   Entitled *Profit or Loss from Business* (Sole Proprietorship)
   (required tax reporting form for Sole Proprietors).

   - **IRS Information Required:** Gross receipts or sales, beginning and ending inventories, labor, materials, goods purchased, returns and allowances, deductible expenses, interest expense, interest income, and net profit or loss.

   - **Benefits of Understanding:** In case you did not catch on, the required information listed above is exactly the same as the list of income and expenses on a Profit & Loss Statement. When the IRS has you fill out a business return, you are merely transferring information from the profit and loss. By understanding this, you can look through a Schedule C and see what categories of information are needed under expenses. This can help you to decide what categories you will use in your Income & Expense Journal. It will also help you after your accountant has sent your return back to you for submission to the IRS. Now you can put your knowledge of a P & L Statement to work and read and check it over for accuracy – a chore too frequently ignored by taxpayers. Since you have the final responsibility for the correctness of your return, knowing how to examine it can prevent mistakes that might prove costly.

   Note: Form 1065, *U.S. Return of Partnership Income*, and Form 1120, *U.S. Corporation Income Tax Returns*, are used for those legal structures.

2. **Schedule SE (Form 1040)**

   Entitled *Computation of Social Security Self Employment Tax.*

   - **IRS Information Required:** Computation of contribution to Social Security.

   - **Benefits of Understanding:** Failure to familiarize yourself with the requirements on how to compute this tax and know what percentage of your net income will be owed will result in a false picture as to the net profit of your business. Don't forget – the IRS is interested in your Net Profit before taxes. You are concerned with Net Profit after taxes.

As you can see from the two examples, examination of required tax forms can lead to the discovery of many types of records that your business will need and that it can profit from.

Federal Taxes for Which You May be Liable

This chapter is devoted to introducing you to the most common federal taxes for which a sole proprietor, partnership, or corporation may be liable. Its purpose is not to guide you through filling out tax returns. It is to make you aware of required reporting, familiarize you with some of the forms, and give you a frame of reference for any questions you have. To do this, I will give you a brief overview of each requirement and include the following:

- Tax to be reported (calendars)
- Sample Tax forms and worksheets
- IRS publications to be used for information

Calendar of Federal Taxes

During the tax year, all businesses must comply with reporting regulations and periodic payments of federal taxes. Familiarize yourself with the federal taxes liabilities. Your legal structure will determine required reporting dates. They are not the same for sole proprietorships and partnerships as they are for S Corporations and C Corporations. Your cash flow statement must reflect these payments. If you fail to account for tax liabilities, you will find yourself with an unbalanced budget and it is possible that a serious cash deficiency could result.

For your convenience, I have provided tax calendars on the next four pages. There is a calendar for each of the four legal structures (sole proprietor, partnership, S Corporation, and corporation). They will serve as guides to tell you when tax and information returns must be filed.

Copy the calendar that is appropriate to your business and post it near your bookkeeping area to remind you to file on the appropriate dates. It will be especially useful combined with your Recordkeeping Schedule which will be presented in the next chapter.

Tax Forms and Information

Following the tax calendars, you will find the most common tax forms for each legal structure as well as various tax worksheets. You will also find pertinent information that applies to each of the forms.

Free IRS Publications, Forms, and Information

What most of us don't know is that the United States government has spent a great deal of time and money to provide you with free publications and forms, as well as tax workshops, forums, videos, etc. On page 150, we will provide you with a list of some of the most frequently requested publications.

Make a conscious decision to send for (or download) publications and forms.

At least once a year, you should update your IRS file with new publications and forms and you should make it a priority to study revisions that take place in U.S. tax laws.

> ☞ ***Use the Index.*** If you are looking for information on a specific tax or form, you will find that the text and forms are referenced three ways in the index at the back of the book: by form number, by subject matter, and by legal structure.

Sole Proprietor

Calendar of Federal Taxes for Which You May be Liable

January	15	Estimated tax	Form 1040ES
	31	Social security (FICA) tax and the withholding of income tax Note: See IRS rulings for deposit - Pub. 334	941, 941E, 942, and 943
	31	Providing information on social security (FICA) tax and the withholding of income tax	W-2 (to employee)
	31	Federal unemployment (FUTA) tax	940-EZ or 940
	31	Federal unemployment (FUTA) tax (only if liability for unpaid taxes exceeds $100)	8109 (to make deposits)
	31	Information returns to non-employees and transactions with other persons	Form 1099 (to recipients)
February	28	Information returns to non-employees and transactions with other persons	Form 1099 (to IRS)
	28	Providing information on social security (FICA) tax and the withholding income tax	W-2 & W-3 (to Social Security Admin.)
April	15	Income tax	Schedule C (Form 1040)
	15	Self-employment tax	Schedule SE (Form 1040)
	15	Estimated tax	Form 1040ES
	30	Social security (FICA) tax and the withholding of income tax Note: See IRS rulings for deposit - Pub. 334	941, 941E, 942, and 943
	30	Federal unemployment (FUTA) tax (only if liability for unpaid taxes exceeds $100)	8109 (to make deposits)
June	15	Estimated tax	Form 1040ES
July	31	Social security (FICA) tax and the withholding of income tax Note: See IRS rulings for deposit - Pub. 334	941, 941E, 942, and 943
	31	Federal unemployment (FUTA) tax (only if liability for unpaid taxes exceeds $100)	8109 (to make deposits)
September	15	Estimated tax	Form 1040ES
October	31	Social security (FICA) tax and the withholding of income tax Note: See IRS rulings for deposit - Pub. 334	941, 941E, 941, and 943
	31	Federal unemployment (FUTA) tax (only if liability for unpaid taxes exceeds $100)	8109 (to make deposits)

If your tax year is not January 1st through December 31st:

- Schedule C (Form 1040) is due the 15th day of the 4th month after end of the tax year. Schedule SE is due same day as Form 1040.

- Estimated tax (1040ES) is due the 15th day of 4th, 6th, and 9th months of tax year, and the 15th day of 1st month after the end of tax year.

Partnership

Calendar of Federal Taxes for Which You My be Liable

January	15	Estimated tax (individual who is a partner)	Form 1040ES
	31	Social security (FICA) tax and the withholding of income tax Note: See IRS rulings for deposit - Pub. 334	941, 941E, 942, and 943
	31	Providing information on soc. security (FICA) tax and the withholding of income tax	W-2 (to employee)
	31	Federal unemployment (FUTA) tax	940-EZ or 940
	31	Federal unemployment (FUTA) tax (only if liability for unpaid taxes exceeds $100)	8109 (to make deposits)
	31	Information returns to non-employees and transactions with other persons	Form 1099 (to recipients)
February	28	Information returns to non-employees and transactions with other persons	Form 1099 (to IRS)
	28	Providing information on social security (FICA) tax and on withholding income tax	W-2 & W-3 (to Social Security Admin.)
April	15	Income tax (individual who is a partner)	Schedule C (Form 1040)
	15	Annual return of income	Form 1065
	15	Self-employment tax (individual who is partner)	Schedule SE (Form 1040)
	15	Estimated tax (individual who is partner)	Form 1040ES
	30	Social security (FICA) tax and the withholding of income tax Note: See IRS rulings for deposit - Pub. 334	941, 941E, 942, and 943
	30	Federal unemployment (FUTA) tax (only if liability for unpaid taxes exceeds $100)	8109 (to make deposits)
June	15	Estimated tax (individual who is a partner)	Form 1040ES
July	31	Social security (FICA) tax and the withholding of income tax Note: See IRS rulings for deposit - Pub. 334	941, 941E, 942, and 943
	31	Federal unemployment (FUTA) tax (only if liability for unpaid taxes exceeds $100)	8109 (to make deposits)
September	15	Estimated tax (individual who is a partner)	Form 1040ES
October	31	Social security (FICA) tax and the withholding of income tax Note: See IRS rulings for deposit - Pub. 334	941, 941E, 941, and 943
	31	Federal unemployment (FUTA) tax (only if liability for unpaid taxes exceeds $100)	8109 (to make deposits)

If your tax year is not January 1st through December 31st:

- Income tax is due the 15th day of the 4th month after end of tax year.
- Self-employment tax is due the same day as income tax (Form 1040).
- Estimated tax (1040ES) is due the 15th day of the 4th, 6th, and 9th month of the tax year and the 15th day of 1st month after end of the tax year.

S Corporation

Calendar of Federal Taxes for Which You May be Liable

January	15	Estimated tax (individual S corp. shareholder)	Form 1040ES
	31	Social security (FICA) tax and the withholding of income tax Note: See IRS rulings for deposit - Pub. 334	941, 941E, 942, and 943
	31	Providing information on social security (FICA) tax and the withholding of income tax	W-2 (to employee)
	31	Federal unemployment (FUTA) tax	940-EZ or 940
	31	Federal unemployment (FUTA) tax (only if liability for unpaid taxes exceeds $100)	8109 (to make deposits)
	31	Information returns to non-employees and transactions with other persons	Form 1099 (to recipients)
February	28	Information returns to non-employees and transactions with other persons	Form 1099 (to IRS)
	28	Providing information on social security (FICA) tax and the withholding of income tax	W-2 & W-3 (to Social Security Admin.)
March	15	Income tax	1120S
April	15	Income tax (individual S corp. shareholder)	Form 1040
	15	Estimated tax (individual S corp. shareholder)	Form 1040ES
	30	Social security (FICA) tax and the withholding of income tax Note: See IRS rulings for deposit - Pub. 334	941, 941E, 942, and 943
	30	Federal unemployment (FUTA) tax (only if liability for unpaid taxes exceeds $100)	8109 (to make deposits)
June	15	Estimated tax (individual S corp. shareholder)	Form 1040ES
July	31	Social security (FICA) tax and the withholding of income tax Note: See IRS rulings for deposit - Pub. 334	941, 941E, 942, and 943
	31	Federal unemployment (FUTA) tax (only if liability for unpaid taxes exceeds $100)	8109 (to make deposits)
September	15	Estimated tax (individual S corp. shareholder)	Form 1040ES
October	31	Social security (FICA) tax and the withholding of income tax Note: See IRS rulings for deposit - Pub. 334	941, 941E, 941, and 943
	31	Federal unemployment (FUTA) tax (only if liability for unpaid taxes exceeds $100)	8109 (to make deposits)

If your tax year is not January 1st through December 31st:

- S corporation income tax (1120S) and individual S corporation shareholder income tax (Form 1040) are due the 15th day of the 4th month after end of tax year.

- Estimated tax of individual shareholder (1040ES) is due 15th day of 4th, 6th, and 9th months of tax year and 15th day of 1st month after end of tax year.

Corporation

Calendar of Federal Taxes for Which You May be Liable

January	31	Social security (FICA) tax and the withholding of income tax Note: See IRS rulings for deposit - Pub. 334	941, 941E, 942, and 943
	31	Providing information on social security (FICA) tax and the withholding of income tax	W-2 (to employee)
	31	Federal unemployment (FUTA) tax	940-EZ or 940
	31	Federal unemployment (FUTA) tax (only if liability for unpaid taxes exceeds $100)	8109 (to make deposits)
	31	Information returns to non-employees and transactions with other persons	Form 1099 (to recipients)
February	28	Information returns to non-employees and transactions with other persons	Form 1099 (to IRS)
	28	Providing information on social security (FICA) tax and the withholding of income tax	W-2 & W-3 (to Social Security Admin.)
March	15	Income tax	1120 or 1120-A
April	15	Estimated tax	1120-W
	30	Social security (FICA) tax and the withholding of income tax Note: See IRS rulings for deposit - Pub. 334	941, 941E, 942, and 943
	30	Federal unemployment (FUTA) tax (only if liability for unpaid taxes exceeds $100)	8109 (to make deposits)
June	15	Estimated tax	1120-W
July	31	Social security (FICA) tax and the withholding of income tax Note: See IRS rulings for deposit - Pub. 334	941, 941E, 942, and 943
	31	Federal unemployment (FUTA) tax (only if liability for unpaid taxes exceeds $100)	8109 (to make deposits)
September	15	Estimated tax	1120-W
October	31	Social security (FICA) tax and the withholding of income tax Note: See IRS rulings for deposit - Pub. 334	941, 941E, 941, and 943
	31	Federal unemployment (FUTA) tax (only if liability for unpaid taxes exceeds $100)	8109 (to make deposits)
December	15	Estimated tax	1120-W

If your tax year is not January 1st through December 31st:

- Income tax (Form 1120 or 1120-A) is due on the 15th day of the 3rd month after the end of the tax year.

- Estimated tax (1120-W) is due the 5th day of the 4th, 6th, 9th, and 12th months of the tax year.

Income Tax (For Sole Proprietors)

File Schedule C (Form 1040), *Profit or Loss from Business (Sole Proprietorship)*.

You are a sole proprietor if you are self-employed and are the sole owner of an unincorporated business.

If you are a sole proprietor, you report your income and expenses from your business or profession on Schedule C. File Schedule C with your Form 1040 and report the amount of net profit or (loss) from Schedule C on your 1040. If you operate more than one business as a sole proprietor, you prepare a separate Schedule C for each business.

Withdrawals. If you are a sole proprietor, there is no tax effect if you take money to or from your business, or transfer money to or from your business. You should set up a drawing account to keep track of amounts that are for personal use and not for business expenses.

Home Office Deductions. If you use part of your home exclusively and regularly as the principal place of business or as the place where you meet or deal with patients, clients, or customers you can deduct the expense for that part of your home. If you claim a home office deduction, you must attach Form 8829. (Sample form is included after Schedule C.) For more information, see Publication 587, *Business Use of Your Home.*

Estimated Tax. If you are a sole proprietor, you will have to make estimated tax payments if the total of your estimated income tax and self-employment tax for the year will exceed your total withholding and credits by $1,000 or more. Form 1040-ES is used to estimate your tax. See "Estimated Tax for Sole Proprietors."

Self-Employment Tax. Generally required if you are a sole proprietor. See "Self-Employment Tax," Schedule SE.

Schedule C and Form 1040

Forms are due by April 15th. If you use a fiscal year, your return is due by the 15th day of the 4th month after the close of your tax year.

IRS Publication. See Publication 334, *Tax Guide for Small Business* for discussion on tax rules and for examples illustrating how to fill in these forms.

 Sample. Schedule C (Form 1040) can be seen on the next two pages.

115

Schedule C (Form 1040)
Profit or Loss from Business (Sole Proprietorship)

SCHEDULE C (Form 1040)	**Profit or Loss From Business** (Sole Proprietorship)	OMB No. 1545-0074
Department of the Treasury Internal Revenue Service (99)	▶ For information on Schedule C and its instructions, go to *www.irs.gov/schedulec*. ▶ Attach to Form 1040, 1040NR, or 1041; partnerships generally must file Form 1065.	20**13** Attachment Sequence No. **09**

Name of proprietor | Social security number (SSN)

A Principal business or profession, including product or service (see instructions) | **B** Enter code from instructions ▶

C Business name. If no separate business name, leave blank. | **D** Employer ID number (EIN), (see instr.)

E Business address (including suite or room no.) ▶
City, town or post office, state, and ZIP code

F Accounting method: **(1)** ☐ Cash **(2)** ☐ Accrual **(3)** ☐ Other (specify) ▶

G Did you "materially participate" in the operation of this business during 2013? If "No," see instructions for limit on losses ☐ Yes ☐ No

H If you started or acquired this business during 2013, check here ▶ ☐

I Did you make any payments in 2013 that would require you to file Form(s) 1099? (see instructions) ☐ Yes ☐ No

J If "Yes," did you or will you file required Forms 1099? ☐ Yes ☐ No

Part I Income

1	Gross receipts or sales. See instructions for line 1 and check the box if this income was reported to you on Form W-2 and the "Statutory employee" box on that form was checked ▶ ☐	1	
2	Returns and allowances	2	
3	Subtract line 2 from line 1	3	
4	Cost of goods sold (from line 42)	4	
5	**Gross profit.** Subtract line 4 from line 3	5	
6	Other income, including federal and state gasoline or fuel tax credit or refund (see instructions)	6	
7	**Gross income.** Add lines 5 and 6 ▶	7	

Part II Expenses   Enter expenses for business use of your home only on line 30.

8	Advertising	8		18	Office expense (see instructions)	18
9	Car and truck expenses (see instructions)	9		19	Pension and profit-sharing plans	19
10	Commissions and fees	10		20	Rent or lease (see instructions):	
11	Contract labor (see instructions)	11		a	Vehicles, machinery, and equipment	20a
12	Depletion	12		b	Other business property	20b
13	Depreciation and section 179 expense deduction (not included in Part III) (see instructions).	13		21	Repairs and maintenance	21
				22	Supplies (not included in Part III)	22
				23	Taxes and licenses	23
				24	Travel, meals, and entertainment:	
14	Employee benefit programs (other than on line 19)	14		a	Travel	24a
15	Insurance (other than health)	15		b	Deductible meals and entertainment (see instructions)	24b
16	Interest:			25	Utilities	25
a	Mortgage (paid to banks, etc.)	16a		26	Wages (less employment credits)	26
b	Other	16b		27a	Other expenses (from line 48)	27a
17	Legal and professional services	17		b	**Reserved for future use**	27b

28	**Total expenses** before expenses for business use of home. Add lines 8 through 27a ▶	28	
29	Tentative profit or (loss). Subtract line 28 from line 7	29	
30	Expenses for business use of your home. Do not report these expenses elsewhere. Attach Form 8829 unless using the simplified method (see instructions). **Simplified method filers only:** enter the total square footage of: (a) your home: _____ and (b) the part of your home used for business: _____. Use the Simplified Method Worksheet in the instructions to figure the amount to enter on line 30	30	
31	**Net profit or (loss).** Subtract line 30 from line 29. • If a profit, enter on both **Form 1040, line 12** (or **Form 1040NR, line 13**) and on **Schedule SE, line 2**. (If you checked the box on line 1, see instructions). Estates and trusts, enter on **Form 1041, line 3**. • If a loss, you **must** go to line 32.	31	
32	If you have a loss, check the box that describes your investment in this activity (see instructions). • If you checked 32a, enter the loss on both **Form 1040, line 12,** (or **Form 1040NR, line 13**) and on **Schedule SE, line 2**. (If you checked the box on line 1, see the line 31 instructions). Estates and trusts, enter on **Form 1041, line 3**. • If you checked 32b, you **must** attach **Form 6198**. Your loss may be limited.	32a ☐ All investment is at risk. 32b ☐ Some investment is not at risk.	

For Paperwork Reduction Act Notice, see the separate instructions. | Cat. No. 11334P | Schedule C (Form 1040) 2013

Schedule C (Form 1040)
Profit or Loss from Business (Sole Proprietorship)
Page 2

Schedule C (Form 1040) 2013   Page **2**

Part III   Cost of Goods Sold (see instructions)

33   Method(s) used to
     value closing inventory: **a** ☐ Cost   **b** ☐ Lower of cost or market   **c** ☐ Other (attach explanation)

34   Was there any change in determining quantities, costs, or valuations between opening and closing inventory?
     If "Yes," attach explanation . . . .   ☐ Yes   ☐ No

35 Inventory at beginning of year. If different from last year's closing inventory, attach explanation . . .	**35**	
36 Purchases less cost of items withdrawn for personal use	**36**	
37 Cost of labor. Do not include any amounts paid to yourself	**37**	
38 Materials and supplies	**38**	
39 Other costs	**39**	
40 Add lines 35 through 39	**40**	
41 Inventory at end of year	**41**	
42 **Cost of goods sold.** Subtract line 41 from line 40. Enter the result here and on line 4	**42**	

Part IV   Information on Your Vehicle. Complete this part **only** if you are claiming car or truck expenses on line 9 and are not required to file Form 4562 for this business. See the instructions for line 13 to find out if you must file Form 4562.

43   When did you place your vehicle in service for business purposes? (month, day, year)   ▶ _____ / _____ / _____

44   Of the total number of miles you drove your vehicle during 2013, enter the number of miles you used your vehicle for:

 a Business _____   **b** Commuting (see instructions) _____   **c** Other _____

45   Was your vehicle available for personal use during off-duty hours? . . . .   ☐ Yes   ☐ No

46   Do you (or your spouse) have another vehicle available for personal use?. . . . .   ☐ Yes   ☐ No

47a Do you have evidence to support your deduction? . . . .   ☐ Yes   ☐ No

 b If "Yes," is the evidence written? . . . .   ☐ Yes   ☐ No

Part V   Other Expenses. List below business expenses not included on lines 8–26 or line 30.

--		
--		
--		
--		
--		
--		
--		
--		
48 **Total other expenses.** Enter here and on line 27a	**48**	

Schedule C (Form 1040) 2013

Home Office Deduction

File Form 8829, *Expenses for Business Use of Your Home* (with Schedule C).

If you use your home for business, you may be able to deduct some of your expenses for its business use. However, you cannot deduct more than you receive in gross income from its business use. The allowable deduction is computed on Form 8829.

Use Tests

To take a deduction for the use of part of your home in business, you must meet certain tests. That part of your home that you deduct must be used *exclusively* and *regularly* as (1) the principal place of business for the trade in which you engage, (2) as a place to meet and deal with customers in the normal course of your trade, or in connection with your trade if you are using a separate structure that is appurtenant to, but not attached to, your house or residence.

Note: The Taxpayer Relief Act of 1997 liberalized the Home Office Deduction for tax years beginning after December 31, 1998. The new law expanded the definition of "principal place of business." Home office expenses will qualify if: (1) the office is used to conduct administrative or management activities of the taxpayer's trade or business; and (2) there is no other fixed location of the trade or business where the administrative or management activities are conducted.

Figure Business Percentage

To figure deductions for the business use of your home, you will have to divide the expenses of operating your home between personal and business use. Some expenses are divided on an area basis. Some are further divided on a time usage basis. To find the business percentage, divide the area used for the business by the total area of your home.

Deductible Expenses

Certain expenses are totally deductible, such as painting or repairs made to the specific area used for business. You can deduct indirect expenses based on percentage of usage, including real estate taxes, mortgage interest, casualty losses, utilities, telephone, insurance and security systems, and depreciation. Unrelated expenses cannot be deducted.

Form 8829

This form, entitled *Expenses for Business Use of Your Home*, is filed with Schedule C (Form 1040) on April 15th.

 Sample: A copy of Form 8829 is provided on the next page.

Form 8829
Expenses for Business Use of Your Home

Form **8829**	**Expenses for Business Use of Your Home**	OMB No. 1545-0074
	▶ File only with Schedule C (Form 1040). Use a separate Form 8829 for each home you used for business during the year.	20**13**
Department of the Treasury Internal Revenue Service (99)	▶ Information about Form 8829 and its separate instructions is at *www.irs.gov/form8829*.	Attachment Sequence No. **176**

Name(s) of proprietor(s) | Your social security number

Part I — Part of Your Home Used for Business

1	Area used regularly and exclusively for business, regularly for daycare, or for storage of inventory or product samples (see instructions)	**1**	
2	Total area of home	**2**	
3	Divide line 1 by line 2. Enter the result as a percentage	**3**	%

For daycare facilities not used exclusively for business, go to line 4. All others go to line 7.

4	Multiply days used for daycare during year by hours used per day	**4**	hr.
5	Total hours available for use during the year (365 days x 24 hours) (see instructions)	**5**	*8,760* hr.
6	Divide line 4 by line 5. Enter the result as a decimal amount . . .	**6**	.
7	Business percentage. For daycare facilities not used exclusively for business, multiply line 6 by line 3 (enter the result as a percentage). All others, enter the amount from line 3 . . . . . ▶	**7**	%

Part II — Figure Your Allowable Deduction

8	Enter the amount from Schedule C, line 29, **plus** any gain derived from the business use of your home and shown on Schedule D or Form 4797, minus any loss from the trade or business not derived from the business use of your home and shown on Schedule D or Form 4797. See instructions . .	**8**	

See instructions for columns (a) and (b) before completing lines 9–21.

		(a) Direct expenses	(b) Indirect expenses		
9	Casualty losses (see instructions)	**9**			
10	Deductible mortgage interest (see instructions)	**10**			
11	Real estate taxes (see instructions)	**11**			
12	Add lines 9, 10, and 11	**12**			
13	Multiply line 12, column (b) by line 7		**13**		
14	Add line 12, column (a) and line 13			**14**	
15	Subtract line 14 from line 8. If zero or less, enter -0-			**15**	
16	Excess mortgage interest (see instructions) .	**16**			
17	Insurance	**17**			
18	Rent	**18**			
19	Repairs and maintenance	**19**			
20	Utilities	**20**			
21	Other expenses (see instructions).	**21**			
22	Add lines 16 through 21	**22**			
23	Multiply line 22, column (b) by line 7	**23**			
24	Carryover of operating expenses from 2012 Form 8829, line 42 . .	**24**			
25	Add line 22, column (a), line 23, and line 24			**25**	
26	Allowable operating expenses. Enter the **smaller** of line 15 or line 25			**26**	
27	Limit on excess casualty losses and depreciation. Subtract line 26 from line 15			**27**	
28	Excess casualty losses (see instructions)	**28**			
29	Depreciation of your home from line 41 below	**29**			
30	Carryover of excess casualty losses and depreciation from 2012 Form 8829, line 43	**30**			
31	Add lines 28 through 30			**31**	
32	Allowable excess casualty losses and depreciation. Enter the **smaller** of line 27 or line 31 . .			**32**	
33	Add lines 14, 26, and 32.			**33**	
34	Casualty loss portion, if any, from lines 14 and 32. Carry amount to **Form 4684** (see instructions)			**34**	
35	**Allowable expenses for business use of your home.** Subtract line 34 from line 33. Enter here and on Schedule C, line 30. If your home was used for more than one business, see instructions ▶			**35**	

Part III — Depreciation of Your Home

36	Enter the **smaller** of your home's adjusted basis or its fair market value (see instructions) . .	**36**	
37	Value of land included on line 36	**37**	
38	Basis of building. Subtract line 37 from line 36	**38**	
39	Business basis of building. Multiply line 38 by line 7.	**39**	
40	Depreciation percentage (see instructions).	**40**	%
41	Depreciation allowable (see instructions). Multiply line 39 by line 40. Enter here and on line 29 above	**41**	

Part IV — Carryover of Unallowed Expenses to 2014

42	Operating expenses. Subtract line 26 from line 25. If less than zero, enter -0-	**42**	
43	Excess casualty losses and depreciation. Subtract line 32 from line 31. If less than zero, enter -0-	**43**	

For Paperwork Reduction Act Notice, see your tax return instructions.   Cat. No. 13232M   Form **8829** (2013)

Income Tax (Partnerships)

File Form 1065, *U.S. Return of Partnership Income.*

A partnership is the relationship between two or more persons who join together to carry on a trade or business with each person contributing money, property, labor, or skill, and each expecting to share in the profits and losses of the business.

Every partnership doing business in or having income from sources within the United States is required to file Form 1065 for its tax year. This is mainly an information return. Partnership profits are not taxed to the partnership. Each partner must take into account his or her distributive share of partnership items and report it on his or her own income tax return (whether distributed or not).

- **Estimated Tax.** Tax is not withheld on partnership distributions and partners may have to make estimated tax payments. See Schedule SE (Form 1040) *Self-Employment Tax.*

- **Self Employment Tax.** A partner's distributive share of income is usually included in figuring net earnings from self-employment. See Schedule SE (Form 1040) *Self-Employment Tax.*

Schedules K and K-1 (Form 1065)

These forms are used to show partners distributive shares of reportable partnership items. Form 1065 and its Schedules K or K-1 are filed separately and not attached to your income tax return.

Schedule E (Form 1040)

Supplemental Income and Loss Schedule, Part II is used to report partnership items on your individual tax return. Failure to treat your individual and partnership returns consistently will allow the IRS to assess and take action to collect deficiencies and penalties.

IRS Publication. See Publication 541, *Partnerships*, for information and for examples of filled-in forms.

Sample. Form 1065 and Schedule K-1 follow on the next two pages.

Form 1065
U.S. Return of Partnership Income

Page 1 only

Form **1065** Department of the Treasury Internal Revenue Service	**U.S. Return of Partnership Income** For calendar year 2013, or tax year beginning _____ , 2013, ending _____ , 20 ____ . ▶ Information about Form 1065 and its separate instructions is at *www.irs.gov/form1065*.	OMB No. 1545-0099 **2013**

A Principal business activity	**Type or Print**	Name of partnership	**D** Employer identification number
B Principal product or service		Number, street, and room or suite no. If a P.O. box, see the instructions.	**E** Date business started
C Business code number		City or town, state or province, country, and ZIP or foreign postal code	**F** Total assets (see the instructions) $

G Check applicable boxes: **(1)** ☐ Initial return   **(2)** ☐ Final return   **(3)** ☐ Name change   **(4)** ☐ Address change   **(5)** ☐ Amended return   **(6)** ☐ Technical termination - also check (1) or (2)

H Check accounting method: **(1)** ☐ Cash   **(2)** ☐ Accrual   **(3)** ☐ Other (specify) ▶ _____

I Number of Schedules K-1. Attach one for each person who was a partner at any time during the tax year ▶ _____

J Check if Schedules C and M-3 are attached . . . . ☐

Caution. Include **only** trade or business income and expenses on lines 1a through 22 below. See the instructions for more information.

Income	**1a**	Gross receipts or sales	**1a**		
	b	Returns and allowances	**1b**		
	c	Balance. Subtract line 1b from line 1a		**1c**	
	2	Cost of goods sold (attach Form 1125-A)		**2**	
	3	Gross profit. Subtract line 2 from line 1c		**3**	
	4	Ordinary income (loss) from other partnerships, estates, and trusts (attach statement) . .		**4**	
	5	Net farm profit (loss) (attach Schedule F (Form 1040))		**5**	
	6	Net gain (loss) from Form 4797, Part II, line 17 (attach Form 4797)		**6**	
	7	Other income (loss) (attach statement)		**7**	
	8	**Total income (loss).** Combine lines 3 through 7		**8**	
Deductions (see the instructions for limitations)	**9**	Salaries and wages (other than to partners) (less employment credits)		**9**	
	10	Guaranteed payments to partners		**10**	
	11	Repairs and maintenance		**11**	
	12	Bad debts		**12**	
	13	Rent		**13**	
	14	Taxes and licenses		**14**	
	15	Interest		**15**	
	16a	Depreciation (if required, attach Form 4562) . . .	**16a**		
	b	Less depreciation reported on Form 1125-A and elsewhere on return	**16b**	**16c**	
	17	Depletion **(Do not deduct oil and gas depletion.)**		**17**	
	18	Retirement plans, etc.		**18**	
	19	Employee benefit programs		**19**	
	20	Other deductions (attach statement)		**20**	
	21	**Total deductions.** Add the amounts shown in the far right column for lines 9 through 20 .		**21**	
	22	**Ordinary business income (loss).** Subtract line 21 from line 8		**22**	

Sign Here	Under penalties of perjury, I declare that I have examined this return, including accompanying schedules and statements, and to the best of my knowledge and belief, it is true, correct, and complete. Declaration of preparer (other than general partner or limited liability company member manager) is based on all information of which preparer has any knowledge.	May the IRS discuss this return with the preparer shown below (see instructions)? ☐ Yes ☐ No
	▶ _____ Signature of general partner or limited liability company member manager ▶ _____ Date	

Paid Preparer Use Only	Print/Type preparer's name	Preparer's signature	Date	Check ☐ if self-employed	PTIN
	Firm's name ▶			Firm's EIN ▶	
	Firm's address ▶			Phone no.	

For Paperwork Reduction Act Notice, see separate instructions.   Cat. No. 11390Z   Form **1065** (2013)

Schedule K-1 (Form 1065)
Partner's Share of Income, Credits, Deductions, etc.

651113

□ Final K-1 □ Amended K-1 OMB No. 1545-0099

Schedule K-1 (Form 1065) 2013

Department of the Treasury
Internal Revenue Service

For calendar year 2013, or tax
year beginning _____ , 2013
ending _____ , 20 _____

Partner's Share of Income, Deductions, Credits, etc. ▶ See back of form and separate instructions.

Part I Information About the Partnership

A Partnership's employer identification number

B Partnership's name, address, city, state, and ZIP code

C IRS Center where partnership filed return

D □ Check if this is a publicly traded partnership (PTP)

Part II Information About the Partner

E Partner's identifying number

F Partner's name, address, city, state, and ZIP code

G □ General partner or LLC member-manager □ Limited partner or other LLC member

H □ Domestic partner □ Foreign partner

I1 What type of entity is this partner? _____

I2 If this partner is a retirement plan (IRA/SEP/Keogh/etc.), check here (see instructions) . . . . □

J Partner's share of profit, loss, and capital (see instructions):

	Beginning	Ending
Profit	%	%
Loss	%	%
Capital	%	%

K Partner's share of liabilities at year end:

Nonrecourse . . . . . . $ _____
Qualified nonrecourse financing . $ _____
Recourse . . . . $ _____

L Partner's capital account analysis:

Beginning capital account . . . $ _____
Capital contributed during the year $ _____
Current year increase (decrease) . $ _____
Withdrawals & distributions . . $ (_____)
Ending capital account . . . . $ _____

□ Tax basis □ GAAP □ Section 704(b) book
□ Other (explain)

M Did the partner contribute property with a built-in gain or loss?
□ Yes □ No
If "Yes," attach statement (see instructions)

Part III Partner's Share of Current Year Income, Deductions, Credits, and Other Items

1	Ordinary business income (loss)	15	Credits
2	Net rental real estate income (loss)		
3	Other net rental income (loss)	16	Foreign transactions
4	Guaranteed payments		
5	Interest income		
6a	Ordinary dividends		
6b	Qualified dividends		
7	Royalties		
8	Net short-term capital gain (loss)		
9a	Net long-term capital gain (loss)	17	Alternative minimum tax (AMT) items
9b	Collectibles (28%) gain (loss)		
9c	Unrecaptured section 1250 gain		
10	Net section 1231 gain (loss)	18	Tax-exempt income and nondeductible expenses
11	Other income (loss)		
		19	Distributions
12	Section 179 deduction		
13	Other deductions		
		20	Other information
14	Self-employment earnings (loss)		

*See attached statement for additional information.

For IRS Use Only

For Paperwork Reduction Act Notice, see Instructions for Form 1065. IRS.gov/form1065 Cat. No. 11394R Schedule K-1 (Form 1065) 2013

Income Tax (S Corporations)

File Form 1120S, *U.S. Income Tax Return for an S Corporation.*

An S Corporation is a corporation that is not subject to income tax. Instead, it passes corporate income, losses, deductions, and credits through to its shareholders for federal tax purposes. The shareholders of the S Corporation are responsible for reporting the flow-through of income and losses on their personal tax returns and are assessed tax at their individual income tax rates. This allows S Corporations to avoid double taxation on the corporate income.

The formation of an S Corporation is only allowable under certain circumstances.

- It must be a domestic corporation either organized in the United States or organized under federal or state law.

- It must have only one class of stock.

- It must have no more than 100 shareholders.

- It must have as shareholders only individuals, estates, and certain trusts. Partnerships and corporations cannot be shareholders in an S Corporation.

- It must have shareholders who are citizens or residents of the United States. Nonresident aliens cannot be shareholders.

The formation of an S Corporation can be an advantageous form of legal structure, but if entered into without careful planning, it can result in more taxes instead of less, as anticipated.

Form 1120S

This form is used to file an income tax return for an S Corporation. Schedule K and K-1 are extremely important parts of Form 1120S. Schedule K summarizes the corporation's income, deductions, credits, etc., reportable by the shareholders. Schedule K-1 shows each shareholder's separate share. The individual shareholders report their income taxes on Form 1040. Form 1120S is due on the 15th day of the third month after the end of the tax year.

IRS Publication. If you need information about S Corporations, see Instructions for Form 1120S.

Sample. A copy of Form 1120S follows.

Form 1120S
U.S. Income Tax Return for an S Corporation
Page 1 only

Form **1120S**	**U.S. Income Tax Return for an S Corporation**	OMB No. 1545-0130
Department of the Treasury Internal Revenue Service	► Do not file this form unless the corporation has filed or is attaching Form 2553 to elect to be an S corporation. ► Information about Form 1120S and its separate instructions is at *www.irs.gov/form1120s*.	20**13**

For calendar year 2013 or tax year beginning _____ , 2013, ending _____ , 20 ___

A S election effective date		Name	**D** Employer identification number
B Business activity code number (see instructions)	**TYPE OR PRINT**	Number, street, and room or suite no. If a P.O. box, see instructions.	**E** Date incorporated
C Check if Sch. M-3 attached ☐		City or town, state or province, country, and ZIP or foreign postal code	**F** Total assets (see instructions) $

G Is the corporation electing to be an S corporation beginning with this tax year? ☐ Yes ☐ No   If "Yes," attach Form 2553 if not already filed

H Check if: **(1)** ☐ Final return **(2)** ☐ Name change **(3)** ☐ Address change **(4)** ☐ Amended return **(5)** ☐ S election termination or revocation

I Enter the number of shareholders who were shareholders during any part of the tax year . . . . ►

Caution. Include **only** trade or business income and expenses on lines 1a through 21. See the instructions for more information.

Income	**1a**	Gross receipts or sales	1a	
	b	Returns and allowances	1b	
	c	Balance. Subtract line 1b from line 1a	1c	
	2	Cost of goods sold (attach Form 1125-A)	2	
	3	Gross profit. Subtract line 2 from line 1c	3	
	4	Net gain (loss) from Form 4797, line 17 (attach Form 4797)	4	
	5	Other income (loss) (see instructions—attach statement)	5	
	6	**Total income (loss).** Add lines 3 through 5 . . . . ►	6	

Deductions (see instructions for limitations)	**7**	Compensation of officers (see instructions—attach Form 1125-E)	7	
	8	Salaries and wages (less employment credits)	8	
	9	Repairs and maintenance	9	
	10	Bad debts	10	
	11	Rents	11	
	12	Taxes and licenses	12	
	13	Interest	13	
	14	Depreciation not claimed on Form 1125-A or elsewhere on return (attach Form 4562)	14	
	15	Depletion **(Do not deduct oil and gas depletion.)**	15	
	16	Advertising	16	
	17	Pension, profit-sharing, etc., plans	17	
	18	Employee benefit programs	18	
	19	Other deductions (attach statement)	19	
	20	**Total deductions.** Add lines 7 through 19 . . . . ►	20	
	21	**Ordinary business income (loss).** Subtract line 20 from line 6	21	

Tax and Payments	**22a**	Excess net passive income or LIFO recapture tax (see instructions) . .	22a	
	b	Tax from Schedule D (Form 1120S)	22b	
	c	Add lines 22a and 22b (see instructions for additional taxes) . . .	22c	
	23a	2013 estimated tax payments and 2012 overpayment credited to 2013	23a	
	b	Tax deposited with Form 7004	23b	
	c	Credit for federal tax paid on fuels (attach Form 4136)	23c	
	d	Add lines 23a through 23c	23d	
	24	Estimated tax penalty (see instructions). Check if Form 2220 is attached . . . . . . ► ☐	24	
	25	**Amount owed.** If line 23d is smaller than the total of lines 22c and 24, enter amount owed . .	25	
	26	**Overpayment.** If line 23d is larger than the total of lines 22c and 24, enter amount overpaid . .	26	
	27	Enter amount from line 26 **Credited to 2014 estimated tax** ► ____ Refunded ►	27	

Sign Here	Under penalties of perjury, I declare that I have examined this return, including accompanying schedules and statements, and to the best of my knowledge and belief, it is true, correct, and complete. Declaration of preparer (other than taxpayer) is based on all information of which preparer has any knowledge.	May the IRS discuss this return with the preparer shown below (see instructions)? ☐ Yes ☐ No
	► Signature of officer _____ Date _____ ► Title _____	

Paid Preparer Use Only	Print/Type preparer's name	Preparer's signature	Date	Check ☐ if self-employed	PTIN
	Firm's name ►			Firm's EIN ►	
	Firm's address ►			Phone no.	

For Paperwork Reduction Act Notice, see separate instructions.   Cat. No. 11510H   Form **1120S** (2013)

Income Tax (Corporations)

File Form 1120, *U.S. Corporation Income Tax Return*.

A corporation is an independent legal entity owned by shareholders. Forming a corporation involves a transfer of either money, property, or both by the prospective shareholders in exchange for capital stock in the corporation. One of the most important aspects of a corporation is limited liability. This means shareholders have the right to participate in the profits, through dividends and/or the appreciation of stock, but are not held personally liable for the company's debts.

Every corporation, unless it is specifically exempt or has dissolved, must file a tax return even if it has no taxable income for the year and regardless of the amount of its gross income. Corporate profits normally are taxed to the corporation. When the profits are distributed as dividends, the dividends are then taxed to the shareholders.

Estimated Tax. Every corporation must make installment payments of estimated tax if it expects its total tax for the year (less applicable credits) to be $500 or more. Corporations whose taxes are over a certain amount (see rules) are required to make electronic deposits by Electronic Federal Tax Payment System (EFTPS). All corporations must use EFTPS and can set up for payments by going to the EFTPS website to provide business information and authorization for payments from the business checking account. New companies receive automatic enrollment to EFTPS when they file an application for an Employer Identification Number (EIN).

Contributions to the Capital of a Corporation. Contributions are "paid in capital" and are not taxable income to the corporation.

Form 1120

The income tax return for ordinary corporations is Form 1120. The form is used to report the income, gains, losses, deductions, credits, and to figure the income tax liability of a corporation.

Corporation returns are due on March 15th. A corporation using a fiscal year not beginning January 1st and ending December 31st will have to file it on or before the 15th of the third month following the close of its fiscal year.

IRS Publication. See Publication 542, *Corporations*, for explanation of the application of various tax provisions to corporations (filing requirements, tax computations, estimated tax payments, corporate distribution and retained earnings, discussion of corporation taxation, as well as liquidations and stock redemptions).

 Sample. See Form 1120 on the following pages.

Form 1120
U.S. Corporation Income Tax Return
Page 1 only

Form **1120** Department of the Treasury Internal Revenue Service	**U.S. Corporation Income Tax Return** For calendar year 2013 or tax year beginning _____, 2013, ending _____, 20 _____ ▶ Information about Form 1120 and its separate instructions is at *www.irs.gov/form1120.*	OMB No. 1545-0123 **2013**

A Check if:			
1a Consolidated return (attach Form 851) . ☐	**TYPE OR PRINT**	Name	**B Employer identification number**
b Life/nonlife consoli- dated return . . . ☐		Number, street, and room or suite no. If a P.O. box, see instructions.	**C Date incorporated**
2 Personal holding co. (attach Sch. PH) . . ☐ **3** Personal service corp. (see instructions) . . ☐		City or town, state, or province, country and ZIP or foreign postal code	**D Total assets** (see instructions) $
4 Schedule M-3 attached ☐	**E** Check if: **(1)** ☐ Initial return **(2)** ☐ Final return **(3)** ☐ Name change **(4)** ☐ Address change		

Income	**1a**	Gross receipts or sales	**1a**	
	b	Returns and allowances	**1b**	
	c	Balance. Subtract line 1b from line 1a	**1c**	
	2	Cost of goods sold (attach Form 1125-A)	**2**	
	3	Gross profit. Subtract line 2 from line 1c	**3**	
	4	Dividends (Schedule C, line 19)	**4**	
	5	Interest	**5**	
	6	Gross rents	**6**	
	7	Gross royalties	**7**	
	8	Capital gain net income (attach Schedule D (Form 1120))	**8**	
	9	Net gain or (loss) from Form 4797, Part II, line 17 (attach Form 4797) . . .	**9**	
	10	Other income (see instructions—attach statement)	**10**	
	11	**Total income.** Add lines 3 through 10 . . . . ▶	**11**	

Deductions (See instructions for limitations on deductions.)	**12**	Compensation of officers (see instructions—attach Form 1125-E) . . . . . ▶	**12**	
	13	Salaries and wages (less employment credits)	**13**	
	14	Repairs and maintenance	**14**	
	15	Bad debts	**15**	
	16	Rents	**16**	
	17	Taxes and licenses	**17**	
	18	Interest	**18**	
	19	Charitable contributions	**19**	
	20	Depreciation from Form 4562 not claimed on Form 1125-A or elsewhere on return (attach Form 4562) . .	**20**	
	21	Depletion	**21**	
	22	Advertising	**22**	
	23	Pension, profit-sharing, etc., plans	**23**	
	24	Employee benefit programs	**24**	
	25	Domestic production activities deduction (attach Form 8903)	**25**	
	26	Other deductions (attach statement)	**26**	
	27	**Total deductions.** Add lines 12 through 26 . . . . ▶	**27**	
	28	Taxable income before net operating loss deduction and special deductions. Subtract line 27 from line 11.	**28**	
	29a	Net operating loss deduction (see instructions)	**29a**	
	b	Special deductions (Schedule C, line 20)	**29b**	
	c	Add lines 29a and 29b	**29c**	

Tax, Refundable Credits, and Payments	**30**	**Taxable income.** Subtract line 29c from line 28 (see instructions)	**30**	
	31	Total tax (Schedule J, Part I, line 11)	**31**	
	32	Total payments and refundable credits (Schedule J, Part II, line 21)	**32**	
	33	Estimated tax penalty (see instructions). Check if Form 2220 is attached . . . . . ▶ ☐	**33**	
	34	**Amount owed.** If line 32 is smaller than the total of lines 31 and 33, enter amount owed . . .	**34**	
	35	**Overpayment.** If line 32 is larger than the total of lines 31 and 33, enter amount overpaid	**35**	
	36	Enter amount from line 35 you want: **Credited to 2014 estimated tax** ▶ _____ **Refunded** ▶	**36**	

Sign Here	Under penalties of perjury, I declare that I have examined this return, including accompanying schedules and statements, and to the best of my knowledge and belief, it is true, correct, and complete. Declaration of preparer (other than taxpayer) is based on all information of which preparer has any knowledge.		May the IRS discuss this return with the preparer shown below (see instructions)? ☐ **Yes** ☐ **No**
	▶ _____ Signature of officer	_____ Date	▶ _____ Title

Paid Preparer Use Only	Print/Type preparer's name	Preparer's signature	Date	Check ☐ if self-employed	PTIN
	Firm's name ▶			Firm's EIN ▶	
	Firm's address ▶			Phone no.	

For Paperwork Reduction Act Notice, see separate instructions.   Cat. No. 11450Q   Form **1120** (2013)

Estimated Tax
(For Sole Proprietor, Individual who is a Partner
or an S Corporation Shareholder)

File Form 1040-ES, *Estimated Tax for Individuals*.

If you are a sole proprietor, an individual who is a partner, or a shareholder in an S Corporation, in most cases, you will have to make estimated tax payments if the total of your estimated income tax and self-employment tax is in excess of a certain amount (if it exceeds your total withholding and credits by $1,000 or more for the year).

Underpayment of Tax. If you do not pay enough income tax and self-employment tax for the current year by withholding or by making estimated tax payments, you may have to pay a penalty on the amount not paid. IRS will figure the penalty and send you a bill.

Form 1040-ES

IRS Form 1040-ES is used to estimate your tax. There are four vouchers and they are filed on April 15th, June 15th, September 15th, and January 15th. (Notice that there are only two months between the first and second payments and four months between the third and fourth payments.)

Your estimated tax payments include both federal income tax and self-employment tax liabilities.

Estimated Tax Worksheet

You can use the Estimated Tax Worksheet to figure your estimated tax liability. Keep it for your own records and revise if your actual income is very far over or under your estimate. After the first filing, Form 1040 ES will be sent to you each year.

Publications. See Publication 505, *Tax Withholding and Estimated Tax*, for information. Also see instructions accompanying Form 1040-ES.

 Samples. On the next three pages, you will find an Estimated Tax Worksheet, Estimated Tax Payment Record, Tax Rate Schedule, and 1040-ES payment vouchers.

Form 1040-ES
Estimated Tax Worksheet

2013 Estimated Tax Worksheet   *Keep for Your Records*

1	Adjusted gross income you expect in 2013 (see instructions)	1
2	• If you plan to itemize deductions, enter the estimated total of your itemized deductions. **Caution:** *If line 1 is over $300,000 if married filing jointly or qualifying widow(er); $275,000 if head of household; $250,000 if single; and $150,000 if married filing separately, your deduction may be reduced. See Pub. 505 for details.*	
	• If you do not plan to itemize deductions, enter your standard deduction.	2
3	Subtract line 2 from line 1.	3
4	Exemptions. Multiply $3,900 by the number of personal exemptions. **Caution:** *See Pub. 505 to figure the amount to enter if line 1 is over: $300,000 if married filing jointly or qualifying widow(er); $275,000 if head of household; $250,000 if single; and $150,000 if married filing separately*	4
5	Subtract line 4 from line 3.	5
6	**Tax.** Figure your tax on the amount on line 5 by using the **2013 Tax Rate Schedules**. **Caution:** *If you will have qualified dividends or a net capital gain, or expect to exclude or deduct foreign earned income or housing, see chapter 2 of Pub. 505 to figure the tax*	6
7	Alternative minimum tax from **Form 6251**	7
8	Add lines 6 and 7. Add to this amount any other taxes you expect to include in the total on Form 1040, line 44	8
9	Credits (see instructions). **Do not** include any income tax withholding on this line	9
10	Subtract line 9 from line 8. If zero or less, enter -0-	10
11	Self-employment tax (see instructions)	11
12	Other taxes including, if applicable, Additional Medicare Tax and/or NIIT (see instructions) . .	12
13a	Add lines 10 through 12	13a
b	Earned income credit, additional child tax credit, fuel tax credit, refundable American opportunity credit, and refundable credit from **Form 8885**	13b
c	**Total 2013 estimated tax.** Subtract line 13b from line 13a. If zero or less, enter -0- . . . ▶	13c
14a	Multiply line 13c by 90% (66⅔% for farmers and fishermen)	14a	
b	Required annual payment based on prior year's tax (see instructions) .	14b	
c	**Required annual payment to avoid a penalty.** Enter the **smaller** of line 14a or 14b . . . ▶	14c
	Caution: *Generally, if you do not prepay (through income tax withholding and estimated tax payments) at least the amount on line 14c, you may owe a penalty for not paying enough estimated tax. To avoid a penalty, make sure your estimate on line 13c is as accurate as possible. Even if you pay the required annual payment, you may still owe tax when you file your return. If you prefer, you can pay the amount shown on line 13c. For details, see chapter 2 of Pub. 505.*	
15	Income tax withheld and estimated to be withheld during 2013 (including income tax withholding on pensions, annuities, certain deferred income, etc.)	15
16a	Subtract line 15 from line 14c	16a	
	Is the result zero or less? ☐ **Yes.** Stop here. You are not required to make estimated tax payments. ☐ **No.** Go to line 16b.	
b	Subtract line 15 from line 13c	16b	
	Is the result less than $1,000? ☐ **Yes.** Stop here. You are not required to make estimated tax payments. ☐ **No.** Go to line 17 to figure your required payment.	
17	If the first payment you are required to make is due April 15, 2013, enter ¼ of line 16a (minus any 2012 overpayment that you are applying to this installment) here, and on your estimated tax payment voucher(s) if you are paying by check or money order.	17

2013 Self-Employment Tax and Deduction Worksheet for Lines 1 and 11 of the Estimated Tax Worksheet   *Keep for Your Records*

1a.	Enter your expected income and profits subject to self-employment tax*	1a. _____
b.	If you will have farm income and also receive social security retirement or disability benefits, enter your expected Conservation Reserve Program payments that will be included on Schedule F (Form 1040) or listed on Schedule K-1 (Form 1065)	b. _____
2.	Subtract line 1b from line 1a	2. _____
3.	Multiply line 2 by 92.35% (.9235)	3. _____
4.	Multiply line 3 by 2.9% (.029)	4. _____
5.	Social security tax maximum income	5. **$113,700**
6.	Enter your expected wages (if subject to social security tax or the 6.2% portion of tier 1 railroad retirement tax)	6. _____
7.	Subtract line 6 from line 5	7. _____
	Note. *If line 7 is zero or less, enter -0- on line 9 and skip to line 10.*	
8.	Enter the **smaller** of line 3 or line 7	8. _____
9.	Multiply line 8 by 12.4% (.124)	9. _____
10.	Add lines 4 and 9. Enter the result here and on line 11 of your 2013 Estimated Tax Worksheet	10. _____
11.	Multiply line 10 by 50% (.50). This is your expected deduction for self-employment tax on Form 1040, line 27. Subtract this amount when figuring your expected AGI on line 1 of your 2013 Estimated Tax Worksheet	11. _____

* Your net profit from self-employment is found on Schedule C (Form 1040), line 31; Schedule F (Form 1040), line 34; Schedule K-1 (Form 1065), box 14, code A; and Schedule K-1 (Form 1065-B), box 9, code J1.

Form 1040-ES
Estimated Tax Payment Record

Record of Estimated Tax Payments (Farmers, fishermen, and fiscal year taxpayers, see page 3 for payment due dates.)   *Keep for Your Records*

Payment number	Payment due date	(a) Amount due		(b) Date paid	(c) Check or money order number, or credit or debit card confirmation number	(d) Amount paid (**do not** include any convenience fee)*		(e) 2012 overpayment credit applied	(f) Total amount paid and credited (add (d) and (e))	
1	4/15/2013									
2	6/17/2013									
3	9/16/2013									
4	1/15/2014**									
Total . . . . ▶										

* You can deduct the convenience fee charged by the service provider in 2013 as a miscellaneous itemized deduction (subject to the 2%-of-AGI limit) on your 2013 income tax return.

** You do not have to make this payment if you file your 2013 tax return by January 31, 2014, **and** pay the entire balance due with your return.

Form 1040-ES
Tax Rate Schedules

2013 Tax Rate Schedules

Caution. Do not use these Tax Rate Schedules to figure your 2012 taxes. Use only to figure your 2013 estimated taxes.

Schedule X—Use if your **2013** filing status is **Single**

If line 5 is: Over—	But not over—	The tax is:			of the amount over—
$0	$8,925	----------	+	10%	$0
8,925	36,250	$892.50	+	15%	8,925
36,250	87,850	4,991.25	+	25%	36,250
87,850	183,250	17,891.25	+	28%	87,850
183,250	398,350	44,603.25	+	33%	183,250
398,350	400,000	115,586.25	+	35%	398,350
400,000	----------	116,163.75	+	39.6%	400,000

Schedule Z—Use if your **2013** filing status is **Head of household**

If line 5 is: Over—	But not over—	The tax is:			of the amount over—
$0	$12,750	----------	+	10%	$0
12,750	48,600	$1,275.00	+	15%	12,750
48,600	125,450	6,652.50	+	25%	48,600
125,450	203,150	25,865.00	+	28%	125,450
203,150	398,350	47,621.00	+	33%	203,150
398,350	425,000	112,037.00	+	35%	398,350
425,000	----------	121,364.50	+	39.6%	425,000

Schedule Y-1— Use if your **2013** filing status is **Married filing jointly or Qualifying widow(er)**

If line 5 is: Over—	But not over—	The tax is:			of the amount over—
$0	$17,850	----------	+	10%	$0
17,850	72,500	$1,785.00	+	15%	17,850
72,500	146,400	9,982.50	+	25%	72,500
146,400	223,050	28,457.50	+	28%	146,400
223,050	398,350	49,919.50	+	33%	223,050
398,350	450,000	107,768.50	+	35%	398,350
450,000	---------	125,846.00	+	39.6%	450,000

Schedule Y-2—Use if your **2013** filing status is **Married filing separately**

If line 5 is: Over—	But not over—	The tax is:			of the amount over—
$0	$8,925	----------	+	10%	$0
8,925	36,250	$892.50	+	15%	8,925
36,250	73,200	4,991.25	+	25%	36,250
73,200	111,525	14,228.75	+	28%	73,200
111,525	199,175	24,959.75	+	33%	111,525
199,175	225,000	53,884.25	+	35%	199,175
225,000	----------	62,923.00	+	39.6%	225,000

Form 1040-ES
Tax Payment Vouchers

Form **1040-ES** Department of the Treasury Internal Revenue Service	20**13 Estimated Tax**	Payment Voucher **3** OMB No. 1545-0074

Calendar year—Due Sept. 16, 2013

File only if you are making a payment of estimated tax by check or money order. Mail this voucher with your check or money order payable to **"United States Treasury."** Write your social security number and "2013 Form 1040-ES" on your check or money order. Do not send cash. Enclose, but do not staple or attach, your payment with this voucher.

Amount of estimated tax you are paying by check or money order.

	Dollars	Cents

Your first name and initial	Your last name	Your social security number

If joint payment, complete for spouse

Spouse's first name and initial	Spouse's last name	Spouse's social security number

Address (number, street, and apt. no.)

City, state, and ZIP code. (If a foreign address, enter city, also complete spaces below.)

Foreign country name	Foreign province/county	Foreign postal code

For Privacy Act and Paperwork Reduction Act Notice, see instructions.

- - - - - - - - - - - **Tear off here** - - - - - - - - - - -

Form **1040-ES** Department of the Treasury Internal Revenue Service	20**13 Estimated Tax**	Payment Voucher **2** OMB No. 1545-0074

Calendar year—Due June 17, 2013

File only if you are making a payment of estimated tax by check or money order. Mail this voucher with your check or money order payable to **"United States Treasury."** Write your social security number and "2013 Form 1040-ES" on your check or money order. Do not send cash. Enclose, but do not staple or attach, your payment with this voucher.

Amount of estimated tax you are paying by check or money order.

	Dollars	Cents

Your first name and initial	Your last name	Your social security number

If joint payment, complete for spouse

Spouse's first name and initial	Spouse's last name	Spouse's social security number

Address (number, street, and apt. no.)

City, state, and ZIP code. (If a foreign address, enter city, also complete spaces below.)

Foreign country name	Foreign province/county	Foreign postal code

For Privacy Act and Paperwork Reduction Act Notice, see instructions.

- - - - - - - - - - - **Tear off here** - - - - - - - - - - -

Form **1040-ES** Department of the Treasury Internal Revenue Service	20**13 Estimated Tax**	Payment Voucher **1** OMB No. 1545-0074

Calendar year—Due April 15, 2013

File only if you are making a payment of estimated tax by check or money order. Mail this voucher with your check or money order payable to **"United States Treasury."** Write your social security number and "2013 Form 1040-ES" on your check or money order. Do not send cash. Enclose, but do not staple or attach, your payment with this voucher.

Amount of estimated tax you are paying by check or money order.

	Dollars	Cents

Your first name and initial	Your last name	Your social security number

If joint payment, complete for spouse

Spouse's first name and initial	Spouse's last name	Spouse's social security number

Address (number, street, and apt. no.)

City, state, and ZIP code. (If a foreign address, enter city, also complete spaces below.)

Foreign country name	Foreign province/county	Foreign postal code

For Privacy Act and Paperwork Reduction Act Notice, see instructions.   **Form 1040-ES (2013)**

Estimated Tax (Corporations)

File Form 1120-W, *Estimated Tax for Corporations* (Worksheet).

Every corporation whose tax is expected to be $500 or more (less applicable credits) must make estimated tax payments. A corporation's estimated tax is the amount of its expected tax liability (including alternative minimum tax and environmental tax) less its allowable tax credits.

Deposits

If a corporation's estimated tax for the year is $500 or more, its estimated tax payments must be made through the Electronic Federal Tax Payment System (EFTPS).

The due dates of deposits are the 15th day of the 4th, 6th, 9th, and 12th day of the of the tax year. Depending on when the $500 requirement is first met, a corporation will make either four, three, two, or one installment deposit. Amounts of estimated tax should be refigured each quarter and amended to reflect changes.

Penalty. A corporation that fails to pay in full a correct installment of estimated tax by the due date is generally subject to a penalty. The penalty is figured at a rate of interest published quarterly by the IRS in the *Internal Revenue Bulletin*.

Note: Corporations are required to make electronic deposits of all depository taxes (such as employment tax, excise tax, and corporate income tax) by Electronic Federal Tax Payment System (EFTPS), a free service provided by the Department of Treasury. If a corporation does not want to use EFTPS, it can chose to have its tax professional, financial institution, payroll service or other third party resource make deposits on its behalf. In the case of using a financial institution, a same day tax wire payment can be arranged.

Form 1120-W (Worksheet)

This form is filled out as an aid in determining the estimated tax and required deposits. The form should be retained and not filed with the IRS. As an aid in determining its estimated alternative minimum tax and environmental tax, a corporation should get a copy of Form 4626. This form should also be retained and not filed with the IRS.

IRS Publication. See Publication 542, *Corporations*. This publication includes discussion of corporation taxation, as well as liquidation and stock redemptions.

 Sample. See sample of Form 1120-W (Worksheet) on the next page.

Form 1120-W
Estimated Tax for Corporations Worksheet

Form **1120-W** (WORKSHEET) Department of the Treasury Internal Revenue Service	**Estimated Tax for Corporations** For calendar year 2014, or tax year beginning _____ , 2014, and ending _____ , 20 _____ ▶ Information about Form 1120-W and its separate instructions is at *www.irs.gov/form1120.* (Keep for the corporation's records—Do *not* send to the Internal Revenue Service.)	OMB No. 1545-0975 **2014**

Estimated Tax Computation

1	Taxable income expected for the tax year	**1**	
	Qualified personal service corporations (defined in the instructions), skip lines 2 through 13 and go to line 14. Members of a controlled group, see instructions.		
2	Enter the **smaller** of line 1 or $50,000	**2**	
3	Multiply line 2 by 15%		**3**
4	Subtract line 2 from line 1	**4**	
5	Enter the **smaller** of line 4 or $25,000	**5**	
6	Multiply line 5 by 25%		**6**
7	Subtract line 5 from line 4	**7**	
8	Enter the **smaller** of line 7 or $9,925,000	**8**	
9	Multiply line 8 by 34%		**9**
10	Subtract line 8 from line 7	**10**	
11	Multiply line 10 by 35%		**11**
12	If line 1 is greater than $100,000, enter the **smaller** of **(a)** 5% of the excess over $100,000 or **(b)** $11,750. Otherwise, enter -0-		**12**
13	If line 1 is greater than $15 million, enter the **smaller** of **(a)** 3% of the excess over $15 million or **(b)** $100,000. Otherwise, enter -0-		**13**
14	Add lines 3, 6, 9, and 11 through 13. (Qualified personal service corporations, multiply line 1 by 35%.)		**14**
15	Alternative minimum tax (see instructions)		**15**
16	**Total.** Add lines 14 and 15		**16**
17	Tax credits (see instructions)		**17**
18	Subtract line 17 from line 16		**18**
19	Other taxes (see instructions)		**19**
20	**Total tax.** Add lines 18 and 19		**20**
21	Credit for federal tax paid on fuels and other refundable credits (see instructions)		**21**
22	Subtract line 21 from line 20. **Note:** *If the result is less than $500, the corporation is not required to make estimated tax payments*		**22**
23a	Enter the tax shown on the corporation's 2013 tax return (see instructions). **Caution:** *If the tax is zero or the tax year was for less than 12 months, skip this line and enter the amount from line 22 on line 23b*		**23a**
b	Enter the **smaller** of line 22 or line 23a. If the corporation is required to skip line 23a, enter the amount from line 22		**23b**

		(a)	(b)	(c)	(d)
24	Installment due dates (see instructions) ▶ **24**				
25	**Required installments.** Enter 25% of line 23b in columns **(a)** through **(d).** If the corporation uses the annualized income installment method or adjusted seasonal installment method or is a "large corporation," see the instructions for the amount to enter **25**				

For Paperwork Reduction Act Notice, see instructions. | Cat. No. 11525G | Form **1120-W** (2014)

Self-Employment Tax

(For Sole Proprietor, Individual Who Is a Partner or an S Corporation Shareholder)

File Schedule SE (Form 1040), *Self-Employment Tax*.

The self-employment tax is a Social Security and Medicare tax for individuals who work for themselves. Social Security benefits are available to the self-employed individual just as they are to wage earners. Your payments of self-employment tax contribute to your coverage under the Social Security system. That coverage provides you with retirement benefits and with medical insurance (Medicare) benefits.

Note: You may be liable for paying self-employment tax even if you are now fully insured under Social Security and are now receiving benefits.

Who Must Pay the Tax?

If you carry on a trade or business, except as an employee, you will have to pay self-employment tax on your self-employment income. A trade or business is generally an activity that is carried on for a livelihood, or in good faith to make a profit. The business does not need to actually make a profit, but the profit motive must exist and there must be ongoing efforts to further the business. Regularity of activities and transactions and the production of income are key elements.

You are self-employed if you are a (1) sole proprietor, (2) independent contractor, (3) member of a partnership, or (4) are otherwise in business for yourself. You do not have to carry on regular full-time business activities to be self-employed. Part-time work, including work you do on the side in addition to your regular job, may also be self-employment.

Income Limits

You must pay self-employment tax if you have net earnings from self-employment of $400 or more. The self-employment tax rate for 2014 is 15.3% (a total of 12.4% for Social Security on net earnings up to a maximum of $117,000 for 2014, and 2.9% for Medicare on net earnings). If you are also a wage earner and those earnings were subject to Social Security tax, you will not be taxed on that amount under self-employment income.

Figuring Self-Employment Tax

There are three steps to figure out the amount of self-employment tax you owe: (1) determine your net earnings from self-employment, (2) determine the amount that is subject to the tax, and (3) multiply that amount by the tax rate.

Note: There are two deductions on your income tax return relating to self-employment tax. Both deductions result in a reduction of your total income tax burden.

1. **On Schedule SE.** A deduction of 7.65% of your net earnings from self-employment is taken directly on Schedule SE, reducing the self-employment tax itself by that percentage.

2. **On Form 1040.** There is a deduction that reduces your adjusted gross income on Form 1040 by allowing one-half the amount of your self-employment tax liability to be deducted as a business expense. This is an income tax adjustment only. It does not affect your net earnings from self-employment or your Schedule SE tax.

Joint Returns

You may not file a joint Schedule SE (Form 1040) even if you file a joint income tax return. Your spouse is not considered self-employed just because you are. If you both have self-employment income, each of you must file a separate Schedule SE (Form 1040).

Social Security Number

You must have a Social Security number if you have to pay self-employment tax. You may apply for one at the nearest Social Security office. Form SS-5, *Application for a Social Security Card*, may be obtained from any Social Security office.

Schedule SE (Form 1040)

Schedule SE, *Self Employment Tax*, is used to compute self-employment tax. If you are required to pay estimated income tax (see Estimated Tax section) you must also figure any self-employment tax you owe and include that amount when you send in your 1040-ES vouchers. If you are not required to pay estimated taxes, the full payment is remitted with your annual tax return.

IRS Publication. See Publication 334, *Tax Guide for Small Business*. For more detailed information, read Publication 533, *Self-Employment Tax*. Included in the publication is an illustrated Schedule SE.

 Sample. A sample of Schedule SE (Form 1040) can be seen on the next page. For information on 1040-ES, refer back to page 127 to the information on Estimated Tax for your legal structure.

Schedule SE (Form 1040)
Computation of Self-Employment Tax

SCHEDULE SE (Form 1040) Department of the Treasury Internal Revenue Service (99)	**Self-Employment Tax** ▶ Information about Schedule SE and its separate instructions is at *www.irs.gov/schedulese.* ▶ **Attach to Form 1040 or Form 1040NR.**	OMB No. 1545-0074 20**13** Attachment Sequence No. **17**
Name of person with **self-employment** income (as shown on Form 1040)	Social security number of person with **self-employment** income ▶	

Before you begin: To determine if you must file Schedule SE, see the instructions.

May I Use Short Schedule SE or Must I Use Long Schedule SE?

Note. Use this flowchart **only if** you must file Schedule SE. If unsure, see *Who Must File Schedule SE* in the instructions.

```
                          ┌────────────────────────────────────────┐
                          │  Did you receive wages or tips in 2013? │
                          └────────────────────────────────────────┘
             No │                                            │ Yes
                ▼                                            ▼
  ┌──────────────────────────────────┐         ┌──────────────────────────────────────┐
  │ Are you a minister, member of a  │         │ Was the total of your wages and tips   │ Yes
  │ religious order, or Christian     │ Yes     │ subject to social security or railroad │───▶
  │ Science practitioner who received │───▶     │ retirement (tier 1) tax plus your net  │
  │ IRS approval not to be taxed on   │         │ earnings from self-employment more     │
  │ earnings from these sources, but  │         │ than $113,700?                         │
  │ you owe self-employment tax on    │         └──────────────────────────────────────┘
  │ other earnings?                   │                         │ No
  └──────────────────────────────────┘                         ▼
             No │                              ┌──────────────────────────────────────┐
                ▼                              │ Did you receive tips subject to social │ Yes
  ┌──────────────────────────────────┐ Yes    │ security or Medicare tax that you did   │───▶
  │ Are you using one of the optional │───▶     │ not report to your employer?           │
  │ methods to figure your net        │         └──────────────────────────────────────┘
  │ earnings (see instructions)?      │                         │ No
  └──────────────────────────────────┘                         ▼
             No │                    No        ┌──────────────────────────────────────┐
                ▼              ◀───────────────│ Did you report any wages on Form 8919, │ Yes
  ┌──────────────────────────────────┐ Yes    │ Uncollected Social Security and        │───▶
  │ Did you receive church employee   │───▶     │ Medicare Tax on Wages?                 │
  │ income (see instructions)         │         └──────────────────────────────────────┘
  │ reported on Form W-2 of $108.28   │
  │ or more?                          │
  └──────────────────────────────────┘
             No │
                ▼
  ┌──────────────────────────────────┐         ┌──────────────────────────────────────┐
  │ You may use Short Schedule SE     │ ◀────── │ You must use Long Schedule SE on page 2│
  │ below                             │         └──────────────────────────────────────┘
  └──────────────────────────────────┘
```

Section A—Short Schedule SE.   Caution. Read above to see if you can use Short Schedule SE.

1a	Net farm profit or (loss) from Schedule F, line 34, and farm partnerships, Schedule K-1 (Form 1065), box 14, code A	**1a**	
b	If you received social security retirement or disability benefits, enter the amount of Conservation Reserve Program payments included on Schedule F, line 4b, or listed on Schedule K-1 (Form 1065), box 20, code Z	**1b**	( )
2	Net profit or (loss) from Schedule C, line 31; Schedule C-EZ, line 3; Schedule K-1 (Form 1065), box 14, code A (other than farming); and Schedule K-1 (Form 1065-B), box 9, code J1. Ministers and members of religious orders, see instructions for types of income to report on this line. See instructions for other income to report	**2**	
3	Combine lines 1a, 1b, and 2	**3**	
4	Multiply line 3 by 92.35% (.9235). If less than $400, you do not owe self-employment tax; **do not** file this schedule unless you have an amount on line 1b . . . . ▶	**4**	
	Note. If line 4 is less than $400 due to Conservation Reserve Program payments on line 1b, see instructions.		
5	**Self-employment tax.** If the amount on line 4 is: • $113,700 or less, multiply line 4 by 15.3% (.153). Enter the result here and on **Form 1040, line 56,** or **Form 1040NR, line 54** • More than $113,700, multiply line 4 by 2.9% (.029). Then, add $14,098.80 to the result. Enter the total here and on **Form 1040, line 56,** or **Form 1040NR, line 54**	**5**	
6	**Deduction for one-half of self-employment tax.** Multiply line 5 by 50% (.50). Enter the result here and on **Form 1040, line 27,** or **Form 1040NR, line 27** . . . . | **6** |		

For Paperwork Reduction Act Notice, see your tax return instructions.	Cat. No. 11358Z	Schedule SE (Form 1040) 2013

Social Security (FICA) Tax and Withholding of Income Tax

File Form 941 (941E or 943), *Employers Quarterly Federal Tax Return*. Also, Forms W-2, W-3, and W-4.

If you have one or more employees, you will be required to withhold federal income tax from their wages. You also must collect and pay the employee's part and your matching share of Social Security (FICA) and Medicare taxes.

You are liable for the payment of these taxes to the federal government whether or not you collect them from your employees. See "Liability for Tax Withheld" on page 137.

Who Are Employees?

Under common law rules, every individual who performs services that are subject to the will and control of an employer, as to both what must be done and how it must be done, is an employee. Two of the usual characteristics of an employer-employee relationship are that the employer has the right to discharge the employee and the employer supplies tools and a place to work. It does not matter if the employee is called an employee, a partner, co-adventurer, agent, or independent contractor. It does not matter how the payments are measured, how they are made, or what they are called. Nor does it matter whether the individual is employed full-time or part-time.

Note: For an in-depth discussion and some examples of employer-employee relationships, see Publication 15-A, *Employer's Supplemental Tax Guide*. If you want the IRS to determine whether a worker is an employee, file Form SS-8 with the District Director for the area in which your business is located.

Social Security and Medicare Taxes

The Federal Insurance Contributions Act (FICA) provides for a federal system of old-age, survivors, disability, and hospital insurance. The old-age, survivors, and disability part is financed through Social Security taxes. The hospital part is financed by the Medicare tax. Each of these taxes is reported separately. Social security taxes are levied on both you and your employees. You as an employer must collect and pay the employee's part of the tax. You must withhold it from wages. You are also liable for your own (employer's) matching share of Social Security taxes.

Tax Rate

The tax rate for social security in 2014 was 6.2% each for employers and employees (12.4% total) with a wage base of $117,000. Self-employed individuals pay the combined rate of 12.4% of their net earnings from self-employment, up to the maximum wage base. The tax rate for Medicare is 1.45% each for employers and employees (2.9% total). As of January 2013, employee's wages in excess of $200,000 ($250,000 for married couples filing jointly) is subject to an additional 0.9% Medicare Tax for a total rate of 2.35% (1.45% + 0.9%). The additional Medicare Tax is not matched by employers. Social Security taxes and withheld income taxes are reported and paid together. For detailed information, read Publication 334, *Tax Guide for Small Business*, and Publication 15, *Circular E, Employer's Tax Guide*.

Withholding of Income Tax

Generally, you must withhold income from wages you pay employees if their wages for any payroll period are more than the amount of their withholding allowances claimed for that period. The amount to be withheld is figured separately for each payroll period. You should figure withholding on gross wages before any deductions for Social Security tax, pension, union dues, insurance, etc. are made. *Circular E, Employer's Tax Guide*, contains the applicable tables and detailed instructions for using withholding methods.

Tax Forms

The following are the forms used to report Social Security taxes and withheld income tax.

- **Form 941, Employer's Quarterly Federal Tax Return**

  Generally, Social Security (FICA) and Medicare taxes and withheld income tax are reported together on Form 941. Forms 943 and 945 are used for other than the usual type of employee. (See Publication 334.) Form 943 (for Agricultural Employees) is an annual return due one month after the end of the calendar year. The other forms are quarterly returns and are due one month after the end of each calendar quarter. Due dates are April 30, July 31, October 31, and January 31. An extra 10 days are given if taxes are deposited on time and in full.

- **Federal Tax Deposits**

  You generally will have to make deposits of Social Security and Medicare taxes and withheld income taxes before the return is due. You must deposit both your part and your employee's part of Social Security taxes using the Electronic Federal Tax Payment System (EFTPS). Deposits are made either semi-weekly or monthly, depending on the average size of deposits for the past year and must be made. See Publication 15, *Circular E, Employer's Tax Guide*, for more detailed information on deposits.

- **Form W-2**

  You must furnish copies of Form W-2 to each employee from whom income tax or Social Security tax has been withheld. Form W-2 shows the total wages subject to Social Security and Medicare taxes, amounts deducted for income, Social Security, and Medicare taxes, and any other information required on the statement. Detailed information for preparation of this form is contained in the instructions for Form W-2. Furnish copies of Form W-2 to employees as soon as possible after December 31, so they may file their income tax returns early. It must be sent to the employee no later than January 31st. W-2s must also be transmitted annually to the Social Security Administration.

- **Form W-3**

  Employers must file Form W-3 annually to transmit forms W-2 and W-2P to the Social Security Administration. These forms will be processed by the Social Security Administration, which will then furnish the Internal Revenue Service with the income tax data that it needs from the forms. Form W-3 and its attachments must be filed separately from Form 941 by the last day of February, following the calendar year for which the Form W-2 is prepared.

- **Form W-4**

  In general, an employee can claim withholding allowances equal to the number of exemptions he or she is entitled to claim on an income tax return. Each new employee should give you a Form W-4, *Employee's Withholding Allowance Certificate*, on or before the first day of work. The certificates must include the employee's Social Security number. Copies of Form W-4 that are required to be submitted because of a large number of allowances or claims of exemption from income tax withholding are sent in with quarterly employment tax returns (Form 941). Withholding is then figured on gross wages before deductions for Social Security, tax pension, insurance, etc.

Liability for Tax Withheld

You are required by law to deduct and withhold income tax from the salaries and wages of your employees. You are liable for payment of that tax to the federal government whether or not you collect it from your employees.

IRS Publication. For detailed information, refer to Publication 15, *Circular E, Employer's Tax Guide*.

 Samples. On the next four pages, you will find samples of Form 941, Form W-2, Form W-3, and Form W-4.

Form 941
Employer's Quarterly Federal Tax Return

Form **941 for 2013:** Employer's QUARTERLY Federal Tax Return   950113
(Rev. January 2013)   Department of the Treasury — Internal Revenue Service   OMB No. 1545-0029

Employer identification number (EIN) ☐☐ – ☐☐☐☐☐☐☐

Name *(not your trade name)* _____

Trade name *(if any)* _____

Address _____
         Number   Street   Suite or room number
         _____
         City   State   ZIP code

Report for this Quarter of 2013
(Check one.)

☐ **1:** January, February, March

☐ **2:** April, May, June

☐ **3:** July, August, September

☐ **4:** October, November, December

Instructions and prior year forms are available at *www.irs.gov/form941*.

Read the separate instructions before you complete Form 941. Type or print within the boxes.

Part 1:	Answer these questions for this quarter.

1 Number of employees who received wages, tips, or other compensation for the pay period
including: *Mar. 12* (Quarter 1), *June 12* (Quarter 2), *Sept. 12* (Quarter 3), or *Dec. 12* (Quarter 4)   **1** ☐

2 Wages, tips, and other compensation . . . .   **2** ☐

3 Income tax withheld from wages, tips, and other compensation . . . .   **3** ☐

4 If no wages, tips, and other compensation are subject to social security or Medicare tax   ☐ Check and go to line 6.

		Column 1		Column 2
5a	Taxable social security wages . .	☐	× .124 =	☐
5b	Taxable social security tips . . .	☐	× .124 =	☐
5c	Taxable Medicare wages & tips. .	☐	× .029 =	☐
5d	Taxable wages & tips subject to Additional Medicare Tax withholding	☐	× .009 =	☐

5e Add Column 2 from lines 5a, 5b, 5c, and 5d . . . .   **5e** ☐

5f Section 3121(q) Notice and Demand—Tax due on unreported tips (see instructions) . .   **5f** ☐

6 Total taxes before adjustments (add lines 3, 5e, and 5f) . . . .   **6** ☐

7 Current quarter's adjustment for fractions of cents . . . .   **7** ☐

8 Current quarter's adjustment for sick pay . . . .   **8** ☐

9 Current quarter's adjustments for tips and group-term life insurance . . . . . .   **9** ☐

10 Total taxes after adjustments. Combine lines 6 through 9 . . . .   **10** ☐

11 Total deposits for this quarter, including overpayment applied from a prior quarter and
overpayment applied from Form 941-X or Form 944-X filed in the current quarter . . .   **11** ☐

12a COBRA premium assistance payments (see instructions) . . . .   **12a** ☐

12b Number of individuals provided COBRA premium assistance . . ☐

13 Add lines 11 and 12a . . . .   **13** ☐

14 Balance due. If line 10 is more than line 13, enter the difference and see instructions . . .   **14** ☐

15 Overpayment. If line 13 is more than line 10, enter the difference ☐   Check one: ☐ Apply to next return. ☐ Send a refund.

▶ You MUST complete both pages of Form 941 and SIGN it.   Next ▶

For Privacy Act and Paperwork Reduction Act Notice, see the back of the Payment Voucher.   Cat. No. 17001Z   Form **941** (Rev. 1-2013)

Form 941
Employer's Quarterly Federal Tax Return
Page 2

950213

Name *(not your trade name)* | **Employer identification number (EIN)**

Part 2:   **Tell us about your deposit schedule and tax liability for this quarter.**

If you are unsure about whether you are a monthly schedule depositor or a semiweekly schedule depositor, see Pub. 15 (Circular E), section 11.

16   Check one: ☐   Line 10 on this return is less than $2,500 or line 10 on the return for the prior quarter was less than $2,500, and you did not incur a $100,000 next-day deposit obligation during the current quarter. If line 10 for the prior quarter was less than $2,500 but line 10 on this return is $100,000 or more, you must provide a record of your federal tax liability. If you are a monthly schedule depositor, complete the deposit schedule below; if you are a semiweekly schedule depositor, attach Schedule B (Form 941). Go to Part 3.

           ☐   **You were a monthly schedule depositor for the entire quarter.** Enter your tax liability for each month and total liability for the quarter, then go to Part 3.

           Tax liability: Month 1   [.]

                           Month 2   [.]

                           Month 3   [.]

           Total liability for quarter   [.]   Total must equal line 10.

           ☐   **You were a semiweekly schedule depositor for any part of this quarter.** Complete Schedule B (Form 941), Report of Tax Liability for Semiweekly Schedule Depositors, and attach it to Form 941.

Part 3:   **Tell us about your business. If a question does NOT apply to your business, leave it blank.**

17   If your business has closed or you stopped paying wages . . . . ☐ Check here, and

      enter the final date you paid wages   [/ /] .

18   If you are a seasonal employer and you do not have to file a return for every quarter of the year . . ☐ Check here.

Part 4:   **May we speak with your third-party designee?**

Do you want to allow an employee, a paid tax preparer, or another person to discuss this return with the IRS? See the instructions for details.

    ☐ Yes. Designee's name and phone number [   ]   [   ]

           Select a 5-digit Personal Identification Number (PIN) to use when talking to the IRS. ☐ ☐ ☐ ☐ ☐

    ☐ No.

Part 5:   **Sign here. You MUST complete both pages of Form 941 and SIGN it.**

Under penalties of perjury, I declare that I have examined this return, including accompanying schedules and statements, and to the best of my knowledge and belief, it is true, correct, and complete. Declaration of preparer (other than taxpayer) is based on all information of which preparer has any knowledge.

X   Sign your name here [   ]   Print your name here [   ]

                                        Print your title here [   ]

           Date [/ /]   Best daytime phone [   ]

Paid Preparer Use Only   Check if you are self-employed . . . ☐

Preparer's name	[ ]	PTIN	[ ]
Preparer's signature	[ ]	Date	[/ /]
Firm's name (or yours if self-employed)	[ ]	EIN	[ ]
Address	[ ]	Phone	[ ]
City	[ ] State [ ]	ZIP code	[ ]

         Form **941** (Rev. 1-2013)

Form W-2
Wage and Tax Statement

a Employee's social security number		

22222	**a** Employee's social security number	OMB No. 1545-0008	

		1 Wages, tips, other compensation	2 Federal income tax withheld
b Employer identification number (EIN)			
c Employer's name, address, and ZIP code		3 Social security wages	4 Social security tax withheld
DO NOT FILE INFORMATION ONLY		5 Medicare wages and tips	6 Medicare tax withheld
		7 Social security tips	8 Allocated tips
d Control number		9	10 Dependent care benefits
e Employee's first name and initial Last name Suff.		11 Nonqualified plans	12a
		13 Statutory employee ☐ Retirement plan ☐ Third-party sick pay ☐	12b
		14 Other	12c
			12d
f Employee's address and ZIP code			

15 State Employer's state ID number	16 State wages, tips, etc.	17 State income tax	18 Local wages, tips, etc.	19 Local income tax	20 Locality name

Form **W-2** Wage and Tax Statement   **2013**   Department of the Treasury—Internal Revenue Service
Copy 1—For State, City, or Local Tax Department

Form W-3
Transmittal of Income and Tax Statements

DO NOT STAPLE

33333	**a** Control number	For Official Use Only ▶ OMB No. 1545-0008	

b Kind of Payer (Check one)	941 ☐ Military ☐ 943 ☐ 944 ☐ CT-1 ☐ Hshld. emp. ☐ Medicare govt. emp. ☐	**Kind of Employer** (Check one)	None apply ☐ 501c non-govt. ☐ State/local non-501c ☐ State/local 501c ☐ Federal govt. ☐	Third-party sick pay (Check if applicable) ☐

c Total number of Forms W-2	**d** Establishment number	1 Wages, tips, other compensation	2 Federal income tax withheld
e Employer identification number (EIN)		3 Social security wages	4 Social security tax withheld
f Employer's name		5 Medicare wages and tips	6 Medicare tax withheld
		7 Social security tips	8 Allocated tips
DO NOT FILE INFORMATION ONLY		9	10 Dependent care benefits
		11 Nonqualified plans	12a Deferred compensation
g Employer's address and ZIP code			
h Other EIN used this year		13 For third-party sick pay use only	12b
15 State Employer's state ID number		14 Income tax withheld by payer of third-party sick pay	
16 State wages, tips, etc.	17 State income tax	18 Local wages, tips, etc.	19 Local income tax
Employer's contact person		Employer's telephone number	For Official Use Only
Employer's fax number		Employer's email address	

Under penalties of perjury, I declare that I have examined this return and accompanying documents and, to the best of my knowledge and belief, they are true, correct, and complete.

Signature ▶   Title ▶   Date ▶

Form **W-3** Transmittal of Wage and Tax Statements   **2014**   Department of the Treasury Internal Revenue Service

Send this entire page with the entire Copy A page of Form(s) W-2 to the Social Security Administration (SSA). Photocopies are not acceptable. Do not send Form W-3 if you filed electronically with the SSA. Do not send any payment (cash, checks, money orders, etc.) with Forms W-2 and W-3.

Form W-4
Employee's Withholding Allowance Certificate

Form W-4 (2014)

Purpose. Complete Form W-4 so that your employer can withhold the correct federal income tax from your pay. Consider completing a new Form W-4 each year and when your personal or financial situation changes.

Exemption from withholding. If you are exempt, complete **only** lines 1, 2, 3, 4, and 7 and sign the form to validate it. Your exemption for 2014 expires February 17, 2015. See Pub. 505, Tax Withholding and Estimated Tax.

Note. If another person can claim you as a dependent on his or her tax return, you cannot claim exemption from withholding if your income exceeds $1,000 and includes more than $350 of unearned income (for example, interest and dividends).

Exceptions. An employee may be able to claim exemption from withholding even if the employee is a dependent, if the employee:

• Is age 65 or older,

• Is blind, or

• Will claim adjustments to income; tax credits; or itemized deductions, on his or her tax return.

The exceptions do not apply to supplemental wages greater than $1,000,000.

Basic instructions. If you are not exempt, complete the **Personal Allowances Worksheet** below. The worksheets on page 2 further adjust your withholding allowances based on itemized deductions, certain credits, adjustments to income, or two-earners/multiple jobs situations.

Complete all worksheets that apply. However, you may claim fewer (or zero) allowances. For regular wages, withholding must be based on allowances you claimed and may not be a flat amount or percentage of wages.

Head of household. Generally, you can claim head of household filing status on your tax return only if you are unmarried and pay more than 50% of the costs of keeping up a home for yourself and your dependent(s) or other qualifying individuals. See Pub. 501, Exemptions, Standard Deduction, and Filing Information, for information.

Tax credits. You can take projected tax credits into account in figuring your allowable number of withholding allowances. Credits for child or dependent care expenses and the child tax credit may be claimed using the **Personal Allowances Worksheet** below. See Pub. 505 for information on converting your other credits into withholding allowances.

Nonwage income. If you have a large amount of nonwage income, such as interest or dividends, consider making estimated tax payments using Form 1040-ES, Estimated Tax for Individuals. Otherwise, you may owe additional tax. If you have pension or annuity income, see Pub. 505 to find out if you should adjust your withholding on Form W-4 or W-4P.

Two earners or multiple jobs. If you have a working spouse or more than one job, figure the total number of allowances you are entitled to claim on all jobs using worksheets from only one Form W-4. Your withholding usually will be most accurate when all allowances are claimed on the Form W-4 for the highest paying job and zero allowances are claimed on the others. See Pub. 505 for details.

Nonresident alien. If you are a nonresident alien, see Notice 1392, Supplemental Form W-4 Instructions for Nonresident Aliens, before completing this form.

Check your withholding. After your Form W-4 takes effect, use Pub. 505 to see how the amount you are having withheld compares to your projected total tax for 2014. See Pub. 505, especially if your earnings exceed $130,000 (Single) or $180,000 (Married).

Future developments. Information about any future developments affecting Form W-4 (such as legislation enacted after we release it) will be posted at *www.irs.gov/w4*.

Personal Allowances Worksheet (Keep for your records.)

A	Enter "1" for **yourself** if no one else can claim you as a dependent	**A** _____
B	Enter "1" if: { • You are single and have only one job; or	
	• You are married, have only one job, and your spouse does not work; or } . . .	**B** _____
	• Your wages from a second job or your spouse's wages (or the total of both) are $1,500 or less.	
C	Enter "1" for your **spouse**. But, you may choose to enter "-0-" if you are married and have either a working spouse or more than one job. (Entering "-0-" may help you avoid having too little tax withheld.) . . . . **C** _____	
D	Enter number of **dependents** (other than your spouse or yourself) you will claim on your tax return . . . . **D** _____	
E	Enter "1" if you will file as **head of household** on your tax return (see conditions under **Head of household** above) . . **E** _____	
F	Enter "1" if you have at least $2,000 of **child or dependent care expenses** for which you plan to claim a credit . . . **F** _____	
	(**Note.** Do **not** include child support payments. See Pub. 503, Child and Dependent Care Expenses, for details.)	
G	**Child Tax Credit** (including additional child tax credit). See Pub. 972, Child Tax Credit, for more information.	
	• If your total income will be less than $65,000 ($95,000 if married), enter "2" for each eligible child; then **less** "1" if you have three to six eligible children or **less** "2" if you have seven or more eligible children.	
	• If your total income will be between $65,000 and $84,000 ($95,000 and $119,000 if married), enter "1" for each eligible child . . . **G** _____	
H	Add lines A through G and enter total here. (**Note.** This may be different from the number of exemptions you claim on your tax return.) ▶ **H** _____	

For accuracy, complete all worksheets that apply. {	• If you plan to **itemize** or **claim adjustments to income** and want to reduce your withholding, see the **Deductions and Adjustments Worksheet** on page 2.
	• If you are **single and have more than one job** or are **married and you and your spouse both work** and the combined earnings from all jobs exceed $50,000 ($20,000 if married), see the **Two-Earners/Multiple Jobs Worksheet** on page 2 to avoid having too little tax withheld.
	• If **neither** of the above situations applies, **stop here** and enter the number from line H on line 5 of Form W-4 below.

---------------------------------- **Separate here and give Form W-4 to your employer. Keep the top part for your records.** ----------------------------------

Form **W-4**	**Employee's Withholding Allowance Certificate**	OMB No. 1545-0074
Department of the Treasury Internal Revenue Service	▶ Whether you are entitled to claim a certain number of allowances or exemption from withholding is subject to review by the IRS. Your employer may be required to send a copy of this form to the IRS.	20**14**

1 Your first name and middle initial	Last name	2 Your social security number

Home address (number and street or rural route)	3 ☐ Single ☐ Married ☐ Married, but withhold at higher Single rate.
	Note. If married, but legally separated, or spouse is a nonresident alien, check the "Single" box.
City or town, state, and ZIP code	4 If your last name differs from that shown on your social security card, check here. You must call 1-800-772-1213 for a replacement card. ▶ ☐

5	Total number of allowances you are claiming (from line **H** above **or** from the applicable worksheet on page 2)	5	
6	Additional amount, if any, you want withheld from each paycheck	6	$
7	I claim exemption from withholding for 2014, and I certify that I meet **both** of the following conditions for exemption.		
	• Last year I had a right to a refund of **all** federal income tax withheld because I had **no** tax liability, **and**		
	• This year I expect a refund of **all** federal income tax withheld because I expect to have **no** tax liability.		
	If you meet both conditions, write "Exempt" here . . . . ▶	7	

Under penalties of perjury, I declare that I have examined this certificate and, to the best of my knowledge and belief, it is true, correct, and complete.

Employee's signature
(This form is not valid unless you sign it.) ▶ _____   Date ▶ _____

8 Employer's name and address (Employer: Complete lines 8 and 10 only if sending to the IRS.)	9 Office code (optional)	10 Employer identification number (EIN)

For Privacy Act and Paperwork Reduction Act Notice, see page 2.   Cat. No. 10220Q   Form **W-4** (2014)

Federal Unemployment (FUTA) Tax

File Form 940, *Employer's Annual Federal Unemployment (FUTA) Tax Return*.

The federal unemployment tax system, together with the state systems, provides for payments of unemployment compensation to workers who have lost their jobs. This tax applies to wages you pay your employees. Most employers pay both a state and the federal unemployment tax.

In general you are subject to FUTA tax on the wages you pay employees who are not farm workers or household workers if: (1) in any calendar quarter, the wages you paid to employees in this category totaled $1,500 or more; or (2) in each of 20 different calendar weeks, there was at least a part of a day in which you had an employee in this category. See *Circular E, Employer's Tax Guide*, for lists of payments excluded from FUTA and types of employment not subject to the tax.

Figuring the Tax

The federal unemployment tax is figured on the first $7,000 in wages paid to each employee annually. The tax is imposed on you as the employer. You must not collect it or deduct it from the wages of your employees.

Tax Rate

The gross federal unemployment tax rate for 2013 was 6.0%. However, you are given a credit of up to 5.4% for the state unemployment tax you pay providing you have paid your state unemployment liability by the due date. The tax rate, therefore, can be as low as 0.6% (6.0% minus 5.4%) if your state is not subject to a credit reduction. Study rules applying to liability for this tax (i.e., credit reduction, success of employer, concurrent employment by related corporations). For information on figuring federal unemployment tax, including special rules for a "successor employer," see Publication 15, *Circular E, Employer's Tax Guide*.

Form 940

Employer's annual FUTA tax return, Form 940, is used for reporting. This form covers one calendar year and is generally due one month after the year ends. However, you may have to make deposits of this tax before filing the return. If you deposit the tax on time and in full, you have an extra ten days to file – until February 10th.

Deposits

If at the end of any calendar quarter, you owe but have not yet deposited, more than $500 in federal unemployment (FUTA) tax for the year, you must make a deposit by the end of the next month.

Deposit Due dates are as follows:	
If undeposited FUTA tax is more than $500 on:	**Deposit full amount by:**
March 31	April 30
June 30	July 31
September 30	October 31
December 31	January 31

If the tax is $500 or less at the end of the quarter, you need not deposit it, but you must add it to the tax for the next quarter and deposit according to the $500 rule. (Publication 15, *Circular E, Employer's Tax Guide*.) The Electronic Federal Tax Payment System (EFTPS) must be used for all tax deposit transactions.

Federal Tax Deposit

Prior to 2011, federal tax deposit coupons were used to make deposits through an authorized financial institution or Federal Reserve Bank. Each deposit was accompanied by a federal tax deposit (FTD) coupon. As of January 1, 2011, the IRS stopped accepting tax payments made using deposit coupons. Instead, all tax deposit transactions must be made through the Electronic Federal Tax Payment System (EFTPS). The system was set up to allow businesses to make payments electronically and to reduce payment errors. Payments can be made at anytime of the day or night, from any location by computer or phone. Payments can also be scheduled in advance. In order to avoid having a payment being considered late, it must be made by 8 p.m. eastern time, the day prior to the due date. For example, if a payment is due on April 15, it must be entered into the system by 8 p.m. eastern time on April 14.

IRS Publication. Form 940, *FUTA Tax Return* (instructions) and Publication 15, *Circular E, Employer's Tax Guide*.

 Sample. The next page shows a sample Form 940, *Employer's Annual Federal Unemployment (FUTA) Tax Return*.

Form 940
Employer's Annual Federal Unemployment (FUTA) Tax Return
Page 1 only + Example 940-V

Form **940 for 2013:** Employer's Annual Federal Unemployment (FUTA) Tax Return
Department of the Treasury — Internal Revenue Service

850113

OMB No. 1545-0028

Employer identification number (EIN) ☐☐ – ☐☐☐☐☐☐☐

Name *(not your trade name)*

Trade name *(if any)*

Address
Number   Street   Suite or room number
City   State   ZIP code
Foreign country name   Foreign province/county   Foreign postal code

Type of Return
(Check all that apply.)
☐ a. Amended
☐ b. Successor employer
☐ c. No payments to employees in 2013
☐ d. Final: Business closed or stopped paying wages

Instructions and prior-year forms are available at *www.irs.gov/form940.*

Read the separate instructions before you complete this form. Please type or print within the boxes.

Part 1:   Tell us about your return. If any line does NOT apply, leave it blank.

1a If you had to pay state unemployment tax in one state only, enter the state abbreviation .   **1a** ☐☐

1b If you had to pay state unemployment tax in more than one state, you are a multi-state employer . . . .   **1b** ☐ Check here. Complete Schedule A (Form 940).

2 If you paid wages in a state that is subject to CREDIT REDUCTION . . . .   **2** ☐ Check here. Complete Schedule A (Form 940).

Part 2:   Determine your FUTA tax before adjustments for 2013. If any line does NOT apply, leave it blank.

3 Total payments to all employees . . . .   **3** ☐ .

4 Payments exempt from FUTA tax . . . .   **4** ☐ .

   Check all that apply: **4a** ☐ Fringe benefits   **4c** ☐ Retirement/Pension   **4e** ☐ Other
                          4b ☐ Group-term life insurance   **4d** ☐ Dependent care

5 Total of payments made to each employee in excess of $7,000 . . . .   **5** ☐ .

6 Subtotal (line 4 + line 5 = line 6) . . . .   **6** ☐ .

7 Total taxable FUTA wages (line 3 – line 6 = line 7) (see instructions) . . . .   **7** ☐ .

8 FUTA tax before adjustments (line 7 x .006 = line 8) . . . .   **8** ☐ .

Part 3:   Determine your adjustments. If any line does NOT apply, leave it blank.

9 If ALL of the taxable FUTA wages you paid were excluded from state unemployment tax, multiply line 7 by .054 (line 7 × .054 = line 9). Go to line 12 . . . .   **9** ☐ .

10 If SOME of the taxable FUTA wages you paid were excluded from state unemployment tax, OR you paid ANY state unemployment tax late (after the due date for filing Form 940), complete the worksheet in the instructions. Enter the amount from line 7 of the worksheet . .   **10** ☐ .

11 If credit reduction applies, enter the total from Schedule A (Form 940) . . . .   **11** ☐ .

Part 4:   Determine your FUTA tax and balance due or overpayment for 2013. If any line does NOT apply, leave it blank.

12 Total FUTA tax after adjustments (lines 8 + 9 + 10 + 11 = line 12) . . . .   **12** ☐ .

13 FUTA tax deposited for the year, including any overpayment applied from a prior year .   **13** ☐ .

14 Balance due (If line 12 is more than line 13, enter the excess on line 14.)
   • If line 14 is more than $500, you must deposit your tax.
   • If line 14 is $500 or less, you may pay with this return. (see instructions) . . . .   **14** ☐ .

15 Overpayment (If line 13 is more than line 12, enter the excess on line 15 and check a box below.) . . . .   **15** ☐ .

▶ You **MUST** complete both pages of this form and **SIGN** it.   Check one: ☐ Apply to next return.   ☐ Send a refund.   **Next ▶**

For Privacy Act and Paperwork Reduction Act Notice, see the back of Form 940-V, Payment Voucher.   Cat. No. 11234O   Form **940** (2013)

✂ - - - - - - - - ▼ **Detach Here and Mail With Your Payment and Form 940.** ▼ - - - - - - - - ✂

Form **940-V**
Department of the Treasury
Internal Revenue Service

Payment Voucher

▶ Do not staple or attach this voucher to your payment.

OMB No. 1545-0028

20**13**

1 Enter your employer identification number (EIN).

2 **Enter the amount of your payment. ▶**
Make your check or money order payable to **"United States Treasury"**

Dollars   Cents

3 Enter your business name (individual name if sole proprietor).

Enter your address.

Enter your city, state, and ZIP code or your city, foreign country name, foreign province/county, and foreign postal code.

Payment to Non-employees for Services Rendered

File Form 1099-MISC, *Statement to Recipients of Miscellaneous Income* together with Form 1096, *Annual Summary and Transmittal of U.S. Information Returns*.

Payments made by you in your trade or business activities that are not for wages must be reported to the IRS. Payments include fees, commissions, prizes, awards, or other forms of compensation for services rendered to your company by an individual who is not your employee. This also includes fair market value of exchanges (bartering) of property or services between individuals in the course of a trade or business. Exempt payments include payments for inventory, payments for rent to a real estate agent, payments for telephone services, utilities, employee travel expense reimbursements, and payments to corporations.

If the following four conditions are met, a payment is generally reported as non-employee compensation: (1) You made the payment to a non-employee; (2) you made the payment for services rendered in your business; (3) you made the payment to a payee who is not a corporation; and (4) you made payments to the payee totaling $600 or more during the year.

Form 1099-MISC

Statement to Recipient of Miscellaneous Income is an information form used to report payments in the course of your trade or business to non-employees (or for which you were a nominee/ middleman, or from which you withheld federal income tax or foreign tax).

When and How to File

File 1099-MISC on or before the last day of February. Transmit these forms to your IRS Service Center with Form 1096, *Annual Summary and Transmittal of U.S. Information Return*. A 1099-MISC copy must be sent to the recipient by January 31st. For payments in the form of barter, file Form 1099-B, *Proceeds From Broker and Barter Exchange*.

IRS Publications. Publication 15-A, *Employer's Supplemental Tax Guide*. For more information on 1099s, see the current year's instructions for Forms 1099 and 1096.

 Samples. The following pages show samples of Form 1099-MISC and 1096.

Independent Contractors Facts versus Myths

Appendix I of Keeping the Books will provide you with comprehensive information regarding independent contractors. That section, entitled "Independent Contractors: Facts versus Myths," includes:

- The "List of 20 Common Law Factors."
- Basic rules regarding independent contractor status.
- Benefits and risks of hiring independent contractors.
- Benefits and risks to the independent contractor.

Form 1099-MISC
Statement to Recipients of Miscellaneous Income

9595 ☐ VOID ☐ CORRECTED		
PAYER'S name, street address, city or town, state or province, country, ZIP or foreign postal code, and telephone no.	**1** Rents $	OMB No. 1545-0115
DO NOT FILE INFORMATION ONLY	**2** Royalties $	2014 Form **1099-MISC**
	3 Other income $	**4** Federal income tax withheld $
PAYER'S federal identification number RECIPIENT'S identification number	**5** Fishing boat proceeds $	**6** Medical and health care payments $
RECIPIENT'S name	**7** Nonemployee compensation $	**8** Substitute payments in lieu of dividends or interest $
Street address (including apt. no.)	**9** Payer made direct sales of $5,000 or more of consumer products to a buyer (recipient) for resale ▶ ☐	**10** Crop insurance proceeds $
City or town, state or province, country, and ZIP or foreign postal code	**11**	**12**
Account number (see instructions) 2nd TIN not. ☐	**13** Excess golden parachute payments $	**14** Gross proceeds paid to an attorney $
15a Section 409A deferrals $ **15b** Section 409A income $	**16** State tax withheld $	**17** State/Payer's state no. **18** State income $

Miscellaneous Income
Copy A
For
Internal Revenue Service Center
File with Form 1096.
For Privacy Act and Paperwork Reduction Act Notice, see the **2014 General Instructions for Certain Information Returns.**

Form **1099-MISC**   Cat. No. 14425J   www.irs.gov/form1099misc   Department of the Treasury - Internal Revenue Service

Do Not Cut or Separate Forms on This Page — Do Not Cut or Separate Forms on This Page

9595 ☐ VOID ☐ CORRECTED		
PAYER'S name, street address, city or town, state or province, country, ZIP or foreign postal code, and telephone no.	**1** Rents $	OMB No. 1545-0115
DO NOT FILE INFORMATION ONLY	**2** Royalties $	2014 Form **1099-MISC**
	3 Other income $	**4** Federal income tax withheld $
PAYER'S federal identification number RECIPIENT'S identification number	**5** Fishing boat proceeds $	**6** Medical and health care payments $
RECIPIENT'S name	**7** Nonemployee compensation $	**8** Substitute payments in lieu of dividends or interest $
Street address (including apt. no.)	**9** Payer made direct sales of $5,000 or more of consumer products to a buyer (recipient) for resale ▶ ☐	**10** Crop insurance proceeds $
City or town, state or province, country, and ZIP or foreign postal code	**11**	**12**
Account number (see instructions) 2nd TIN not. ☐	**13** Excess golden parachute payments $	**14** Gross proceeds paid to an attorney $
15a Section 409A deferrals $ **15b** Section 409A income $	**16** State tax withheld $	**17** State/Payer's state no. **18** State income $

Miscellaneous Income
Copy A
For
Internal Revenue Service Center
File with Form 1096.
For Privacy Act and Paperwork Reduction Act Notice, see the **2014 General Instructions for Certain Information Returns.**

Form **1099-MISC**   Cat. No. 14425J   www.irs.gov/form1099misc   Department of the Treasury - Internal Revenue Service

Do Not Cut or Separate Forms on This Page — Do Not Cut or Separate Forms on This Page

Form 1096
Annual Summary and Transmittal of
U.S. Information Returns

Do Not Staple   6969

Form **1096** Department of the Treasury Internal Revenue Service	**Annual Summary and Transmittal of U.S. Information Returns**	OMB No. 1545-0108 20**13**

FILER'S name

Street address (including room or suite number)

City or town, province or state, country, and ZIP or foreign postal code

DO NOT FILE
INFORMATION ONLY

For Official Use Only

Name of person to contact	Telephone number
Email address	Fax number

1 Employer identification number	2 Social security number	3 Total number of forms	4 Federal income tax withheld $	5 Total amount reported with this Form 1096 $

6 Enter an "X" in only one box below to indicate the type of form being filed.

7 If this is your **final return**, enter an "X" here . . . . . ▶ ☐

W-2G 32	1097-BTC 50	1098 81	1096-C 78	1098-E 84	1098-T 83	1099-A 80	1099-B 79	1099-C 85	1099-CAP 73	1099-DIV 91	1099-G 86	1099-H 71	1099-INT 92	1099-K 10	1099-LTC 93	1099- MISC 95	1099-OID 96
☐	☐	☐	☐	☐	☐	☐	☐	☐	☐	☐	☐	☐	☐	☐	☐		☐

1099- PATR 97	1099-Q 31	1099-R 98	1099-S 75	1099-SA 94	3921 25	3922 26	5498 28	5498-ESA 72	5498-SA 27
☐	☐	☐	☐	☐	☐	☐	☐	☐	☐

Return this entire page to the Internal Revenue Service. Photocopies are not acceptable.

Under penalties of perjury, I declare that I have examined this return and accompanying documents, and, to the best of my knowledge and belief, they are true, correct, and complete.

Signature ▶   Title ▶   Date ▶

Instructions

Future developments. For the latest information about developments related to Form 1096, such as legislation enacted after they were published, go to *www.irs.gov/form1096*.

Reminder. The only acceptable method of filing information returns with Internal Revenue Service/Information Returns Branch is electronically through the FIRE system. See Pub. 1220, Specifications for Filing Forms 1097, 1098, 1099, 3921, 3922, 5498, 8935, and W-2G Electronically.

Purpose of form. Use this form to transmit paper Forms 1097, 1098, 1099, 3921, 3922, 5498, and W-2G to the Internal Revenue Service. Do not use Form 1096 to transmit electronically. For electronic submissions, see Pub. 1220.

Caution. If you are required to file 250 or more information returns of any one type, you must file electronically. If you are required to file electronically but fail to do so, and you do not have an approved waiver, you may be subject to a penalty. For more information, see part F in the 2013 General Instructions for Certain Information Returns.

Who must file. The name, address, and TIN of the filer on this form must be the same as those you enter in the upper left area of Forms 1097, 1098, 1099, 3921, 3922, 5498, or W-2G. A filer is any person or entity who files any of the forms shown in line 6 above.

Enter the filer's name, address (including room, suite, or other unit number), and TIN in the spaces provided on the form.

When to file. File Form 1096 as follows.
- With Forms 1097, 1098, 1099, 3921, 3922, or W-2G, file by February 28, 2014.
- With Forms 5498, file by June 2, 2014.

Where To File

Send all information returns filed on paper with Form 1096 to the following:

If your principal business, office or agency, or legal residence in the case of an individual, is located in	Use the following three-line address
Alabama, Arizona, Arkansas, Connecticut, Delaware, Florida, Georgia, Kentucky, Louisiana, Maine, Massachusetts, Mississippi, New Hampshire, New Jersey, New Mexico, New York, North Carolina, Ohio, Pennsylvania, Rhode Island, Texas, Vermont, Virginia, West Virginia	Department of the Treasury Internal Revenue Service Center Austin, TX 73301

For more information and the Privacy Act and Paperwork Reduction Act Notice,   Cat. No. 14400O   Form **1096** (2013)

Taxpayer Identification Number (EIN)

Form SS-4, *Application for Employer Identification Number.*

Social Security Number

If you are a sole proprietor, you will generally use your Social Security number as your taxpayer identification number. You must put this number on each of your individual income tax forms, such as Form 1040 and its schedules.

Taxpayer Identification Number (EIN)

Every partnership, S corporation, corporation, and certain sole proprietors must have an employer identification number (EIN) to use as a taxpayer identification number.

Sole proprietors must have EINs if they pay wages to one or more employees or must file pension or excise tax returns. Otherwise they can use their Social Security numbers.

New EIN

You may need to get a new EIN if either the form or the ownership of your business changes.

- **Change in Organization.** A new EIN is required if: a sole proprietor incorporates; a sole proprietorship takes in partners and operates as a partnership; a partnership incorporates; a partnership is taken over by one of the partners and is operated as a sole proprietorship; or a corporation changes to a partnership or to a sole proprietorship.

- **Change in Ownership.** A new EIN is required if: you buy or inherit an existing business that you will operate as a sole proprietorship; you represent an estate that operates a business after the owner's death; or you terminate an old partnership and begin a new one.

Application for an EIN or Social Security Number

To apply for an EIN, use Form SS-4, *Application for Employer Identification Number.* This form is available from the IRS and Social Security Administration offices. You can also download the form online. Go to http://www.irs.gov and type "Form SS-4" in the search box. This will take you to a page where the form can be downloaded as a PDF file. There is a copy of the form in Appendix II on page 195.

Form SS-5 is used to apply for a Social Security number card. This form is available online or directly from Social Security Administration offices. If you are under 18 years of age, you must furnish evidence, along with this form, of age, identity, and U.S. citizenship. If you are 18 or older, you must appear in person with this evidence at a Social Security office. If you are an alien, you must appear in person and bring your birth certificate and either your alien registration card or your U.S. immigration form.

Quick and Easy Access to
IRS Tax Help and Tax Products

The IRS has provided us with several ways to access its publications, forms, and tax information. They are as follows:

Internet. Access the IRS website 24 hours a day, 7 days a week, at **www.irs.gov** to:

- Access commercial tax preparation and e-file services available free to eligible taxpayers;
- Download forms, instructions, and publications;
- Order IRS products online;
- Research your tax questions online;
- Search publications online by topic or keyword;
- Use the online Internal Revenue Code, Regulations, or other official guidance;
- View Internal Revenue Bulletins (IRBs) published in the last few years;
- Send comments or request help by e-mail; and
- Sign up to receive local and national tax news by e-mail.

Phone. Order current year forms, instructions, and publications and prior year forms and instructions by calling **1-800-TAX-FORM (1-800-829-3676)**. You should receive your order within 10 days.

Walk-In. You can pick up some of the most requested forms, instructions, and publications at many IRS offices, post offices, and libraries. Some grocery stores, copy centers, city and county government offices, credit unions, and office supply stores have a collection of reproducible tax forms available to photocopy or print from a CD-ROM.

Mail. Send your order for tax products to: Internal Revenue Service, National Distribution Center, 1201 N. Mitsubishi Motorway, Bloomington, IL 61705–6613. You should receive your products within 15 days after they receive your order. If you wish to order publications or forms by mail, you will find an order form on the last page of this chapter.

DVD For Tax Products. You can order Publication 1796, IRS Tax Products DVD, and obtain:

- Current-year forms, instructions, and publications.
- Prior-year forms, instructions, and publications.
- Tax Map: an electronic research tool and finding aid.
- Tax law frequently asked questions.
- Tax Topics from the IRS telephone response system.
- Internal Revenue Code – Title 26
- Fill-in, print, and save features for most tax forms.
- Internal Revenue Bulletins.
- Toll-free and email technical support.

The DVD is released twice during the year. Purchase the DVD from the National Technical Information Service at www.ntis.gov/products/irsdvd.aspx for $30 (no handling fee) or call 1-877-CDFORMS (1-877-233-6767) toll-free to buy the DVD for $30 (plus a $6 handling fee). The price is subject to change.

A Suggested List of IRS Publications

The following is a list of IRS Publications that may prove helpful to you in the course of
your business. Keep a file of tax information. Send for these publications and update your
file with new publications at least once a year.

Tax Guide for Small Business
(For Individuals Who Use Schedule C or C-EZ)

Sole proprietors should begin by reading Publication 334, *Tax Guide for Small Business*. It
is a general guide to all areas of small business and will give you comprehensive
information.

Listing of Publications for Small Business

If you are a business owner, the following IRS publications will provide you with fairly
detailed information on specific tax-related topics.

1	Your Rights as a Taxpayer
15	*Circular E., Employer's Tax Guide*
15A	*Employers Supplemental Tax Guide*
17	*Your Federal Income Tax*
463	*Travel, Entertainment, Gift and Car Expenses*
505	*Tax Withholding and Estimated Tax*
509	*Tax Calendars*
535	*Business Expenses*
536	*Net Operating Losses*
538	*Accounting Periods & Methods*
541	*Partnerships*
542	*Corporations (S Corporations get instructions for 1120S)*
544	*Sales and Other Dispositions of Assets*
551	*Basis of Assets*
553	*Highlights of Tax Changes*
556	*Examination of Returns, Appeal Rights, and Claims for Refund*
557	*Tax-Exempt Status for Your Organization (SEP, SIMPLE, and Qualified Plans)*
560	*Retirement Plans for the Small Business*
583	*Starting a Business and Keeping Records*
587	*Business Use of Your Home (including Use by Day-Care Providers)*
594	*The IRS Collection Process*
910	*IRS Guide to Free Tax Services*
925	*Passive Activity & At Risk Rules*
946	*How to Depreciate Your Property*
947	*Practice Before the IRS and Power of Attorney*
1066	*Small Business Tax Workshop Workbook*
1544	*Reporting Cash Payments of Over $10,000 (Received in a Trade or Business)*
1546	*The Taxpayer Advocate Service of the IRS*
1779	*Independent Contractor or Employee Brochure*

Order Information
IRS Forms and Publications

Order Blank for Forms and Publications

The most frequently ordered forms and publications are listed on the order blank below. You will receive two copies of each form, one copy of the instructions, and one copy of each publication you order. To help reduce waste, please order only the items you need to prepare your return. Please order no more than ten items.

 For faster ways of getting the items you need, go to www.irs.gov and click on the Forms and Pubs folder.

How To Use the Order Blank

Circle the items you need on the order blank below. Use the blank spaces to order items not listed. If you need more space, attach a separate sheet of paper.

Print or type your name and address accurately in the space provided below to en-sure delivery of your order. Enclose the order blank in an envelope and mail it to the IRS address shown on this page. You should receive your order within 7 to 10 days after receipt of your request.

Do not send your tax return to the address shown here. Instead, see the back cover.

Mail Your Order Blank To:

Internal Revenue Service
National Distribution Center
1201 N. Mitsubishi Motorway
Bloomington, IL 61705-6613

▲ *Cut here* ▲

Save Money and Time by Going Online!
Download or order these and other tax products at www.irs.gov

Order Blank

Please print

Name

Postal mailing address   Apt./Suite/Room

City   State   ZIP code

Foreign country   International postal code

Daytime phone number
(   )

Circle the forms and publications you need. The instructions for any form you order will be included.

The items in bold are also available at many IRS offices, U.S. Post Offices, and various libraries.

Use the **blank spaces** to order items not listed.

1040	Schedule H (1040)	1040-ES (2007)	4684	8863	Pub. 505	Pub. 554	
Schedules A&B (1040)	Schedule J (1040)	1040-V	4868	8913	Pub. 523	Pub. 575	
Schedule C (1040)	Schedule R (1040)	1040X	5695	9465	Pub. 525	Pub. 587	
Schedule C-EZ (1040)	Schedule SE (1040)	2106	6251	Pub. 1	Pub. 526	Pub. 590	
Schedule D (1040)	**1040A**	2106-EZ	8283	Pub. 17	Pub. 527	Pub. 596	
Schedule D-1 (1040)	Schedule 1 (1040A)	2441	8606	Pub. 334	Pub. 529	Pub. 910	
Schedule E (1040)	Schedule 2 (1040A)	4506	8812	Pub. 463	Pub. 535	Pub. 915	
Schedule EIC (1040A or 1040)	Schedule 3 (1040A)	4506-T	8822	Pub. 501	Pub. 547	Pub. 970	
Schedule F (1040)	**1040EZ**	4562	8829	Pub. 502	Pub. 550	Pub. 972	

N

Summary

The purpose of this chapter has been to introduce you to the tax requirements pertaining to your business. It is important to keep abreast of revisions in the tax laws that will affect your business.

IRS Workshops

The IRS holds tax seminars on a regular basis for small business owners who would like to learn more about current regulations and requirements. You can call the local IRS office and ask it to mail you a schedule of upcoming workshops.

Know What is Happening

Planning for your business is an ongoing process requiring the implementation of many changes. You may rest assured that many of those changes will be a direct result of new tax laws. Today, many small businesses are carefully examining their hiring policies because of the regulatory legislation that is being passed or considered regarding employee benefits (such as insurance and pensions), workers' compensation, contract services, etc. Business owners need to understand what is happening and take active positions to impact legislation that is pertinent to their operations and can ultimately lead to their success or failure.

You have taken the first step. You would not be reading this book unless you had already committed yourself to organizing and understanding your recordkeeping and accounting. You are one of the lucky ones -- the entrepreneurs who know that every decision makes an impact on the bottom line.

What's Next?

Now that you are familiar with basic records, financial statements and tax returns, it is time to combine your information and utilize it to formulate recordkeeping and tax reporting schedules for your business. Setting up your records and keeping them current are two different pieces of the same pie.

To help you get started, the next chapter will be devoted to providing you with written guides to follow while you are getting into the habit of doing all the unfamiliar chores required to keep your records current.

Recordkeeping and Tax Reporting Schedules

You should now have a basic understanding of the interrelationship of each of the phases of recordkeeping. Up to this point, you have been introduced to the following:

- **The Basics of Recordkeeping**

- **Income and Expenses**

- **Cash vs. Accrual Accounting**

- **Essential Records for Small Business**

- **Financial Statements**

- **Financial Statement Analysis**

- **Taxes and Bookkeeping**

Organizing Your Recordkeeping

Just as timing is important to all other phases of your business, it also is important when you deal with recordkeeping. You cannot haphazardly throw all of your paperwork into a basket and deal with it in a sporadic nature. You will have to organize your recordkeeping into a system that will allow you to proceed through the tax year in an orderly fashion. That system will have to provide for retrieval and verification of tax information and, at the same time, form a picture of your business that will help you to analyze trends and implement changes to make your venture grow and become more profitable.

Building Your System

The information in this book has been presented in a particular order for a specific reason. Just as a home builder must first lay the foundation, do the framing, put up the walls, and then do the finish work, you, too, must build your foundation first and learn the basics of recordkeeping. The frame can be likened to your General Records. They are the underlying material without which there could be no walls. In the same way, General Records are the basis (source of information) for forming Financial Statements. At last, the builder finishes the home and makes some rooms into a limited space for each family member and other rooms into common areas where the whole family will meet. This is Tax Accounting, with different legal structures functioning within their limited areas, but meeting in areas common to all businesses. The house is complete – and so is your recordkeeping. Now a schedule needs to be made to maintain your home or it will soon be a shambles. To keep your business in a maintained state, it too must have scheduled upkeep. To keep maintenance at an optimum, you will need to set up a Recordkeeping and Tax Reporting Schedule.

Proceeding on the assumption that you have never done recordkeeping and that you have no idea in what order it must be done, I will give you a basic format to follow while you learn this task.

Doing Tasks in Sequence

There is a specific order to recordkeeping, and you must follow that order if your records are going to be effective. Because the two goals of recordkeeping are retrieval for tax purposes and the analyzing of information for internal planning, your schedule will have to provide for the reaching of those goals.

I have provided a General Recordkeeping and a Tax Reporting Schedule on the following pages to help you. There are two things that you must keep in mind to ensure success:

- Do not fail to do any of the tasks.
- Be sure to do them on time.

POST your schedule on the wall in your office and refer to it every day for what needs to be done. Before long, those chores will become automatic. All of the information presented in this book will have assimilated in your mind and you will begin to see the overall picture. At the end of the year, if you have followed the schedules, you will have every piece of financial information at your fingertips. It can be done – and you can do it!

Schedule Formats

The General Recordkeeping Schedule is divided into tasks according to frequency. There are two basic divisions:

1. General Recordkeeping

- **Daily:** Tasks you should be aware of and do every day.

- **Weekly:** The tasks you do when you do your regular bookkeeping. Timing may vary according to the needs of your business.

- **Monthly:** Closing out your books at the end of the month.

- **Quarterly:** Analysis of past quarter and revision of budget.

- **End of Year:** Closing out your books for the current year and setting up records for the new year.

2. Tax Reporting

- **Monthly:** Payroll reporting and deposits, Sales Tax Reporting (sales tax may be monthly, quarterly, or annually)

- **Quarterly:** Sending in required tax reports.

- **Annually:** Filing information and tax returns.

Every business has individual needs. You may have to shift the frequency of some tasks. To begin with, however, follow the progression in the schedules I have provided, and they should adequately cover most of your needs.

Sample schedules. The next five pages contain General Recordkeeping and Tax Reporting Schedules. Copy them! Post them!

Note for Different Legal Structures

Because some recordkeeping tasks are different for different legal structures (i.e., sole proprietorship, partnership, S corporation, and corporation), it will be noted as to which apply. If there is no notation accompanying the task, it applies to all legal structures.

If you need help, refer back. *Keep in mind when you are using the General Recordkeeping Schedule that all the items on the schedule have been covered in one of the previous sections. You need only refer back to the appropriate record, statement, or tax return information to refresh your memory and complete your task. Be sure to keep reference materials mentioned in those sections close at hand in case you need more detailed information.*

Use These Schedules!

The following schedules are meant to serve as guides for you until you are familiar with the recordkeeping process. There may be other jobs for you to do, but this should get you off to a good start.

Recordkeeping Schedule

Daily

1. Go through mail and file for appropriate action.

2. Unpack and put away incoming inventory.

3. Record inventory information in Inventory Record.

4. Pay any invoices (Accounts Payable) necessary to meet discount deadlines.

5. Record daily invoices sent out in Accounts Receivable.

   Note: It would be a good idea to keep invoice copies in an envelope or folder behind its corresponding Accounts Receivable record. *

* **Accounting software.** Invoices generated from within your software will be automatically posted to the proper accounts.

Weekly

1. Prepare bank deposit for income received and take it to the bank.

2. Enter deposit in checkbook and Income & Expense Journal.*

3. Enter sales information in Inventory Record.*

4. Enter week's checking transactions in Income & Expense Journal.*

5. Record petty cash purchases in Petty Cash Record and file receipts.*

6. Pay invoices due. Be aware of discount dates.

7. Record any depreciable purchases in your Fixed Asset Log.*

* **Accounting software.** Enter deposits, checks written, and petty cash expenditures for the week. This will record all of the above.

cont. – next page

Monthly

1. Balance checkbook (reconcile with bank statement).*

2. Enter any interest earned and any bank charges in checkbook and in your Income & Expense Journal.

3. Total and balance all Income & Expense Journal columns.*

4. Enter monthly income and expense totals on 12-month P&L Statement. Prepare a separate one-month Profit & Loss if you wish.*

5. If you wish to look at assets and liabilities, prepare a Balance Sheet. It is only required at year end for those who are not sole proprietors or filers of Schedule C (see End of the Year).

6. Check Accounts Payable and send statements to open accounts.

* **Accounting software.** Perform bank reconciliation. Generate a monthly and year-to-date P&L Statement and a current Balance Sheet.

Quarterly

1. Do a Quarterly Budget Analysis. Compare actual income and expenses with projections.

2. Revise your cash flow statement (budget) accordingly.

End of Tax Year

1. Pay all invoices, sales taxes and other expenses that you wish to use as deductions for the current tax year.

2. Prepare annual Profit & Loss Statement. (Add income and expense totals from the 12 monthly reports.)*

3. Prepare a Balance Sheet for your business. A Balance Sheet is required for all but sole proprietors or filers of Schedule C.*

4. Prepare a Pro Forma Cash Flow Statement (budget) for next year. Use your Profit & Loss information from the current year to help you make decisions.

5. Set up your new records for the coming year. It is a good idea to buy new journals and files early before the supply runs out. Begin recordkeeping in the first week. Do not get behind.*

* **Accounting software.** Generate an annual Profit & Loss Statement and an end-of-year Balance Sheet. Accounting for the new year does not need to be set up again. It will continue from previous year.

Tax Reporting Schedule

Warning!

The following Tax Reporting Schedule is not meant for use as a final authority. Requirements may change. Also you may be responsible for reports and returns that are not listed below. This is meant only to be used as a general guide to help keep you on track until you become familiar with the specific requirements for your business.

This schedule refers to tax reports and reporting dates. In the tax chapter, there are tax-reporting calendars for all legal structures. Post your calendar with this schedule and refer to it for required forms and dates. Also refer to information on individual forms that are listed in the index by subject and by form number.

Monthly

1. **Check your payroll tax liability.** If it equals or exceeds $2,500 for any quarter, a deposit is due on the 15th of the month for the taxes of the previous month. (If you work with an accountant or payroll service, information on payments and withholding amounts needs to be provided to them as early in the month as possible so you can receive information back as to what your deposits should be). See information on "Payroll Records" in Chapter 4.

2. **Sales tax reports.** You may be required to file monthly, quarterly, or annually, according to your sales volume. In some cases, you may be required to be bonded or prepay sales tax. Fill out and send in your sales tax report to the State Board of Equalization (or in some states sales tax may be administered through the Department of Revenue) with a check for monies collected (or due) for the sale of taxable goods or services for the previous period. This is for those businesses holding a Seller's Permit. The subject of sales tax is not covered in this book. (See our business start-up book, *Steps to Small Business Start- Up*, Kaplan Publishing.) Report forms are furnished by the collecting agency and will generally be due somewhere around 30 days after the end of the reporting period.

cont. – next page

Quarterly

1. **Estimated Taxes (Form 1040Es):** File estimated taxes with the Internal Revenue Service. You must also file with your state, if applicable.

    - Sole proprietor, individual who is a partner, or S corporation shareholder file on 15th day of the 4th, 6th, and 9th months of tax year, and 15th day of the 1st month after the end of tax year. For most business the due dates would be April 15, June 15, September 15, and January 15. If the due date falls on a weekend day, the due date will be the following Monday.

    - Corporations file the 15th day of the 4th, 6th, 9th, and 12th months of the tax year. For most business this will be April 15, June 15, September 15, and December 15; the same weekend rules apply.

    Note: *Take special notice that only two months lapse between 1st and 2nd quarter filing dates. There will be four months between the third and fourth quarter filings.*

2. **FICA & Withholding Returns (Form 941):** File *Employer's Quarterly Federal Tax Returns* reporting Social Security (FICA) tax and the withholding of income tax. Check early to see if you are required to make deposits.

3. **FUTA Deposits (Form 8109):** Make Federal Unemployment (FUTA) tax deposits. Make deposits on April 30th, July 31st, October 31st, and January 31st, but only if the liability for unpaid tax is more than $500.

4. **Sales Tax Reports:** If you are on a quarterly reporting basis, reports will be due by April 30th, July 31st, October 31st, and January 31st for the previous quarter. If you are only required to file annually, it will generally be due on January 31st for the previous calendar year.

cont. – next page

Annually

1. **FICA and Withholding Information Returns:** Provide information on Social Security (FICA) tax and the withholding of income tax. (Also, make it your business to be aware of any additional state requirements.)

    - W-2 to employees on January 31st.

    - W-2 and W-3 to Social Security Administration on the last day of February.

2. **1099 Information Returns:** Send information for payments to non-employees and transactions with other persons.

    - Forms 1099 due to recipient by January 31st.

    - Forms 1099 and transmittals 1096 due to IRS on the last day of February.

3. **FUTA Tax Returns:** File federal unemployment (FUTA) tax returns with the IRS. Due date is January 31st.

4. **Income Tax Returns (Form 1040):** File income tax returns with the IRS. (and your state, if applicable)

    - Sole Proprietor, individual who is a partner, S Corporation shareholder file on 15th day of 4th month after end of tax year (generally April 15th, Schedule C, Form 1040).

    - Partnership returns due on the 15th day of the 4th month after the end of tax year (generally April 15th, Form 1065).

    - S corporations (Form 1120S) and corporations (Form 1120) file on the 15th day of the 3rd month after end of the tax year (generally March 15th).

5. **Self-Employment Tax Forms (Form SE):** Self-Employment tax forms are filed with Form 1040 (see above).

    - For sole proprietors or individuals who are partners.

    - Self-employment forms are applicable if your business has net earnings from self-employment of $400 or more.

CHAPTER

9

Preparing for Uncle Sam

This book would not be complete without giving you information on getting ready to prepare your income tax returns. As was stated earlier, one of the two main purposes of recordkeeping is for income tax retrieval and verification.

When all your end-of-the-year work has been done, it is time to begin work on income taxes. By no means am I suggesting that you do it all yourself. As a matter of fact, I strongly suggested that you hire a CPA, Enrolled Agent, or other tax professional to do the final preparation and aid you in maximizing your tax benefits. Not very many of us are well enough informed to have a good command of all the tax regulations and changes. However, you can do a great deal of the preliminary work. This will be of benefit to you in two different ways: (1) You will save on accounting fees, and (2) you will learn a lot about your business by working on your taxes.

There will be a great deal of variation in what you can do yourself, due not only to the complexity of your particular business, but also to the abilities of the individual doing your recordkeeping. For this reason, we will not attempt to give directions for preliminary tax preparations. However, there is some sound advice that we can give you at this point.

You have spent the year keeping general records and developing financial statements. These are the records that provide all the information you need for income tax accounting. In fact, if the IRS regulations weren't so fast changing and complicated, you could probably fill out your own tax return.

However, because you will need a professional preparer to make sure that your return is correct and to maximize your benefits, your task is to gather and pass on the information that is needed to get the job done.

Many tax preparers complain that the assignment is made difficult because customers do not prepare their material. They bring in bags full of receipts and disorganized information. What do you need in order to be prepared for the accountant?

What to Give Your Accountant

The information needed by your accountant will come from sources that you should already have if you have kept your general records and generated financial statements as presented in Chapters 3 and 4.

All Businesses

There are two things that your accountant will need from you regardless of your type of business:

1. **Annual Profit & Loss Statement:** This gives your accountant a list of all of the income and expenses your business has had for the tax year. If you are in a product industry, your accountant will need to compute your cost of goods sold for your return. You are required to do a beginning and ending inventory every year. Before you complete your P&L Statement, you will need the following three items:

   • **Beginning Inventory.** Inventory as of January 1st of the current year. It must match the figure you listed as "Ending Inventory" last year.

   • **Ending Inventory.** Inventory as of December 31st of this year. This is done by physical inventory. It will become your beginning inventory for next year.

   • **Amount of Inventory Purchased.** List the cost of all inventory purchased by your company during the tax year.

   Note: *If you develop your own P&L Statement, you can compute "Cost of Goods Sold." However, giving your accountant a list of the above three items will help in checking your understanding and accuracy. If you use software, your P&L Statement will probably not include beginning and ending inventory. You will still need to give these numbers to your accountant for computation of "Cost of Goods Sold."*

2. **Copy of Your Fixed Asset Log:** This document lists all of the depreciable assets your company has purchased during the current year, with date purchased, purchase price, etc. Your accountant needs to know whether you have listed any of these costs as expenses (instead of cost of goods) in your P&L Statement. Both of you can then decide whether to depreciate these items or expense them under Section 179.

Home-Based Businesses

List of Home-Office Expenses: Because these items are generally paid with personal checks, you will have to gather information on taxes, insurance, and interest paid (rent, if you are not a homeowner). You will also need amounts on maintenance and utilities. Before you decide to depreciate your home as a home-office deduction, ask your accountant to explain the recapture if you subsequently sell. You must also measure your office space and calculate the percentage of your home that is used exclusively for your business. Your accountant will need this information to fill out the required form that must accompany your income tax return if you are claiming home-office deduction.

Partnerships, S Corporations, and Full Corporations

Record of Owner Equity Deposits and Owner Draws: The three legal structures listed are required to have a balance sheet as part of the return, listing the equity of each owner. In order to compute equity, your accountant will have to have the total contributed and withdrawn by each owner. Using last year's equity account balances as a base, deposits will be added and withdrawals subtracted to arrive at the owners' new balances. These tools will be automatically generated by accounting software users.

It is best to provide the accountant with the above information as soon as possible after the end of the tax year. This allows extra time for any questions that might arise while your returns are being prepared. It also allows you to forget about income taxes and get on with the new business year.

The Last Chore

The IRS, in general, requires us to keep all income tax information for a period of three years from the date the return is filed. During that time (and longer, in some cases, such as fraud) past returns are subject to audit. In addition, several records are retained for longer periods, mostly determined by administrative decision. It is a good idea to keep many of them for the life of your business. Remember that the other purpose of records is that of analyzing trends and implementing changes. They are only useful if they are still in your possession.

I have found it to be very effective to file all of the information together for one year. Put the following things in your file, mark it with the year date, and put it away.

- Income tax returns
- All receipts
- Bank statements
- Annual Profit and Loss (Income) Statement
- Fixed Assets Record, Inventory Record, etc.
- All information pertinent to verification of your return

Records Retention Schedule

This schedule will help you to decide what records you should keep and how long you should keep them.

RETENTION PERIOD	AUTHORITY TO DISPOSE
1-10 Number of Years to be Retained **PR** Retain Permanently **EOY** Retain Until End of Year **CJ** Retain Until Completion of Job **EXP** Retain Until Expiration **ED** Retain Until Equipment Disposal	**AD** Administrative Decision **FLSA** Fair Labor Standards Act **CFR** Code of Federal Regulators **IR** Insurance Regulators

TYPE OR RECORD	RETAIN FOR	BY WHOSE AUTHORITY
Bank Deposit Records	7	AD
Bank Statements	7	AD
Business Licenses	EXP	AD
Catalogs	EXP	AD
Check Register	PR	AD
Checks (Cancelled)	3	FLSA, STATE
Contracts	EXP	AD
Correspondence	5	AD
Depreciation Records	PR	CFR
Estimated Tax Records	PR	AD
Expense Records and Travel Records	7	AD
Insurance (Claims Records)	11	IR
Insurance Policies	EXP	AD
Inventory Records	10	AD
Inventory Reports	PR	CFR
Invoices (Accounts Payable)	3	FLSA, STATE
Invoices (Accounts Receivable)	7	AD
Ledger (General) or Electronic Files	PR	CFR
Maintenance Records	ED	AD
Office Equipment Records	5	AD
Patents, Copyrights, Trademarks	PR	AD
Petty Cash Record	PR	AD
Postal Records	1	AD, CFR
Purchase Orders	3	CFR
Sales Tax Reports to State	PR	STATE
Shipping Documents	2-10	AD, CFR
Tax Bills and Statements	PR	AD
Tax Returns (Federal and State)	PR	AD
Work Papers / Projects	CJ	AD
Year-End Reports	PR	AD

Independent Contractors
Facts versus Myths

© 2014
Judee Slack, Enrolled Agent

Judee Slack is a designated Enrolled Agent (licensed by the IRS). She is the owner of SlackTax, Inc., a tax accounting firm located in Fountain Valley, California. Ms. Slack has been active on both the federal and state (CA) level, promoting changes in legislation that will clarify and simplify the classification process regarding independent contractors.

Independent contractors are independent business people who are hired to perform specific tasks. They are just like any other vendor, except they perform services rather than provide tangible goods. Independent contractors are in business for themselves. Thus, they are not the hiring firm's employees. They are not eligible for unemployment, disability, or workers' compensation benefits. The hiring firm does not have to pay employee-employer taxes or provide workers' compensation insurance, and usually is not liable for the contractor's actions.

Benefits and Risks
Of Hiring Independent Contractors

Benefits

1. Save money, hiring firms don't have to pay:

- Social Security taxes (2014 rate: 6.2% of an employee's wages, up to $117,000 and 1.45% of an employee's total wages.)
- Workers compensation premiums.
- Unemployment insurance (rate for new businesses, state and federal taxes total 6.2% of an employee's wages, up to $434 per employee)
- California Employment Training taxes (currently $7 per employee)
- Health insurance and retirement benefits.

2. **Avoid a long-term employee commitment**

3. **Avoid liability for the worker's actions**

4. **Avoid dealing with labor unions and their accompanying demands for union scale wages, benefits, and hiring/firing practices.**

Risks

1. Government fines

-   The government looks negatively at the misclassification of bona-fide employees as Independent Contractors for two reasons. Independent Contractors can contribute to the underground economy by not paying taxes. They are responsible for withholding their own taxes and Social Security. Many do not report their earnings and thus rob the system and the other taxpayers of tax dollars.

-   The government also wants to protect workers. The Social Security, disability, and unemployment insurance programs were all designed to protect average workers. The government does not want businesses to circumvent these programs (and their costs) simply by calling their workers Independent Contractors.

2. Lawsuits from Independent Contractors

-   When workers are injured, employees can usually only receive only workers' compensation benefits. However, Independent Contractors may sue their hiring firm.

3. No control over the work

-   A hiring firm cannot control an Independent Contractor's work. If it does, the worker's legal status will automatically convert to an employer-employee relationship and the hiring firm will be liable for employment taxes and benefits. Because hiring firms can't control their contracts, deadlines may be missed, customers may become angry, or other situations may arise that are detrimental to the hiring firm.

4. Limited right to fire Independent Contractors

-   Hiring firms can fire Independent Contractors only if they breach their contract or if the completed work is unacceptable. If a hiring firm keeps the right to fire the worker at will, the worker's legal status usually converts to an employer-employee relationship.

Benefits and Risks
To Independent Contractors

Benefits

1. **Personal flexibility; they are their own boss**

2. **Business expenses are tax deductible**

Risks

1. **No disability or workers' compensation insurance**

    *   If Independent Contractors are injured, they can't collect disability or workers' compensation insurance.

2. **No unemployment insurance**

    *   Independent Contractors may develop tax troubles.

    *   Independent Contractors must pay quarterly income tax and Social Security self-employment taxes. Social Security self-employment tax is currently 15.3% of net taxable income; a big shock to people who don't plan ahead. When you add federal income tax (10-35%) plus state income tax, the total bill can be huge. If Independent Contractors spend that money before tax time, they get into BIG trouble with the government.

3. **Independent Contractors can be held liable**

    *   Independent Contractors can be held liable for their actions, instead of being protected by the hiring firm (or its insurance).

The Basic Rules

Government Rules (Not Written Agreements)
Determine If a Worker Is an Independent Contractor

The IRS' rules and laws of individual state determine whether a worker is an Independent Contractor or an employee, not the written or oral agreement between the hiring firm and the person hired. A contract in a file is not proof of an Independent Contractor relationship.

Workers Are Employees,
Unless a Hiring Firm Can Prove Otherwise

Statutory Employees

According to IRS Code Section 3121(d), the following workers are automatically employees:

- Officers of corporations who provide services to that corporation.

- Food and laundry drivers.

- Full-time traveling or city salespeople who sell goods to people (or firms) for resale.

- Full-time life insurance agents, working mainly for one company (IRS only).

- At-home workers who are supplied with materials or goods and are given specifications for the work to be done.

Statutory Non-employees

The 1982 Tax Equity and Fiscal Responsibility Act (TEFRA) created new Code Section 3508 that defines two categories of workers who are statutorily not to be treated as employees:

- Direct sellers who sell a product to the final user. Basically, this applies to door-to-door and home demonstration salespeople.

- Licensed real estate agents.

20 Common Law Factors (Rev Rule 87-41)

If workers don't fall into the special categories above, the **20 Common Law Factors** should be used. Independent Contractors do not have to satisfy all 20 common law factors. The courts have given different weights for each factor according to the industry and job and the courts have not always been consistent in weighing these factors.

What Are The
"20 Common Law Factors"?

At the end of this chapter, you will find a **"List of the 20 Common Law Factors"** that are used to determine whether a worker is an "employee" or an "independent contractor." It would be wise to familiarize yourself with the 20 factors and refer to them when you are considering the hiring of independent contractors. The list may help you to avoid misclassification and costly penalties.

Federal "Safe Harbor" Rules (IRS Code Section 530)

The IRS has special Independent Contractors rules which "exempt" certain workers from the 20 common law factors if all of the following three statements are true:

- Since December 31, 1977, the hiring firm and its predecessors have consistently treated individuals doing similar work as Independent Contractors.

- The hiring firm and its predecessors have never treated the current Independent Contractors as employees and have filed all the required federal tax returns (form 1099-MISC) for Independent Contractors.

- There was a reasonable basis for treating the worker as an Independent Contractor. Reasonable basis means:

    − A reliance on judicial rulings, IRS rulings, or IRS technical advice;

    - or -

    − In a prior audit, no penalties were assessed for treating workers doing a similar type of work as Independent Contractors;

    - or -

    − It is a recognized practice for a large segment of the industry to treat certain types of workers as Independent Contractors.

 Note: *If a firm cannot meet the three "safe harbor" rules, it may still be entitled to exemption if it can demonstrate, in some other manner, a reasonable basis for not treating the individual as an employee. IRS Rev. Proc 85-18 indicates that agents should liberally construe what constitutes a "reasonable basis" in favor of the taxpayer.*

Penalties for Misclassification

TEFRA added new Section 3509 that sets rules for any assessments after 1982 resulting from a reclassification of an Independent Contractor to employee status. The employer will be assessed a liability for:

- 1.5% of the gross wages (federal withholding)

    - and -

- 20% of the amount that would have been the employee's share of FICA taxes

    - and −

- The appropriate employer's share of FICA.

- providing -

- Information returns (form 1099-MISC) were filed

- and -

- Such failure to deduct was not intentional disregard of the requirement.

Employer Disregard

In the case of an employer who fails to file information returns on services rendered and direct sellers, or fails to provide W-2's to employees the penalty is doubled to:

- 3% of the gross wages (federal withholding); and

- 40% of the amount that would have been the employee's share of FICA taxes; and

- The appropriate employer's share of FICA.

Relief from Retroactive Assessment

IRS Code Section 3402(d)(1) offers an employer relief from a retroactive assessment of income tax withholding liability if the employer can adequately demonstrate that the worker reported the income covered by the assessment on his Form 1040 return and paid the tax. Form 4669 is designed for this purpose. This relief is not available if the special tax rates (employer disregard) apply.

Summarized Version
20 Common Law Factors

(Rev. Rule 87-41)

1. **No instructions.** Contractors are not required to follow, nor are they furnished with instructions to accomplish a job. They can be provided job specifications by the hiring firm.

2. **No training.** Contractors typically do not receive training by the hiring firm. They use their own methods to accomplish the work.

3. **Services don't have to be rendered personally.** Contractors are hired to provide a result and usually have the right to hire others to do the actual work.

4. **Work not essential to the hiring firm.** A company's success or continuation should not depend on the service of outside contractors. An example violating this would be a law firm which called their lawyers Independent Contractors.

5. **Own work hours.** Contractors set their own work hours.

6. **Not a continuing relationship.** Usually contractors don't have a continuing relationship with a hiring company. The relationship can be frequent, but it must be at irregular intervals, on call, or whenever work is available. *Warning:* Part-time, seasonal, or short duration relationships have nothing to do with Independent Contractor status.

7. **Control their own assistants.** Contractors shouldn't hire, supervise, or pay assistants at the direction of the hiring company. If assistants are hired, it should be at the contractor's sole discretion.

8. **Time to pursue other work.** Contractors should have enough time available to pursue other gainful work.

9. **Job location.** Contractors control where they work. If they work on the premises of the hiring company, it is not under that company's direction or supervision.

10. **Order of work set.** Contractors determine the order and sequence that they will perform their work.

11. **No interim reports.** Contractors are hired for the final result – and, therefore, should not be asked for progress or interim reports.

12. **Payment timing.** Contractors are paid by the job, not by time. Payment by the job can include periodic payments based on a percentage of job completed. Payment can be based on the number of hours needed to do the job times a fixed hourly rate. However, this should be determined before the job commences.

13. **Working for multiple firms.** Contractors often work for more than one firm at a time.

14. **Business expenses.** Contractors are generally responsible for their incidental expenses.

15. **Own tools.** Usually contractors furnish their own tools. Some hiring firms have leased equipment to their Independent Contractors, so that they could show the contractor had their own tools and an investment in their business (see #16). This strategy won't work if the lease is for a nominal amount or can be voided by the hiring firm at will. In short, the lease must be equivalent to what an independent business person could have obtained in the open market.

16. **Significant investment.** Contractors should be able to perform their services without the hiring company's facilities (equipment, office furniture, machinery, etc.). The contractor's investment in his trade must be real, essential, and adequate. *(See #15 above)*

17. **Services available to general public.** Contractors make their services available to the general public by one or more of the following:

    - Having an office and assistants
    - Having business signs
    - Having a business license
    - Listing their services in a business directory
    - Advertising their services

18. **Limited right to discharge.** Contractors can't be fired so long as they produce a result which meets the contract specifications.

19. **No compensation for non-completion.** Contractors are responsible for the satisfactory completion of a job or they may be legally obligated to compensate the hiring firm for failure to complete.

20. **Possible profit or loss.** Contractors should be able to make a profit or a loss. Employees can't suffer a loss. Five circumstances show that a profit or loss is possible:

    - If the contractor hires, directs, and pays assistants
    - If the contractor has his own office, equipment, materials or facilities
    - If the contractor has continuing and reoccurring liabilities
    - If the contractor has agreed to perform specific jobs for prices agreed upon in advance
    - If the contractors services affect his own business reputation

Blank Forms
and Worksheets

The worksheets and forms on the following pages have been provided for you to copy and use for your own recordkeeping purposes.

I have included worksheets for all of the general records and financial statements. You will also find an example of the SS-4, Application for Employer Identification Number, discussed, but not included in the tax chapter.

General record worksheets and financial statement forms can be copied and used if your business is small and you do not use a software accounting application. Some of the financial statement forms contain "Income", "Variable Expense", and "Fixed Expense" headings and have spaces for you to fill in your own income and expense categories in order to customize them for your particular business. You will need to decide on the appropriate categories and use the same ones throughout all financial statements containing these headings.

Beginning Journal

Date	1. Check # 2. Cash 3. C/Card	Paid To or Received From	Explanation of Income or Expense	Income		Expense	
Total Income and Expenses							

Income & Expense Journal

Month: _____   20 ____, page ____

CHECK NO.	DATE	TRANSACTION	REVENUE	EXPENSE	Customize headings to match the business											MISC
		Balance forward →														
TOTALS																

Petty Cash Record

PETTY CASH - 20___						Page ___
DATE	PAID TO WHOM	EXPENSE ACCOUNT DEBITED	DEPOSIT	AMOUNT OF EXPENSE		BALANCE
	BALANCE FORWARD					

Inventory Record
Identifiable Stock

WHOLESALER:_____   Page____

PURCH DATE	Stock #	Description	PURCH. PRICE	DATE SOLD	SALE PRICE	NAME OF BUYER (Optional)

The header "INVENTORY PURCHASED" spans Stock # and Description columns.

Inventory Record

Non-Identifiable Stock

DEPARTMENT/CATEGORY: _____

PRODUCTION OR PURCHASE DATE	INVENTORY PURCHASED OR MANUFACTURED		NUMBER OF UNITS	UNIT COST	VALUE ON DATE OF INVENTORY (Unit Cost X Units on Hand)	
	Stock #	Description			Value	Date

Fixed Assets Log

COMPANY NAME: _____

ASSET PURCHASED	DATE PLACED IN SERVICE	COST OF ASSET	% USED FOR BUSINESS	RECOVERY PERIOD	METHOD OF DEPRECIATION	DEPRECIATION PREVIOUSLY ALLOWED	DATE SOLD	SALE PRICE

Accounts Receivable
Account Record

CUSTOMER: _____

ADDRESS: _____

_____

TEL. NO: _____   ACCOUNT NO. _____

INVOICE DATE	INVOICE NO.	INVOICE AMOUNT		TERMS	DATE PAID	AMOUNT PAID		INVOICE BALANCE	

Accounts Payable
Account Record

CREDITOR: _____

ADDRESS: _____

_____

TEL. NO: _____   ACCOUNT NO. _____

INVOICE DATE	INVOICE NO.	INVOICE AMOUNT	TERMS	DATE PAID	AMOUNT PAID	INVOICE BALANCE

Mileage Log

NAME: _____

DATED: From_____To_____

DATE	CITY OF DESTINATION	NAME OR OTHER DESIGNATION	BUSINESS PURPOSE	NO. OF MILES
		TOTAL MILES THIS SHEET		

Entertainment Expense Record

NAME: _____

DATED: From _____ To _____

DATE	PLACE OF ENTERTAINMENT	BUSINESS PURPOSE	NAME OF PERSON ENTERTAINED	AMOUNT SPENT	

Travel Record

TRIP TO: _____

Dated From: _____ To: _____

Business Purpose: _____

No. Days Spent on Business _____

DATE	LOCATION	EXPENSE PAID TO	MEALS				HOTEL TAXIS, ETC.	AUTOMOBILE			MISC EXP
			Breakfast	Lunch	Dinner	Misc.		Gas	Parking	Tolls	
TOTALS →											

Balance Sheet

Business Name: Date: _____ ___, _____

ASSETS

Current Assets
Cash $ _____
Petty Cash $ _____
Accounts Receivable $ _____
Inventory $ _____
Short-Term Investments $ _____
Prepaid Expenses $ _____

Long-Term Investments $ _____

Fixed Assets
Land (valued at cost) $ _____

Buildings $ _____
  1. Cost   _____
  2. Less Acc. Depr.   _____

Improvements $ _____
  1. Cost   _____
  2. Less Acc. Depr.   _____

Equipment $ _____
  1. Cost   _____
  2. Less Acc. Depr.   _____

Furniture $ _____
  1. Cost   _____
  2. Less Acc. Depr.   _____

Autos/Vehicles $ _____
  1. Cost   _____
  2. Less Acc. Depr.   _____

Other Assets
  1. $ _____
  2. $ _____

TOTAL ASSETS $ _____

LIABILITIES

Current Liabilities
Accounts Payable $ _____
Notes Payable $ _____
Interest Payable $ _____

Taxes Payable
  Federal Income Tax $ _____
  Self-Employment Tax $ _____
  State Income Tax $ _____
  Sales Tax Accrual $ _____
  Property Tax $ _____

Payroll Accrual $ _____

Long-Term Liabilities
Notes Payable $ _____

TOTAL LIABILITIES $ _____

NET WORTH (EQUITY)

Proprietorship $ _____
          or
Partnership
  name_____, ___% Equity $ _____
  name_____, ___% Equity $ _____
          or
Corporation
  Capital Stock $ _____
  Surplus Paid In $ _____
  Retained Earnings $ _____

TOTAL NET WORTH $ _____

Assets - Liabilities = Net Worth
and
Liabilities + Equity = Total Assets

Profit & Loss (Income) Statement

Business Name: _____

For the Year: 20___

	Jan	Feb	Mar	Apr	May	Jun	6-MONTH TOTALS	Jul	Aug	Sep	Oct	Nov	Dec	12-MONTH TOTALS
INCOME														
1. NET SALES (Gr - R&A)														
2. Cost of Goods to be Sold														
a. Beginning Inventory														
b. Purchases														
c. C.O.G. available for sale														
d. Less ending inventory														
3. GROSS PROFIT														
EXPENSES														
1. Variable (Selling) Expenses														
a.														
b.														
c.														
d.														
e.														
f.														
g. Misc. Variable Expense														
h. Depreciation														
Total Variable Expenses														
1. Fixed (Admin) Expenses														
a.														
b.														
c.														
d.														
e.														
f.														
g. Misc. Fixed Expense														
h. Depreciation														
Total Fixed Expenses														
Total Operating Expense														
Net Income From Operations														
Other Income (Interest)														
Other Expense (Interest)														
Net Profit (Loss) Before Tax														
Taxes: a. Federal														
b. State														
c. Local														
NET PROFIT (LOSS) AFTER TAX														

Profit & Loss (Income) Statement
Business Name: _____

Beginning: _____ ___, _____   **Ending:** _____ ___, _____

INCOME		
1. Sales Revenues		$
2. Cost of Goods Sold (c-d)		
a. Beginning Inventory (1/01)		
b. Purchases		
c. C.O.G. Avail. Sale (a+b)		
d. Less Ending Inventory (12/31)		
3. Gross Profit on Sales (1-2)		$
EXPENSES		
1. Variable (Selling) (a thru h)		
a.		
b.		
c.		
d.		
e.		
f.		
g. Misc. Variable (Selling) Expense		
h. Depreciation (Prod/Serv Assets)		
2. Fixed (Administrative) (a thru h)		
a.		
b.		
c.		
d.		
e.		
f.		
g. Misc. Fixed (Administrative) Expense		
h. Depreciation (Office Equipment)		
Total Operating Expenses (1+2)		
Net Income from Operations (GP-Exp)		$
Other Income (Interest Income)		
Other Expense (Interest Expense)		
Net Profit (Loss) Before Taxes		$
Taxes		
a. Federal		
b. State		
c. Local		
NET PROFIT (LOSS) AFTER TAXES		$

Cash to Be Paid Out Worksheet

Business Name: _____   Time Period:_____ to _____

---

1. **Start-Up Costs:** $ _____
   Business License   _____
   Corporation Filing   _____
   Legal Fees   _____
   Other start-up costs:
       a.   _____
       b.   _____
       c.   _____
       d.   _____

2. **Inventory Purchases**   _____
   Cash out for goods intended for resale

2. **Variable Expenses (Selling)**
       a.   _____
       b.   _____
       c.   _____
       d.   _____
       e.   _____
   Miscellaneous Variable Expense   _____
   Total Selling Expenses   _____

4. **Fixed Expenses (Administrative**
       a.   _____
       b.   _____
       c.   _____
       d.   _____
       e.   _____
       f.   _____
   Miscellaneous Fixed Expense   _____
   Total Operating Expenses   _____

5. **Assets (Long-Term Purchases)**   _____
   Cash to be paid out in current period

6. **Liabilities**   _____
   Cash outlay for retiring debts, loans, and/or
   accounts payable

7. **Owner Equity**   _____
   Cash to be withdrawn by owner

Total Cash to Be Paid Out $ _____

Sources of Cash Worksheet

Business Name: _____

Time Period Covered: _____ to _____

---

    1. Cash On Hand $ _____

    2. Sales (Revenues)

        Sales   _____

        Service Income   _____

        Deposits on Sales or Services   _____

        Collections on Accounts Receivable   _____

    3. Miscellaneous Income

        Interest Income   _____

        Payments to be Received on Loans   _____

    4. Sale of Long-Term Assets   _____

    5. Liabilities

        Loan Funds (Banks, Lending Inst., SBA, etc.)   _____

    6. Equity

        Owner Investments (Sole Prop. or Partnership)   _____

        Contributed Capital (Corporation)   _____

        Venture Capital   _____

                A. Without sales = $ _____

Total Cash Available

                B. With sales = $ _____

Pro Forma Cash Flow Statement

Business Name _____

Year: _____

	Jan	Feb	Mar	Apr	May	Jun	6-MONTH TOTALS	Jul	Aug	Sep	Oct	Nov	Dec	12-MONTH TOTALS
BEGINNING CASH BALANCE														
CASH RECEIPTS														
A. Sales/Revenues														
B. Receivables														
C. Interest Income														
D. Sale of Long-Term Assets														
TOTAL CASH AVAILABLE														
CASH PAYMENTS														
A. Cost of goods to be sold														
1. Purchases														
2. Material														
3. Labor														
Total Cost of Goods														
B. Variable (Selling) Expenses														
1.														
2.														
3.														
4.														
5.														
6.														
7. Misc. Variable Expense														
Total Variable Expenses														
C. Fixed Expenses														
1.														
2.														
3.														
4.														
5.														
6.														
7. Misc. Fixed Expense														
Total Fixed Expenses														
D. Interest Expense														
E. Federal Income Tax														
F. Other Uses														
G. Long-Term Asset Payts														
H. Loan Payments														
I. Owner Draws														
TOTAL CASH PAID OUT														
CASH BALANCE/DEFICIENCY														
LOANS TO BE RECEIVED														
EQUITY DEPOSITS														
ENDING CASH BALANCE														

Quarterly Budget Analysis

Business Name: _____   For the Quarter Ending: _____ ___, 2_____

BUDGET ITEM	THIS QUARTER			YEAR-TO-DATE		
	Budget	Actual	Variation	Budget	Actual	Variation
SALES REVENUES						
Less Cost of Goods						
GROSS PROFITS						
VARIABLE EXPENSES						
1.						
2.						
3.						
4.						
5.						
6.						
7. Miscellaneous						
FIXED EXPENSES						
1.						
2.						
3.						
4.						
5.						
6.						
7.						
NET INCOME FROM OPERATIONS						
INTEREST INCOME						
INTEREST EXPENSE						
NET PROFIT (Pretax)						
TAXES						
NET PROFIT (After Tax)						

NON-INCOME STATEMENT ITEMS

1. Long-term Asset Repayments						
2. Loan Repayments						
3. Owner Draws						

BUDGET DEVIATIONS

	This Quarter	Year-To-Date
1. Income Statement Items:		
2. Non-Income Statement Items:		
3. Total Deviation		

Three-Year Income Projection

Business Name: _____   Updated: _____ ___, _____

	YEAR 1 _____	YEAR 2 _____	YEAR 3 _____	TOTAL 3 YEARS
INCOME				
1. SALES REVENUES				
2. Cost of Goods Sold (c-d)				
a. Beginning Inventory				
b. Purchases				
c. C.O.G. Avail. Sale (a+b)				
d. Less Ending Inventory (12/31)				
3. GROSS PROFIT ON SALES (1-2)				
EXPENSES				
1. VARIABLE (Selling) (a thru h)				
a.				
b.				
c.				
d.				
e.				
f.				
g. Miscellaneous Selling Expense				
h. Depreciation (Prod/Serv Assets)				
2. FIXED (Administrative) (a thru h)				
a.				
b.				
c.				
d.				
e.				
f.				
g. Miscellaneous Fixed Expense				
h. Depreciation (Office Equipment)				
TOTAL OPERATING EXPENSES (1+2)				
NET INCOME OPERATIONS (GPr - Exp)				
OTHER INCOME (Interest Income)				
OTHER EXPENSE (Interest Expense)				
NET PROFIT (LOSS) BEFORE TAXES				
TAXES 1. Federal, S-Employment				
2. State				
3. Local				
NET PROFIT (LOSS) AFTER TAXES				

Break-Even Analysis Graph

Business Name: _____

Analysis Date: _____ ___, ____

Note: Figures shown in ___ of thousands of dollars (Ex: 2 = $_____)

Break-Even Point Calculation

B-E Point (Sales) = Fixed Costs + [(Variable Costs/Estimated Revenues) x Sales]

1. B-E Point (Sales) = $_____ + [($_____ /$ _____) x Sales]

2. B-E Point (Sales) = $_____ + (_____ x Sales)

3. Sales = $_____ + _____ x Sales

4. Sales - _____ Sales = $_____

5. _____ Sales = $_____

6. Sales (S) = $_____ / _____

Break-Even Point

S = $ [   ]

Financial Statement Analysis
Ratio Table

Business Name:

Type of Analysis	Formula	Projected: 2____	Historical: 2____
1. Liquidity Analysis a. Net Working Capital	**Balance Sheet** Current Assets − Current Liabilities	Current Assets _____ Current Liabilities _____ Net Working Capital $ _____	Current Assets _____ Current Liabilities _____ Net Working Capital $ _____
b. Current Ratio	**Balance Sheet** Current Assets Current Liabilities	Current Assets _____ Current Liabilities _____ Current Ratio ____.__	Current Assets _____ Current Liabilities _____ Current Ratio ____.__
c. Quick Ratio	**Balance Sheet** Current Assets minus Inventory Current Liabilities	Current Assets _____ Inventory _____ Current Liabilities _____ Quick Ratio ____.__	Current Assets _____ Inventory _____ Current Liabilities _____ Quick Ratio ____.__
2. Profitability Analysis a. Gross Profit Margin	**Income Statement** Gross Profits Sales	Gross Profits _____ Sales _____ Gross Profit Margin ____.__ %	Gross Profits _____ Sales _____ Gross Profit Margin ____.__ %
b. Operating Profit Margin	Income From Operations Sales	Income From Ops. _____ Sales _____ Op. Profit Margin ____.__ %	Income From Ops. _____ Sales _____ Op. Profit Margin ____.__ %
c. Net Profit Margin	Net Profits Sales	Net Profits _____ Sales _____ Net Profit Margin ____.__ %	Net Profits _____ Sales _____ Net Profit Margin ____.__ %
4. Debt Ratios a. Debt to Assets	**Balance Sheet** Total Liabilities Total Assets	Total Liabilities _____ Total Assets _____ Debt to Assets Ratio ____.__ %	Total Liabilities _____ Total Assets _____ Debt to Assets Ratio ____.__ %
b. Debt to Equity	Total Liabilities Total Owners' Equity	Total Liabilities _____ Total Owners' Equity _____ Debt to Equity Ratio ____.__ %	Total Liabilities _____ Total Owners' Equity _____ Debt to Equity Ratio ____.__ %
4. Investment Measures a. ROI *(Return on Investment)*	**Balance Sheet** Net Profits Total Assets	Net Profits _____ Total Assets _____ ROI (Ret. on Invest.) ____.__ %	Net Profits _____ Total Assets _____ ROI (Ret. on Invest.) ____.__ %
5. Vertical Financial Statement Analysis	**Balance Sheet** 1. Each asset % of Total Assets 2. Liability & Equity % Total L&E **Income Statement** 3. All items % of Total Revenues	**NOTE:** *See Attached* **Projected Balance Analysis** **Projected Income Analysis**	**NOTE:** *See* **Balance Sheet &** **Income Statement**
6. Horizontal Financial Statement Analysis	**Balance Sheet** 1. Assets, Liab & Equity measured against 2nd year. Increases and decreases stated as amount & % **Income Statement** 2. Revenues & Expenses measured against 2nd year. Increases and decreases stated as amount & %	**NOTE:** *See Attached* **Balance Sheet** **&** **Income Statement (P&L)**	**NOTE:** *See Attached* **Balance Sheet** **&** **Income Statement (P&L)**

Form SS-4
Application for Employer Identification Number

Form **SS-4** (Rev. January 2010) Department of the Treasury Internal Revenue Service	**Application for Employer Identification Number** (For use by employers, corporations, partnerships, trusts, estates, churches, government agencies, Indian tribal entities, certain individuals, and others.) ▶ See separate instructions for each line. ▶ Keep a copy for your records.	OMB No. 1545-0003 **EIN**

Type or print clearly.

1 Legal name of entity (or individual) for whom the EIN is being requested

2 Trade name of business (if different from name on line 1)	**3** Executor, administrator, trustee, "care of" name

4a Mailing address (room, apt., suite no. and street, or P.O. box)	**5a** Street address (if different) (Do not enter a P.O. box.)
4b City, state, and ZIP code (if foreign, see instructions)	**5b** City, state, and ZIP code (if foreign, see instructions)

6 County and state where principal business is located

7a Name of responsible party	**7b** SSN, ITIN, or EIN

8a Is this application for a limited liability company (LLC) (or a foreign equivalent)? . . . . ☐ Yes ☐ No	**8b** If 8a is "Yes," enter the number of LLC members . . . . ▶

8c If 8a is "Yes," was the LLC organized in the United States? . . . . ☐ Yes ☐ No

9a **Type of entity** (check only one box). **Caution.** If 8a is "Yes," see the instructions for the correct box to check.

☐ Sole proprietor (SSN) _____
☐ Partnership
☐ Corporation (enter form number to be filed) ▶_____
☐ Personal service corporation
☐ Church or church-controlled organization
☐ Other nonprofit organization (specify) ▶_____
☐ Other (specify) ▶

☐ Estate (SSN of decedent) _____
☐ Plan administrator (TIN) _____
☐ Trust (TIN of grantor) _____
☐ National Guard   ☐ State/local government
☐ Farmers' cooperative   ☐ Federal government/military
☐ REMIC   ☐ Indian tribal governments/enterprises
Group Exemption Number (GEN) if any ▶

9b If a corporation, name the state or foreign country (if applicable) where incorporated	State	Foreign country

10 **Reason for applying** (check only one box)

☐ Started new business (specify type) ▶ _____
_____
☐ Hired employees (Check the box and see line 13.)
☐ Compliance with IRS withholding regulations
☐ Other (specify) ▶

☐ Banking purpose (specify purpose) ▶_____
☐ Changed type of organization (specify new type) ▶_____
☐ Purchased going business
☐ Created a trust (specify type) ▶_____
☐ Created a pension plan (specify type) ▶_____

11 Date business started or acquired (month, day, year). See instructions.	**12** Closing month of accounting year
13 Highest number of employees expected in the next 12 months (enter -0- if none). If no employees expected, skip line 14.	**14** If you expect your employment tax liability to be $1,000 or less in a full calendar year **and** want to file Form 944 annually instead of Forms 941 quarterly, check here. (Your employment tax liability generally will be $1,000 or less if you expect to pay $4,000 or less in total wages.) If you do not check this box, you must file Form 941 for every quarter. ☐

Agricultural	Household	Other

15 First date wages or annuities were paid (month, day, year). **Note.** If applicant is a withholding agent, enter date income will first be paid to nonresident alien (month, day, year). . . . . ▶

16 Check **one** box that best describes the principal activity of your business.
☐ Construction ☐ Rental & leasing ☐ Transportation & warehousing
☐ Real estate ☐ Manufacturing ☐ Finance & insurance
☐ Health care & social assistance ☐ Wholesale-agent/broker
☐ Accommodation & food service ☐ Wholesale-other ☐ Retail
☐ Other (specify)

17 Indicate principal line of merchandise sold, specific construction work done, products produced, or services provided.

18 Has the applicant entity shown on line 1 ever applied for and received an EIN? ☐ Yes ☐ No
If "Yes," write previous EIN here ▶

Third Party Designee	Complete this section **only** if you want to authorize the named individual to receive the entity's EIN and answer questions about the completion of this form.	
	Designee's name	Designee's telephone number (include area code) ( )
	Address and ZIP code	Designee's fax number (include area code) ( )

Under penalties of perjury, I declare that I have examined this application, and to the best of my knowledge and belief, it is true, correct, and complete. | Applicant's telephone number (include area code) ( )

Name and title (type or print clearly) ▶

Applicant's fax number (include area code) ( )

Signature ▶   Date ▶

For Privacy Act and Paperwork Reduction Act Notice, see separate instructions.   Cat. No. 16055N   Form **SS-4** (Rev. 1-2010)

Small Business
Resources

The Small Business Administration - www.sba.gov

The United States SBA is an independent federal agency that was created by Congress in 1953 to assist, council, and represent small business. Statistics show that most small business failures are due to poor management. For this reason, the SBA places special emphasis on individual counseling, courses, conferences, workshops, and publications to train the new and existing business owner in all facets of business development with special emphasis on improving the management ability of the owner.

Counseling is provided through Business Information Centers (BICs), the Service Corps of Retired Executives (SCORE), Small Business Development Centers (SBDCs), and numerous professional associations.

Business management training covers such topics as planning, finance, organization, and marketing and is held in cooperation with educational institutions, chambers of commerce, and trade associations. Pre-business workshops are held on a regular basis for prospective business owners. The following is a brief summary of what these programs include:

Service Corp of Retired Executives (SCORE) - www.score.org

SCORE is a 13,000-person volunteer program with over 364 chapters throughout the United States. SCORE help small businesses solve their operating, marketing, and financial problems through one-on-one counseling and through a well-developed system of workshops and training sessions. SCORE counseling is available at no charge.

Small Business Development Centers (SBDCs) - www.sba.gov/sbdc

These centers draw their resources from local, state, and federal government programs, the private sector, and university facilities. They provide managerial and technical help, research studies, and other types of specialized assistance. These centers are generally located or headquartered in academic institutions and provide individual counseling and practical training for small business owners.

Small Business Training Network - www.sba.gov/training

The Small Business Training Network is a virtual campus that houses free training courses, workshops, and knowledge resources designed to assist entrepreneurs and other students of enterprise. The network is a dynamic learning center designed to help small businesses compete in a constantly changing, global environment. Through the network, the SBA makes business management resources available anytime and anywhere.

Federal Agencies

Many federal agencies offer publications of interest to small businesses. There is a nominal fee for some, but most are free. Below is a partial list of government agencies that provide publications and other services targeted to small businesses. To get their publications, go to their web sites, contact the regional offices listed in the telephone directory, or write to the addresses below:

Consumer Information Center (CIC) - www.usa.gov
USA.gov
1800 F Street, NW
Washington, DC 20405
(800) 333-4636
The CIC offers a consumer information catalog of federal publications.

Federal Trade Commission - www.ftc.gov
600 Pennsylvania Avenue, NW
Washington, DC 20580
(202) 326-2222

Internal Revenue Service - www.irs.gov
The IRS web site offers all tax related contacts, information, and downloads of forms and publications.

U.S. Department of Commerce (DOC) - www.commerce.gov
1401 Constitution Avenue, NW
Washington, D.C. 20230
(202) 482-2000

U.S. Department of Labor (DOL) - www.dol.gov
200 Constitution Avenue, NW
Washington, DC 20210
(866) 487-2365

U.S. Department of the Treasury - www.treasury.gov
1500 Pennsylvania Avenue, NW
Washington, D.C. 20220
(202) 622-2000

Glossary
Business and Financial Terms

The following glossary will define business and financial terms with which you may not be familiar. Use of these terms will help you to speak and write in a language that will be understood by potential lenders and investors as well as business associates with whom you may be dealing.

Account. A separate record showing the increases and decreases in each asset, liability, owner's equity, revenue, and expense item.

Accounting. The process by which financial information about a business is recorded, classified, summarized, and interpreted by a business.

Accounting period. The period of time covered by the income statement and other financial statements that report operating results.

Accounts payable. Amounts owed by a business to its creditors on open account for goods purchased or services rendered.

Accounts receivable. Amounts owed to the business on open account as a result of extending credit to a customer who purchases your products or services.

Accrual basis of accounting. The method of accounting in which all revenues and expenses are recognized on the income statement in the period when they are earned and incurred, regardless of when the cash related to the transactions is received or paid.

Accrued expenses. Expenses that have been incurred but not paid (such as employee salaries, commissions, taxes, interest, etc.)

Accrued income. Income that has been earned but not received.

Aging accounts receivable. The classification of accounts receivable according to how long they have been outstanding. An appropriate rate of loss can then be applied to each age group in order to estimate probable loss from uncollectible accounts.

Assets. Everything owned by or owed to a business that has cash value.

Audit trail. A chain of references that makes it possible to trace information about transactions through an accounting system.

Balance sheet. The financial statement that shows the financial position of a business as of a fixed date. It is usually done at the close of an accounting period by summarizing business assets, liabilities, and owners' equity.

Bottom line. A business's net profit or loss after taxes for a specific accounting period.

Break-even point. That point at which a business no longer incurs a loss but has yet to make a profit. The break-even point can be expressed in total dollars of revenue exactly offset by total expenses, or total units of production, the cost of which exactly equals the income derived from their sale.

Budget. The development of a set of financial goals. A business is then evaluated by measuring its performance in terms of these goals. The budget contains projections for cash inflow and outflow and other balance sheet items. Also known as "Cash Flow Statement".

Business financial history. A summary of financial information about a company from its start to the present.

Capital. See "Owner's equity".

Capital expenditure. An expenditure for a purchase of an item of property, plant or equipment that has a useful life of more than one year. (Fixed assets)

Cash flow statement. See "Budget."

Chart of accounts. A list of the numbers and titles of a business's general ledger accounts.

Closing entries. Entries made at the end of an accounting period to reduce the balances of the revenue and expense accounts to zero. Most businesses close books at the end of each month and at the end of the year.

Comparative financial statements. Financial statements that include information for two or more periods or two or more companies.

Corporation. A business structure that is granted separate legal status under state law and whose owners are stockholders of the corporation.

Cost of goods sold. The cost of inventory sold during an accounting period. It is equal to the beginning inventory for the period, plus the cost of purchases made during the period, minus the ending inventory for the period.

Credit. An amount entered on the right side of an account in double-entry accounting. A decrease in asset and expense accounts. An increase in liability, capital, and income accounts.

Creditor. A company or individual to whom a business owes money.

Current assets. Cash plus any assets that will be converted into cash within one year plus any assets that you plan to use up within one year.

Current liabilities. Debts that must be paid within one year.

Current ratio. A dependable indication of liquidity computed by dividing current assets by current liabilities. A ratio of 2.0 is acceptable for most businesses.

Debit. An amount entered on the left side of an account in double-entry accounting. A decrease in liabilities, capital, and income accounts. An increase in asset and expense accounts.

Debt measures. The indication of the amount of other people's money that is being used to generate profits for a business. The more indebtedness, the greater the risk of failure.

Debt ratio. The key financial ratio used by creditors in determining how indebted a business is and how able it is to service the debts. The debt ratio is calculated by dividing total liabilities by total assets. The higher the ratio, the more risk of failure. The acceptable ratio is dependent upon the policies of your creditors and bankers.

Declining-balance method. An accelerated method of depreciation in which the book value of an asset at the beginning of the year is multiplied by an appropriate percentage to obtain the depreciation to be taken for that year.

Depreciable base of an asset. The cost of an asset used in the computation of yearly depreciation expense.

Direct expenses. Those expenses that relate directly to your product or service.

Double-entry accounting. A system of accounting under which each transaction is recorded twice. This is based on the premise that every transaction has two sides. At least one account must be debited and one account must be credited and the debit and credit totals for each transaction must be equal.

Expenses. The costs of producing revenue through the sale of goods or services.

Financial statements. The periodic reports that summarize the financial affairs of a business.

First in, first out method (FIFO). A method of valuing inventory which assumes that the first items purchased are the first items to be sold. When ending inventory is computed, the costs of the latest purchases are used.

Fiscal year. Any 12-month accounting period used by a business.

Fixed assets. Items purchased for use in a business which are depreciable over a fixed period of time determined by the expected useful life of the purchase. Usually includes land, buildings, vehicles, and equipment not intended for resale. Land is not depreciable, but is listed as a fixed asset.

Fixed asset log. A record used to keep track of the fixed assets purchased by a business during the current financial year. This record can be used by an accountant to determine depreciation expense to be taken for tax purposes.

Fixed costs. Costs that do not vary in total during a period even though the volume of goods manufactured may be higher or lower than anticipated.

General journal. Used to record all the transactions of a business. Transactions are listed in chronological order and transferred or posted to individual accounts in the general ledger.

General ledger. In double-entry accounting, the master reference file for the accounting system. A permanent, classified record is kept for each business account. The forms used for the accounts are on separate sheets in a book or binder and are then referred to as the general ledger.

Gross profit margin. An indicator of the percentage of each sales dollar remaining after a business has paid for its goods. It is computed by dividing the gross profit by the sales.

Gross profit on sales. The difference between net sales and the cost of goods sold.

Horizontal analysis. A percentage analysis of the increases and decreases on the items on comparative financial statements. A horizontal financial statement analysis involves comparison of data for the current period with the same data of a company for previous periods. The percentage of increase or decrease is listed.

Income & expense journal. In single-entry accounting, the record used to keep track of all checks written by a business and all income received for the sale of goods or services.

Indirect expenses. Operating expenses that are not directly related to the sale of your product or service.

Interest. The price charged or paid for the use of money or credit.

Inventory. The stock of goods that a business has on hand for sale to its customers.

Investment measures. Ratios used to measure an owner's earnings for his or her investment in the company. See "Return on investment (ROI)."

Invoice. A bill for the sale of goods or services sent by the seller to the purchaser.

Last in, first out method (LIFO). A method of valuing inventory which assumes that the last items purchased are the first items to be sold. The cost of the ending inventory is computed by using the cost of the earliest purchases.

Liabilities. Amounts owed by a business to its creditors. The debts of a business.

Liquidity. The ability of a company to meet its financial obligations. A liquidity analysis focuses on the balance sheet relationships for current assets and current liabilities.

Long-term liabilities. Liabilities that will not be due for more than a year in the future.

Mileage log. The recording of business miles traveled during an accounting period.

Modified accelerated cost recovery system (MACRS). A method of depreciation or cost recovery used for federal income tax purposes for long-term assets purchased after January 1, 1987. Under MACRS, long-term assets fall automatically into certain classes, and the costs of all assets in a class are charged to expense through a standard formula.

Net income. The amount by which revenue is greater than expenses. On an income statement this usually expressed as both a pre-tax and after-tax figure.

Net loss. The amount by which expenses are greater than revenue. On an income statement this figure is usually listed as both a pre-tax and after-tax figure.

Net profit margin. The measure of a business's success with respect to earnings on sales. It is derived by dividing the net profit by sales. A higher margin means the firm is more profitable.

Net sales. Gross sales less returns and allowances and sales discounts.

Net worth. See "Owners' equity."

Note. A written promise with terms for payment of a debt.

Operating expenses. Normal expenses incurred in the running of a business

Operating profit margin. The ratio representing the pure operations profits, ignoring interest and taxes. It is derived by dividing the income from operations by the sales. The higher the percentage of operating profit margin the better.

Other expenses. Expenses that are not directly connected with the operation of a business. The most common is interest expense.

Other income. Income that is earned from non operating sources. The most common is interest income.

Owners' equity. The financial interest of the owner of a business. The total of all owner equity is equal to the business's assets minus its liabilities. The owner's equity represents total investments in the business plus or minus any profits or losses the business has accrued to date.

Partnership. The form of business legal structure that is owned by two or more persons.

Personal financial history. A summary of personal financial information about the owner of a business. The personal financial history is often required by a potential lender or investor.

Petty cash fund. A cash fund from which non-check expenditures are reimbursed.

Physical inventory. The process of counting inventory on hand at the end of an accounting period. The number of units of each item is multiplied by the cost per item resulting in inventory value.

Posting. The process of transferring data from a journal to a ledger

Prepaid expanses. Expense items that are paid for prior to their use. Some examples are insurance, rent, prepaid inventory purchases, etc.

Principal. The amount shown on the face of a note or a bond. Unpaid principal is the portion of the face amount remaining at any given time.

Profit & loss statement. See "Income statement."

Property, plant, and equipment. Assets such as land, buildings, vehicles, and equipment that will be used for a number of years in the operation of a business and (with the exception of land) are subject to depreciation.

Quarterly budget analysis. A method used to measure actual income and expenditures against projections for the current quarter of the financial year and for the total quarters completed. The difference is usually expressed as the amount and percentage over or under budget.

Quick ratio. A test of liquidity subtracting inventory from current assets and dividing the result by current liabilities. A quick ratio of 1.0 or greater is usually recommended.

Ratio analysis. An analysis involving the comparison of two individual items on financial statements. One item is divided by the other and the relationship is expressed as a ratio.

Real property. Land, land improvements, buildings, and other structures attached to the land.

Reconciling the bank statement. The process used to bring the bank's records, the accounts, and the business's checkbook into agreement at the end of a banking period.

Retail business. A business that sells goods and services directly to individual consumers.

Retained earnings. Earnings of a corporation that are kept in the business and not paid out in dividends. This amount represents the accumulated, undistributed profits of the corporation.

Return on investment (ROI). The rate of profit an investment will earn. The ROI is equal to the annual net income divided by total assets. The higher the ROI, the better. Business owners should set a target for the ROI and decide what they want their investments to earn.

Revenue. The income that results from the sale of products or services or from the use of investments or property.

Salvage value. The amount that an asset can be sold for at the end of its useful life.

Service business. A business that provides services rather than products to its customers.

Single-entry accounting. The term referring to a recordkeeping system that uses only income and expense accounts. Now generally used by many smaller businesses, this system is easier to maintain and understand, extremely effective, and 100% verifiable.

Sole proprietorship. A legal structure of a business having one person as the owner.

Stockholders. Owners of a corporation whose investment is represented by shares of stock.

Stockholders' equity. The stockholders' shares of stock in a corporation plus any retained earnings.

Straight-line method of depreciation. A method of depreciating assets by allocating an equal amount of depreciation for each year of its useful life.

Sum-of-the-year's-digits method. An accelerated method of depreciation in which a fractional part of the depreciable cost of an asset is charged to expense each year. The denominator of the fraction is the sum of the numbers representing the years of the asset's useful life. The numerator is the number of years remaining in the asset's useful life.

Tangible personal property. Machinery, equipment, furniture, and fixtures not attached to the land.

Three-year income projection. A pro forma (projected) income statement showing anticipated revenues and expenses for a business.
Travel record. The record used to keep track of expenses for a business-related trip away from the home business area.

Trial balance. A listing of all the accounts in the general ledger and their balances used to prove the equality of debits and credits in accounts.

Unearned income. Revenue that has been received, but not yet earned.

Variable costs. Expenses that vary in relationship to the volume of activity of a business.

Vertical analysis. A percentage analysis used to show the relationship of the components in a single financial statement. In vertical analysis of an income statement, each item on the statement is expressed as a percentage of net sales.

Wholesale business. A business that sells its products to other wholesalers, retailers, or volume customers at a discount.

Work in progress. Manufactured products that are only partially completed at the end of the accounting cycle.

Working capital. Current assets minus current liabilities. This is a basic measure of a company's ability to pay its current obligations.

Index

AUTOMATE YOUR BUSINESS PLAN *for Windows®*

from Linda Pinson
Author of the SBA Publication, "How to Write a Business Plan"

WRITE YOUR BUSINESS PLAN WITH AN EXPERT AT YOUR SIDE

Write a winning business plan that is professional and credible..
- Cover Sheet
- Table of Contents
- Executive Summary
- Organizational Plan
- Advanced or Basic Marketing Plan
- Financial Document
- Supporting Documents

"Simply put, **Automate Your Business Plan** is the best step-by-step software for starting, building, and raising capital for your business. We have raised over $20 million for our clients by using AYBP. Use it - it works!"
Tom Wacker
Centaur Holdings Corporation

"Automate Your Business Plan" assumes you know nothing about writing a business plan. We walk you through the process and make your job easier.

□ *Our step-by-step planning process will enable you to organize your industry expertise into a working business plan that will attract capital and ensure success.*
   ■ Complete instructions guide you through each part of your plan.
   Bonus *Special Web page "hot links"* you to marketing & financial research sites.
   ■ Five complete real business plans (1 product, 2 services, a dot.com, and a nonprofit organization) will help you overcome writer's block.
   ■ **Automate Your Business Plan** is a stand-alone software program. It is not a set of templates depending on someone else's software for compatibility and support. If you have questions, call us.

ATTRACT LENDERS & INVESTORS WITH A CUSTOMIZED BUSINESS PLAN

We guide you step-by-step through the entire business plan process.
- Instructions
- Examples
- Pre-formatted text templates
- Integrated spreadsheet workbook
- Ratio Analysis
- Supplementary worksheets

Investors are turned off by canned plans that look and sound like everyone else's. A customized working business plan is a plan to succeed.

□ *Your plan will be tailored to your specific industry and to your situation.*
   ■ We help you research and write a winning executive summary and marketing plan.
   ■ We help you develop <u>valid</u> financial assumptions and projections for your business.

□ *These are some of the great features you will like about our software:*
   ■ Instructions, examples, formatted files for all parts of your plan; Word® & Excel® compatible
   ■ All files set with headers, fonts, margins, and print commands (including Print Plan to PDF)
   ■ Multiple plans; import/export projects between computers; create P-Point Presentations

SAVE 100+ HOURS WITH OUR INTEGRATED (LINKED) FINANCIAL SPREADSHEETS

Profit & Loss Statement
ABC Corporation

We help you develop realistic financial projections so you can make the right decisions for a successful and profitable business future.

□ *You will move with ease through your entire financial plan.*
   ■ We set up and formulate all of your financial spreadsheets.
   ■ Our Chart of Accounts Wizard generates a customized spreadsheet workbook.
   ■ Numbers input in one spreadsheet flow to all related spreadsheets.
   Bonus *Amortizing Software* calculates loan principal & interest payments.

□ *Your lender will be happy to see the following financial information:*
   ■ Sources & Uses of Funds   ■ Quarterly Budget Analysis
   ■ Pro-Forma Cash Flow Statement   ■ P&L Statement & Balance Sheet
   ■ Three-Year Income Projection   ■ Financial Ratio Analysis
   ■ Break-Even Analysis   ■ Charts & Graphs

"Automate Your Business Plan and *Anatomy of a Business Plan* are thorough, practical, and easy-to-understand."
Sandy Sutton, District Director (ret.)
Santa Ana District Office, U.S. Small Business Administration

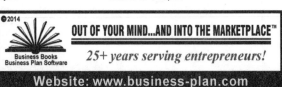